"I LOVED IT! Absolutely loved it. Erik and Emily Orton engagingly narrate the exploits of their family as they disrupt their conventional New York City life for an adventure at sea, unfazed by the challenges of five children, one with special needs. They can't imagine everything that might go wrong, but it will anyway. They won't persuade you to spend a year on a boat—at least, they didn't persuade me—but they will seduce you into imagining boldly and envisioning setting sail on an adventure of your own. They will persuade you that 'unconventional' is a synonym for 'individual' and have you contemplating why you would accept an off-the-rack version of your life when you can tailor-make your own. You'll finish *Seven at Sea* daring to seek a discovery-driven voyage to your dream life, or the dream-of-a-lifetime. A fun, inspiring read."

—WHITNEY JOHNSON
Best-Selling Author of *Disrupt Yourself* and *Dare, Dream, Do*

"We're all on a journey. The Ortons' storytelling of their particular path guides all readers—not just those who dream of seafaring—through lessons on living, loving, and life. They share their hurdles with candor and warmth, and just enough discomfort to remind you they're real: stretching beyond their comfort zone in the joyful and daunting extremes of life on an adventure. The way that Erik and Emily consider, evaluate, and take on challenges they face is instructive for all, and required reading for those who dream of adventuring as a family."

—BEHAN GIFFORD
Coauthor of *Voyaging with Kids—A Guide to Family Life*, featured on the *Today Show*, *CNN*, *Business Insider*, and *Inside Edition*

"I love nothing more than seeing someone put his or her mind to something, and then make it happen. Well, that's not entirely true—I love nothing more than seeing a family put their mind to something, and then make it happen. This is a great story of a loving family working together to fulfill dreams that one of them had—and that the others just didn't realize they had yet."

—PATRICK SCHULTE
Head Writing Bum at Bumfuzzle.com and
Cofounder of Wanderer Financial

SEVEN
at SEA

WHY A NEW YORK CITY FAMILY
CAST OFF CONVENTION FOR A
LIFE-CHANGING YEAR ON A SAILBOAT

SEVEN
at SEA

ERIK ORTON & EMILY ORTON

SHADOW
MOUNTAIN

All photos courtesy of the authors except as noted below.

Pages 4–5: mandritoiu/shutterstock.com; pages 62–63: BlueOrange Studio/shutterstock.com; pages 102–103: Uladzik Kryhin/shutterstock.com; pages 156–57: ju.hrozian/shutterstock.com; pages 252–53: pisaphotography/shutterstock.com; photo section: Lisa Torkelson, John Alonso, and © Ty LaMont Mecham.

Visit us at shadowmountain.com

Library of Congress Cataloging-in-Publication Data
Names: Orton, Erik, 1974– author. | Orton, Emily, 1974– author.
Title: Seven at sea : why a New York City family cast off convention for a life-changing
    year on a sailboat / Erik and Emily Orton.
Description: Salt Lake City, Utah : Shadow Mountain, [2019]
Identifiers: LCCN 2018047098 | ISBN 9781629725512 (hardbound : alk. paper)
Subjects: LCSH: Orton, Erik, 1974—Travel. | Orton, Emily, 1974—Travel. | Sailing—
    Caribbean Area. | Sailing—Atlantic Coast (U.S.) | Caribbean Area—Description and
    travel. | Atlantic Coast (U.S.)—Description and travel. | LCGFT: Travel writing.
Classification: LCC GV776.23 .O75 2019 | DDC 797.12409163/65—dc23
LC record available at https://lccn.loc.gov/2018047098

Printed in the United States of America
Lake Book Manufacturing, Inc., Melrose Park, IL

10   9   8   7   6   5   4   3   2   1

For our crew:
Karina, Alison, Sarah Jane, Eli, and Lily.
You will always be our greatest adventure.

INTRODUCTION

OYSTER POND, SAINT MARTIN, CARIBBEAN

20 Days aboard *Fezywig*

ERIK

I pointed *Fezywig* out of the channel for the third time in three weeks. "Okay, kids, hang on," I called across the deck. Before we arrived at Oyster Pond in Saint Martin, I'd had no idea we were picking up our boat from one of the most treacherous coves in the whole Caribbean: a narrow channel weaving through jagged cliffs, submerged reefs, meandering buoys, and direct exposure to waves rolling in across the Atlantic Ocean. Now I knew what was coming, and I was scared spitless.

Emily turned up the music, and all five of our kids started singing "Rox in the Box" by the Decemberists. We'd been singing this haunting, jaunty song for years as our family had learned to sail. Karina, our oldest at sixteen, dusty blonde and round-faced, stood across the cockpit, her eyes riveted on the channel. Alison, fourteen, with cropped copper hair, looked up the mast to check the wind indicator. Sarah Jane (or SJ or Jane, but never Sarah). twelve and already turning platinum blonde, swung from the canvased bars covering the cockpit. Eli, eight and gangly, was our one boy. Lily, six, with her almond eyes and apple cheeks, was the end of the line. Eli and Lily couldn't swim. That's why they were tethered with harnesses to jack lines running the length of the boat. Emily steadied herself in the doorframe between the galley and the cockpit. Her smile was confident, but her blue eyes were full of questions. I did my best to smile back.

We sang loudly as the boat pitched and the bow pounded into the oncoming waves. Singing kept our minds busy and nausea at bay. We got through the pin buoys and out into open water. I turned the boat toward the island of Tintamarre, which put us sideways to the waves. That's when my queasiness returned, but I was determined. Even with only one working engine, we weren't spending another night in that hot, stuffy anchorage waiting for a mechanic who might never show up.

Putting up the sails would have moved my nausea to the next step, and it was a short trip, so we motored the few miles to Tintamarre. A bunch of boats were already tied to mooring balls along the main beach. There was one ball free, so we went for it. Karina and Alison were at the bow with the boat hook ready to snag the line. Getting the mooring ball on the first try had become a source of pride for me. We'd practiced it constantly since our earliest family sails. Karina and Alison were our best snaggers. But despite my, ahem, nearly impeccable driving, they missed it. I wasn't a good enough captain yet to stay calm. I had something to prove. With the wind pushing the boat sideways and only one engine, I wasn't about to go around for another pass. I shouted up front, "I can't believe you guys! Alison, take the helm!" Emily conveyed the second half of the message, and Alison took the wheel. Jane kept Eli and Lily out of the way. She knew the "Mad Dad" look when she saw it. I jumped down to the stern and grabbed the mooring ball with my bare hands.

"Bring me a docking line!" I ordered. A docking line was fire-brigaded to me. "And another one!" I demanded. Another one appeared in my hand. I did a Herculean move, pulling the lines together and tying them to the stern. I didn't even deign to shoot my kids a nasty look. We were now "anchored"—backward. Boats at anchor are supposed to point forward into the wind, not backward.

We spent the next thirty minutes putting on a circus for the boaters moored near us. I imagined the other boaters' mocking thoughts as they sat quietly poised in their cockpits, their bows bobbing up and down, annoyingly pointed into the wind. Meanwhile I was running around untying lines, retying lines, trying to give Emily and the kids the silent treatment but also needing their help, as we painstakingly pivoted our boat to point into the wind. The correct direction. The direction we would have been if they had gotten the line the first time. If both engines had worked. If we all hadn't felt nauseous. If, if, if.

The sun went down but the wind picked up. It was going to be a long, rolly night. The nausea was not going away. Everyone lay still, looking pale and trying not to puke. Despite her own nausea, Emily rallied to heat broth for dinner. We all took a few sips.

I looked around the ten-by-sixteen-foot cabin at Emily and our five kids, ages six to sixteen. Eli and Lily lay splayed on the floor in a pile. The older girls flopped face-first on the table. Not one of them was happy.

"Whose dumb idea was this?" I asked. Their heads lifted and looked at me. I wasn't asking about this anchorage or this little overnight stay. I was talking about the whole trip: quitting my job, packing up our stuff, leaving our apartment and friends in New York City, flying to the Caribbean, moving aboard a fixer-upper boat we'd never seen before, and imagining we could sail all over the planet for the next year.

All their fingers pointed at me. "It was your idea, Dad!" They burst out laughing. I couldn't help but crack a smile too.

Emily clarified. "Hey, that's not entirely true."

PART
ONE

6 Years

to

1 Month before *Fezywig*

CHAPTER 1

BETTER DONE THAN PERFECT

UPPER MANHATTAN, NEW YORK

6 Years before *Fezywig*

EMILY

I'm not sure why Erik first fell in love with sailing. His first sail wasn't pleasant. He and two buddies sweltered on a blazing, windless day up the Hudson River. Erik threw up five times between his friend's boat, his friend's car, and our apartment. Still, he loved the water, being on the water, and traveling by water rather than being hemmed in by it. He figured he could work around the seasickness.

Twenty miles down the Hudson, Erik worked a graveyard shift managing desktop publishing jobs for investment bankers in a skyscraper in Manhattan's financial district. But we hadn't come to New York City so Erik could sit in a windowless office from four to midnight five nights a week. We came for Broadway. Erik writes musicals, plays, novels, and songs. He has a degree in music. He's also analytical—creating budgets, timelines, and contracts. He's one of those right-brained *and* left-brained people.

We moved to New York City, straight out of college, with our toddler, Karina, and our newborn, Alison. We rented a two-bedroom, one-bathroom apartment in northern Manhattan. Erik had his first Broadway management job. In theatre, each show is a business. Over the years he worked on several different shows, progressing from payroll to producer. My responsibilities expanded as well. Every time we had a baby, Erik called it a promotion. Our daughter Sarah Jane was born shortly after the 9/11 terrorist attack.

Erik quit his job managing national tours for *Wicked*, one of the most stable and prestigious shows in the theatre industry, to produce a new off-Broadway musical. He picked the project, raised the money, hired all the actors, directors, and designers. The show closed after five weeks and was a complete financial loss. Erik was featured on the cover of *Crain's New York Business* magazine; his cleft chin facing forward, his unruly blond hair defying the gel he used to slick it back—literally the poster boy for failure. People who think all producers are rich have probably never produced anything. When we took the risk, our chins were barely above water financially. We were unemployed when we welcomed our fourth child, our only boy, Eli. Simultaneously in love with our son and heartbroken over the show closing, Erik got a nighttime office temp job.

During the day, he obtained the rights to produce a musical on Broadway and started fundraising. He produced workshop readings of two of his plays. I called his creative efforts his day job. "Don't quit your day job," I'd say. Usually, that means, "You'll never earn a living in the arts." I meant, *I believe in you.* No matter how often we called his cubicle work a disposable job, it morphed into a permanent position. Two years later, our last child, Lily, was born.

Erik was never excited to go to his job in the glass tower, but he liked paying the rent and filling the cupboards. He made friends and studied investing, despite his supervisor's advice not to bother understanding the bankers' deals. He was happy to have his days free to write and explore creative opportunities. At the end of the shift, he was always happy to come home. But that first blazing sail opened his eyes to the water. He'd seen the marina adjacent to his office building on hundreds of dinner breaks. He'd seen the sailing school. The first warm season after he'd actually been sailing, he decided to cross the invisible barrier—the paradigm that sailing is for rich people—and ask about classes.

Every night, around eight o'clock, he took a dinner break and called me.

"They're scanning our thumbs now when we clock in," Erik said.

"Sounds like a spy movie. Next they'll be scanning your eyeballs," I said.

"Pretty soon they're gonna start paying us by the minute."

"The fact you don't want promotions tells me you don't want to grow there. You're not in the right place," I said. We'd had this conversation before.

"Speaking of going places," Erik changed the subject. "I talked to a guy at the sailing school today. He said they will form a daytime class if I get three other students to join me."

"You'll love that!" I said. "Do you know anyone who wants to learn to sail?"

Erik couldn't find any friends or coworkers to take the class. A couple of weeks later he hopped out of the shower, a towel around his waist.

"I've got a brilliant idea. You, Karina, and Alison can fill the other three slots. Then we'll all know how to sail."

"I'm scared of deep water," I said. "Six feet deep in a swimming pool and I get irrational."

"That's why you need to learn to sail. You can stay in the boat."

I knew he couldn't do it without us. "What about Sarah Jane, Eli, and Lily?"

"We'll hire a babysitter. It's *one* afternoon a week for five weeks."

"Five hundred dollars each for the class, plus childcare . . . that'll be like twenty-five hundred dollars. How are we going to pay for that?" I asked. Erik countered my money concern by taking on a short-term second job reviewing theatrical contracts for a previous employer. He was embarrassed to go back for this temporary demotion but grateful to be able to learn to sail.

Eleven-year-old Karina and nine-year-old Alison counted down the days until class started. The course was the American Sailing Association 101, Basic Keelboat Sailing Certification. The first week, we mastered basic vocabulary. The second week, our instructor motored us into New York Harbor, raised the sails, and cut the engine. We were sailing.

I stood at the bow smiling into the wind. Under a bright blue sky, the Statue of Liberty presided over a busy harbor filled with water taxis, tankers, and us. I turned to smile at my family and saw Erik upright at the tiller, grimly concentrating on not vomiting. Karina was unusually quiet. Her blonde head rested on the starboard deck, and Alison's red head rested on the portside deck.

"How much longer until class is over?" Karina asked. Alison moved only her eyeballs to look at me. I wasn't seasick at all. I wondered if I had a knack for sailing.

The third week we arrived with generic motion sickness pills, ginger gum, and wristbands that tell your brain you're not queasy.

Things evened out. I got seasick, too. We learned to manage our seasickness when it came. I kept my eyes on the horizon and kept the conversations light. We pulled ropes tight, cleated them off, winched them, released them, raised and lowered sails, and best of all, turned into the wind. Our instructor ensured we didn't catch our thumbs in the winch or cut in front of a water taxi.

Erik was the best sailor. Alison had a knack for wind direction and what to do with it. Karina was mildly surprised to be bested by her younger sister. I aced my written test, but I was the worst sailor in our family. That was no surprise. Erik seems to have been born with an internal compass. *I* usually don't know what direction I'm facing. When we first moved to New York City it once took me so long to parallel park that a stranger got off his front stoop, asked for the keys, and parked for me. For me, sailing was an exciting exercise, a cool learning experience, a one-off.

Erik, however, wasn't done sailing. After all that effort, he wanted to see if we could sail a boat without an instructor. Being in a boat wasn't as bad as being in the water, but it certainly wasn't my idea of a comfort zone. I talked myself into one more outing to support him and to extend the experience to Sarah Jane, Eli, and Lily. They'd never set foot on a boat. Like any mom who wants her child to taste a new food, I wanted them to try it. Erik shopped the tristate area for a budget-friendly rental. His persistence paid off.

"My wife and I are ASA 101 certified, and we'd like to rent one of your boats," he said into the phone. When he hung up, he hugged me.

"No instructor. No charter captain. Just us. We're all going sailing!" he said. That's my soft spot right there, a happy Erik. He's been my best friend since our freshman year of college. He cheered me through graduation and my first year of teaching middle school before Karina was born. Even though he was raised in a dual-income family, he shifted his paradigm to support and truly value my ambitions as a stay-at-home mom. What exhilarated Erik sometimes exposed me—usually in a good way. His aspirations expanded my horizons. I didn't want my fears to hold him back.

"Awesome!" I hugged him. "Which direction is Toms River, New Jersey?"

Maybe if you flew a helicopter from New York City to the Jersey coast it would be fun, but the same trip in a minivan in mid-August is no fun. After a couple of hours the kids were all motion sick.

"Finally!" Karina said, stepping into the gravel parking lot. I unbuckled the little kids while Erik checked in at the office. He returned with a preppy employee who guided us to a twenty-foot open cockpit daysailer, the same size as our sailing class boat but much nicer. It had long white benches down each side—perfect for a family of seven. The tiller was made out of teak, beautifully sealed and polished. Striped ropes lay in flat coils on the dock or passed through shiny shackles. The mainsail wrapped snugly around the boom, tied down with crisp square knots. Too bad we weren't dressed for a Ralph Lauren photo shoot.

The employee handed us a stack of stiff life jackets in all the right sizes. The three older girls managed their own while I snapped Eli and Lily into theirs.

"This jacket makes me look fat," said Sarah Jane. At six, SJ was already too feisty to play the mild middle child. Nothing about this trip excited her. "Let's get this over with so we can go home," she said.

Karina and Alison went to the bow to hank the jib, which means they attached the small triangular sail to a cable at the front of the boat. Eli was nearly three and so scared that he wanted to sit right next to me. He was so close our life jackets rubbed every time I leaned forward. Lily was eight months old, but she couldn't yet sit up on her own. I put her Bumbo seat on the cockpit floor, where she could face me, and held it steady between my feet. After supervising the jib work, Erik reached out to remove the rope from the dock cleat.

"This boat is really nice," he said. "I feel a little guilty, like they're giving me keys to a Porsche when I barely got my driver's license."

"We passed the class," I said wrapping my arm around Eli, his face buried in my ribs.

"Let's do this," Erik said, pulling in the rope and shoving off the dock. "Alison, coil up the docking line. Karina, grab the mainsheet. Heading up."

"Heading up," Karina repeated, rope in hand and ready to trim the sails. Eli started to cry. Several poles marked the entrance channel. To inexperienced sailors like us, they posed a big challenge, because on our way out Erik was trying to captain and steer the boat while sorting out all the rigging. He got tangled in the lines.

"Karina, trim your line," Erik snapped.

"I can't! Alison has to release her line first," Karina snapped back.

"Alison!" Erik yelled.

"I'm trying. It's really tight," Alison said.

We nearly ran into the pylons on our way out of the marina toward the main channel. I rubbed Eli's chubby arm and looked for Lily's pacifier to prevent her from starting a sympathy howl. I could at least try to keep the noise down.

Instead of the predictable professionally piloted ferries and tankers of New York Harbor, we shared the river with deeply tanned weekend amateurs in motorboats, powerboats, speedboats, and jet skis. Everyone, except us, had an engine.

"Do you think they can tell we don't know what we're doing?" Erik asked over Eli's sobs.

"I'm sure they're thinking about themselves and their boats," I said.

Karina and Alison untied half a dozen square knots to release the mainsail. Karina dropped a sail tie. She lunged to catch it and slumped as it slipped into the water. Erik ran into one of the channel posts trying to recover it. Alison's hat blew into the water.

"I'm not going back for that," Erik said. Alison's usual rosebud mouth made a slim line across her pale face. She nodded, stoic under pressure. When Erik was flustered, the savvy kids went quiet so he could think.

"It'll be our offering to Poseidon today," I said extra cheerfully. Nobody laughed. My job was to boost morale. Whatever the task, relationships are my goal. I didn't care whether the kids liked sailing or not. I wanted them to like being a family. Karina slid her eyes to one side, flared her nostrils, and sighed. Alison maintained her straight-line mouth. SJ curled into the fetal position and rested her face on the bench seat. If Eli was scared in the marina, he was terrified in the channel. He started wailing. Screaming.

"What is wrong with Eli?" Erik snapped. Lily cried too, but it was only the frustrated, hungry cry that follows a long drive. It's hard to nurse a baby through two life vests. We rocked through the wake of the most recent speedboat crossing. We probably looked like we were bobbing a little aimlessly, but it felt like we were in the movie *The Perfect Storm*.

Jane clung to the deck repeating, "I want to go home. I want to go home. I want to go home." The boat leaned deeply to the right. That's called heeling. I didn't like it any better than Sarah Jane. I nearly touched the choppy surface of the water. Salt sprayed me in the face. I doubted Erik's claim that sailing would keep me out of deep water. Eli's scream modulated up. The deeply tanned people aboard the speedboat were pointing at us and laughing.

"They *are* looking at us," SJ glared. I laughed, hoping to keep the mood afloat. This was supposed to be a fun, memorable, family adventure. I hushed and snuggled the babies. I hollered praise to Karina and Alison as they winched or released ropes to control the triangular jib sail. I hugged Sarah Jane. Erik sat stiff on the bench across from me, his right hand on the tiller, brows furrowed behind mirrored sunglasses. We escaped the wake of the main thoroughfare. Beginners need lots of room to make mistakes.

Eli and Lily calmed. The boat stopped threatening to dump us out. With one arm still around Eli, I set my hand on Erik's knee for a moment. He lifted his sunglasses to see my smile better. He winked at me. We were going to be okay. I may not be a great sailor, but when it comes to our family, I know which way the wind is blowing.

Erik regained his bearing and apologized to the crew. We were all new. There is more to captaining than tillers and mainsails. The captain has to look ahead, think ahead, and decide ahead. On a boat, it's essential to have one person in command to prevent confusion and injury.

Erik ran ideas past us, asked for our opinions, and then told our young crew what to expect. With this preparation, Karina and Alison learned to identify conditions and anticipate commands. Each of them took a turn at the tiller. Erik issued clear orders in a calm voice. I figured out how to trim the sails while nursing a baby through two life jackets on a tippy boat. I'm still waiting for my tiara for that one.

We zigzagged our way up and down the river, jerky and making wide turns, but without crashing into anyone. We did not run into any more poles. We did not run aground. We kept all the Ortons inside the boat. Most importantly, we still loved each other.

"It wasn't as boring as I thought it would be," Sarah Jane pronounced as she tossed parking lot pebbles from the pier into the water.

"We just did that," I said, congratulating Erik with a hug.

"I wish that *had* been more boring. That was rough," Erik said, still glassy in the eyeballs. "Not sure I want to take the family again."

Better done than perfect.

ERIK

The summer ended and winter set in. I spent those down months trying to find ways to practice sailing within our budget. My best idea was sharing the cost. None of my coworkers or friends wanted to pony up for sailing lessons, but plenty of them wanted to go sailing. I found a place out in the Bronx called City Island that rented sailboats: $100 for half a day. As spring rolled around we drove out as a family to check it out. It was a mash-up of Cape Cod and, well, the Bronx. Most people in the city don't own a car, so with our minivan, I could be both chauffeur and captain to my friends. I put together a group of three or four people a couple times a month between spring and fall and charged my friends $20 to $25 per sail. My friends got a steal of a deal on sailing. I got to practice, have fun, and stay within budget. I

Better done than perfect.

managed one sail with just Karina and Alison. I'd become a much better captain since our first family sail, and they were on point as crew.

That's how I passed the first season after sailing lessons. The main bummer was we weren't sailing as a family. I hadn't officially said that was something I wanted to do, but I felt pulled in that direction.

The following winter, on a cold February day, I wrote in my journal, "Sail as a family." It was part of a far-fetched "blue-sky" exercise I did with a friend who wanted to practice her life coaching course. In my mind I imagined a whole year relaxing on a sailboat, probably in the Mediterranean. I'd grown up in Europe as a kid when my dad was stationed there with the military. The question my friend had asked was, "What would you do if you weren't afraid?" or "What would you do if money were no object?" I forget which. It was probably both. Later that month I had some downtime at work. I found myself googling "sailing as a family."

I'd spent a lot of time over the previous year taking stock of my life. When the show I produced folded, I felt professionally embarrassed, emotionally vulnerable, and financially scared. I wanted to disappear but I needed to provide for my family. I found an anonymous job where I didn't know anyone and no one could find me. My family knew what I did for work, but to others I kept quiet. I earned enough for us to live on.

When I was a teenager I delivered newspapers and looked up at the stars each morning. They were always there, timeless. Throughout history, people sailed the planet guided by stars that still move across the sky in the same rhythms and patterns. I wanted to connect with that.

Looking back on my anonymous, disposable job, I can see what sailing meant to me. I needed to feel safe. I needed to feel hope. I needed something to look forward to. Too many aspects of my former dreams depended on the decisions and choices of others. Sailing as a family for a year was something we could control. It wasn't dependent on the decisions and actions of others—or so I thought. It was a big enough dream to give me hope. It was something to look forward to. That was what I needed.

My google searching turned up some good results. In March, the Orton family—that's us—started following the Norton family website. They were a British couple with two young daughters and a son. They lived on a sailboat, *Miss Tippy*, and were planning to take two years to sail around the world. We caught up with their blog after they'd started their trip. They were still close to home. We quickly watched everything they'd already posted: videos of their boat being built, their farewell party, receiving a big box of nautical charts, getting their dental work done. The first leg of their journey was from England to Gibraltar. The son looked over the bow and said, "There's Africa!"

Emily turned to me and asked, "You can *see* Africa from Spain?" We were learning all kinds of things.

I checked every day for new posts and videos. Every time something went up, we gathered the kids around the TV to watch and read together. We found other families already out there on boats: *Bumfuzzle* in Mexico, *Totem* in Papua New Guinea, *Galactic* in the

South Pacific.[1] These weren't families with big budgets. They lived simple, lean lives. They valued time with their families over careers and over stuff. They parted ways with nine-to-five jobs, minivans, suburbs, and other mainstays of a culture Emily and I knew well. They figured out their actual physical needs were minimal and found ways to earn enough to provide those. They were learning about the world by being out in it. They knew their "prime earning years" were also the same precious years they would be healthy and active enough to be out there with their children. For them, waiting to retire at sixty-five made no sense, and retirement wasn't an all-or-nothing proposition. They talked about mini-retirements, mobile jobs, and unconventional solutions. Each family took a custom approach. Their lives were made by hand, from scratch, based on their own recipes. They knew what mattered most to them, and their life choices reflected that. They weren't saying everyone should do what they were doing, but what they were doing was working for them. They shared it openly, and Emily and I liked what we saw. Maybe we could do it too.

EMILY

Maybe our family was already a little unconventional before we considered living on a sailboat. While washing our clothes in the basement laundry room, a gentleman folding his towels told me about growing up in our neighborhood. In the 1960s, a family with five children and a stay-at-home mom was not rare in New York City. Forty years later, I knew only three other women like me. In that sense, my old-fashioned choices made me unusual. I didn't know *any* other

---

1. All three of these families are awesome and, as of this printing, are still living mobile lives. You can find them at bumfuzzle.com, sailingtotem.com, and thelifegalactic.blogspot.com. Tell them the Fezywigs sent you. :)

families of seven trying to pull it off in a two-bedroom, one-bathroom apartment.

After the birth of each new child, Erik's parents would say, "Now you'll have to move." They live in a typical suburban home with a driveway and a yard. We figured out how to be happy right where we were. I was grateful for my marriage, my growing family, my friends, and good health, but it was easy to want more. Once, I took Karina to Target. Before we left for the store, I asked her if she needed anything, and she said she didn't. After we arrived, she asked me to buy her an armful of items.

"I thought you didn't need anything," I said.

"I didn't know I needed it until I saw it," she replied.

"Me too," I said. I had moved to New York with the conventional mindset that having more stuff and more space to put it would make my life better. But my apartment wasn't getting any bigger.

Back at home, I had just stepped on a wooden alphabet block and wished for the hundredth time that we had a basement playroom when a thought occurred to me: *What could I subtract from my life to make it better?* Adding was difficult. Adding a closet organizer, a bookshelf, or even a new pair of shoes required money, which meant a budget strategy meeting. Subtracting could be simpler. I started by subtracting toys instead of adding storage containers. The kids and I assessed, sorted, and kept what mattered most. Our apartment felt bigger. I was learning to curate my space.

I wondered if I could curate my calendar, too. I wanted our whole family to spend more time together. Erik's night job didn't allow him to see Karina and Alison on weekdays. He left for work before they got home from school. He wasn't in a position to quit. We tried an unconventional route: homeschool. Subtracting public school was a thoughtful, protracted process that involved research, discussions with administrators, and prayer. I had a clear vision of why I would fail at homeschooling. Our home was tiny. Erik's day job was at home. I had three small children at home. I didn't think I had enough space, stamina, or patience to have everyone home all day. Through books, conversations, and an unshakable buoyant feeling, God showed me that we could thrive: we would be together as a family.

We departed from conventional wisdom again when it came to Lily's birth. With each child, my labor time was half that of the previous child. If the standard held, and my labor with Lily was half of what it had been with Eli, I'd have only one hour's warning before she was born. I wanted the professionals to come to me, so Lily was born in our apartment. That old-fashioned birth and bonding experience was calmer and more comfortable than my previous hospital births, and I had delivered at four different hospitals.

The road less traveled was less crowded. We traveled in September when the summer tourists returned to work. Erik asked for sabbaticals instead of promotions. When Brigham Young University produced one of his musicals for TV, we took eight weeks to be on set for the shoot. Erik earned enough to replace his lost wages. The TV show won some awards. They didn't change our lives and only came up if someone saw them on our living room bookshelf, but ditching work for a creative project was way more satisfying than getting promoted. Promotions meant less flexibility. We were not on the same schedule as everyone else, but we were on the same schedule as each other. The autonomy was delicious.

Erik proposed Family Day: one day a month with just members of our immediate family, usually without an agenda. I liked it, and we went for it. It was hard. We had to put Family Day on the calendar before anything else. We had to turn down birthday parties, baby showers, babysitting jobs, and sometimes even church meetings. But as we made it a priority, the kids looked forward to it. They would rather have their parents' full attention than earn a few dollars or go to a party. Our friends started to catch on too. They'd preface their invitations with, "If it's not Family Day . . . "

Erik and I regularly evaluated but couldn't always control what to add to or subtract from our lives. Shortly before our Toms River family sail, we discovered a tiny addition—the size of a microscopic chromosome. That one extra chromosome explained why Lily didn't hold up her head and why she slept so much. I'd spent six months researching and worrying, even though her pediatrician had assured me she was fine. I told God that if Lily needed something extra then I needed to be a more substantial person. I felt spiritual ballast enter my soul. Lily was diagnosed with Down syndrome. Erik wrapped me in his arms as we sat on the steps outside Columbia hospital.

"We can make T-shirts that say, 'We put the O in chromosome,'" he said. O for Orton. I smiled through my tears. I quit wasting time worrying and started learning. Along with Lily's diagnosis came speech therapy, occupational therapy, physical therapy, and play therapy. Over the next two years, while Erik created by day, earned by night, and occasionally chauffeured buddies to sail, the older kids and I fitted our lives to Lily's eight weekly therapy appointments.

We had taken two steps forward toward autonomy. This therapy schedule felt like one step back, but we were all happy to take it. Lily's siblings were her biggest cheerleaders. Karina read and sang to her. Alison tickled her. SJ bounced with her on an exercise ball. Eli loved to hold her. They all mimicked her squishy faces. We raved about every incremental success—not only Lily's success; each child's success. Obviously, Lily's path would be atypical. She helped me realize *each* of my children would progress at his or her own pace. I quit expecting them to achieve on a predetermined schedule. This meant less worry about timed milestones and more focus on interests and strengths.

With therapy, the kids and I stayed close to home on weekdays. In between, we bounced from co-op to playdates, playgrounds to the local library. Saturdays were our family days. Sometimes, Erik took a vanload of friends sailing. It wasn't much to ask. On Sundays, we all attended church. Erik and I volunteered in our local congregation. That was part of what made life abundant. Our days were full and our routine worked—for now.

ERIK

I was born in late March. March is technically still winter, but—inspired by the Nortons—I thought a great way to celebrate my birthday would be to go sailing. Emily thought I was crazy. Steve, who rented out boats in the Bronx, was always happy to make a buck, so he kept one twenty-three-foot boat in the water that time of year. Emily wanted to make my birthday dreams come true, so she joined me in City Island on the last day of winter, which I prefer to think of as the first day of spring.

There was another, equally "enthusiastic" guy who also wanted to sail. Steve insisted we take him with us on our date. Steve didn't want anyone sailing alone in the still-very-cold water. It wasn't the most romantic date, but we did get a good piece of intel. Our new sailing buddy told us about another sailing option that might be a better fit for our family.

The New York Sailing School was farther up the Long Island Sound. They offered classes but were mostly a club. Members could sail as often as they liked for a flat monthly fee: $160 a month between April and October.

I did some research and pitched it to Emily. "Since we've already done ASA 101, our entire family could join for roughly the cost of basic cable TV. Did I mention it's a flat monthly fee?"

"Really?" she said. "So anyone could give up cable and join a yacht club?!"

"Pretty much." We didn't have cable, but that was beside the point. "And you do realize, since we don't mind sailing when it's colder, we could *really* get our money's worth."

"You mean, since *you* don't mind," Emily said. I seemed to be the only one who liked bundling up in coats, scarves, gloves, and hats to go sailing. Weird.

We splurged on a full set of life vests and started taking the kids sailing nearly every week.

People assumed we were loaded. In reality, I had an average income that Emily stretched to fit a larger-than-average family in an expensive city. We weren't money-rich, but we figured time with our kids was its own kind of wealth. We did the math on the intangibles and decided it was worth it.

The boats at NYSS were called Sonars and were a lot like the boat at Toms River—about twenty-three feet long, a small jib sail at the bow, and a mainsail in the middle. The varnish on the wooden tiller was weather-worn and sometimes gave me splinters, but it did the job. Parallel benches lined the open cockpit. There was a small "below-deck" cubby that held a couple of sail bags, a bailing bucket, and some extra life vests. Jane would tuck in there with Eli and Lily to keep them out of the way while Emily and I rigged the sails with Karina and Alison.

Those day sails were a bit of a production: getting five kids ready with snacks, first aid kit, ginger candies, seven life vests, sunscreen, etc. Emily and I hiked to wherever we'd most recently found parking on the street and piled the kids into the van. Then there was getting from the van to the dock: stairs, vending machines, random cats wandering the docks, coils of rope, hoses. Any distraction could derail our train. Then we piled into the launch for a ride out to the boats in the mooring field. Lily had learned to walk, so the main goal was to keep her seated. After pulling up alongside, we transferred everybody and everything to a sailboat. Once we finished our sail, we repeated the whole thing in reverse.

Getting cable would have been easier.

We sailed with the NYSS for the next three years.

I came to love those sailing days. Cell service was lousy, so Emily and I didn't worry about getting calls or checking emails. The kids didn't have phones yet. There was nowhere else to go and nothing else to do except be together for three hours. We read books aloud. We played question games. We sang a lot of songs, preferably ones that involved nautical terms and stomping. We all became better sailors.

Everyone had a chance to steer the boat and trim the sails. I gave Alison control of the tiller and said, "Okay, you're driving." She sat up a little straighter and did her best not to smile too wide. We practiced man-overboard drills and heaving to.[2] One week we'd head up the sound. The next week we'd head down the sound. We tacked and jibbed, sailed wing-on-wing.[3] Karina became expert at snagging the mooring ball on our first pass. She got low on the forward deck as I eased us up to the mooring ball. Once within reach, she grabbed the mooring ball line and quickly looped it over the deck cleat. She smiled big when she got it right.

One bright, crisp afternoon, Lily knelt on the bench, facing out and dragging a bit of extra rope in the water. "I do ropes," she said, looking back at me and Emily with happy eyes. Our kids were growing up on the water.

EMILY

Over those three seasons of family sailing, Lily grew from a wobbly baby into a running toddler. The kids and I had spent hours walking her up and down our building stairwells with therapeutic weights

---

2. Heaving to: a maneuver in which the boat is stopped by setting the jib sail and tiller in opposition to each other. Nothing to do with vomit.
3. Tacking, jibing, wing-on-wing: not dance moves; rather, sailing maneuvers. Tacking = sailing with the wind in front of you. Jibing = sailing with the wind behind you. Wing-on-wing = sailing with the wind *directly* behind you.

Velcroed around her ankles. We all took pleasure in her progress. She was into everything, as any toddler would be, but the messes didn't bother me as much. When we took Lily into new environments, like a weekend at Grandma Orton's, I noticed her natural curiosity catapulted learning. Her motor skills and language skills

Our kids were growing up on the water.

jumped. The kids and I were still tethered to our same, boring apartment thirty-two times per month for therapy. I wondered if Lily was getting too much therapy and if it was actually holding her back. The rhythm of the routine wore thin. I persuaded her team to run a trial month cutting back to twenty-five percent of her normal therapy so we could take more field trips. Afterward, Lily's therapists agreed she was continuing to progress at the same rate or better. All of the kids were thrilled.

After a few more months of prayerful consideration, Erik and I decided Lily would quit therapy altogether. That is not the answer for everyone, but we were able to provide a language-rich environment where Lily got constant feedback and encouragement from her siblings and me. The world of special education puts a lot of emphasis on kids with special needs being allowed to progress in the "least restrictive environment," and we totally agreed. When I discovered that what was best for our whole family was also best for Lily, I happily threw off the restrictions of therapy. We went to the Jersey Shore for the day. Lily built sandcastles—well, she mostly ate sand, but it was a tactile experience. We saw dolphins. We met new people. We had our life back.

The older kids were working on their homeschool assignments one morning when Erik leaned against the wall next to me and said, "I think the seven of us on a boat would be enough universe to keep me engaged for the rest of my life."

"Really?" I asked. "You wouldn't get bored with just us?"

"I don't think so."

"And you'd want to live on a boat?" I asked.

"We'd be together," Erik said. "I would be with you and the kids full-time. We could explore the world together. There would be no packing and unpacking. We wouldn't have to leave home, because we'd take our home wherever we went." Erik strummed all of my major heartstrings at once: family, home, and firsthand experiences. I was happy with my life. Even without sailing, having a family is an epic adventure—a long-term, high stakes proposition with daily surprises and unpredictable outcomes. If I stood our children in a row from youngest to oldest, each was a head taller than the last. But I could see where this was going, and it was going too fast.

At Karina's recommendation, I read *A Million Miles in a Thousand Years: How I Learned to Live a Better Story*. The author, Donald Miller, says the same elements that make a great story—dreams, struggle, risk—also make a great life. If I were watching a movie of my life and I were the hero, what would I want myself to do? I wanted to create memories that would strengthen and sustain us individually and as a family. I wanted to live a more dynamic story. I wanted to pursue a dream so big there was room for my whole family. I wanted us to deliberately disrupt our family, not just to do more or see more, but to *become* more.

I wrapped one arm around Erik's waist and rested my head on his chest. Lily pressed the buttons on her musical pop-up toy. Eli rolled a red car across the floor. Karina and Alison read on the couch while Jane drew at the table. I liked this universe of seven.

"When should we go?" I asked.

"Sometime before Karina leaves for college," he said. She was fourteen. We had four years.

"I guess we'd better get cracking."

Erik didn't waste any time. Driving home from another day of family sailing, he said, "We should take some more ASA classes. 103 and 104. Then we can take out bigger boats. Maybe even overnight." He'd looked into this.

"Do they have home study?" I asked. "Or daytime classes?" Erik still worked nights.

"No. You can't learn that stuff home study," he said. Clearly, I knew nothing about it. "But we could finish both classes in a week if we take them in the Caribbean."

My usual questions sprang up: time, money, and childcare.

I said, "That's a lot to pack into one week."

CHAPTER 2

WHAT COULD GO RIGHT?

ROAD TOWN, TORTOLA, BRITISH VIRGIN ISLANDS

3 Years, 6 Months before *Fezywig*

ERIK

"I packed too much," Emily said, unzipping her duffle. At least we avoided the most obvious boat newbie mistake: hard-shell luggage. Our duffles tucked nicely under the V-berth.[4] My parents agreed to watch our kids, so Emily and I were now in the British Virgin Islands (BVI) . . . in July. My secret desire was to sail as a family in the Mediterranean, but turns out the Caribbean is a lot closer and more affordable, especially—we would learn—during hurricane season. We were nervous about the cost, about $1,250 per person plus airfare, but Emily and I were also both a little nervous about spending the whole week on a boat with strangers. But, if we were actually going to sail as a family, we had to take some risks.

The other students turned out to be a lovely couple from New

---

4. V-berth: a bed and/or cabin at the forepeak of a boat.

Jersey. Our instructor, Matt, was the best. He had red hair and wore the biggest broad-brimmed hat I'd ever seen short of a sombrero. I immediately vowed to someday own a hat like that. Everyone on the dock called him Big Red. He put Emily and me at ease right off the bat. We would all spend the next six days sailing the BVI on *Barnaby*, a forty-six-foot monohull. After some book work on shore and making sure everything was properly stowed in its precise location, we tossed off the lines. Matt asked for a volunteer to take the helm. I raised my hand. We pulled out of our slip and headed for Peter Island.

Matt was all calm positivity. You could, hypothetically speaking, be pulling a forty-six-foot monohull out of a slip for the first time. You could, ostensibly, be about to slam this forty-six-foot sailboat into the dock or another boat, and he'd say, "Why don't you just turn the wheel a bit that way to make sure we don't bump into anything?" He was my kind of teacher.

EMILY

The first night, Matt, Erik, and the other couple pulled on their fins and slid into the water—in the dark—at night—when you couldn't see anything. They all went on about how bathtub-warm the water was. Miniscule bioluminescent creatures sparkled after every kick or stroke, making this terrifying night swim in thirty feet of opaque water look like a Disney cartoon romance. I didn't care what anybody thought of me. Well, I did care, but I was more scared than embarrassed. I stayed on the boat.

Every day started with a snorkel as well. I was learning to sail so I wouldn't have to be *in* the deep water. By daylight, I was more embarrassed than scared. I didn't want to be the wimp of the group. I pulled on fins and hopped in. Everyone else was way ahead of me. I was alone. I saw the underside of the boat. I saw the thick metal chain running straight to the anchor. There was plenty of room for a pod of dolphins or a frenzy of sharks to sneak up behind me. I looked straight ahead at the island and kicked as fast as I could. In my head, I sang a children's song over and over again. I slowed my breathing. A giant turtle glided past me. I stopped singing. I followed it with my eyes until it was out of view. I continued to the rim of the undeveloped island. Fish were everywhere, yellow ones the size of my hand, tiny purple ones, so many vibrant colors. I followed a multicolored fish with a friendly turquoise face. Lacy plants I'd never seen before fanned out, waving in the current. I was on a different planet. I'd seen nature movies, but to experience it myself was a revelation. I'd never realized this world was here on the other side of the water's surface. Will death be like that? Passing through some permeable surface, suddenly able to see strange and amazing things that immediately engage my attention and distract me from thoughts of land, safety, and my former life?

"Ready to head back?" Erik asked when we both came up for air.

"Not really," I said. "Snorkeling is my new favorite thing." What other favorites were hiding inside my fears?

The week felt long because everything was new. Learning slows time. Hurricane season is hot, muggy, and sometimes rainy. When it was clear, Matt kept us at the helm practicing maneuvers. When it was inclement, he kept us in our textbooks. Matt gently drilled us on navigation techniques, chart reading, sail trimming, emergency procedures, propane safety, plumbing procedures, diesel engine maintenance, and countless other topics I'd never imagined had anything to do with sailing. Erik regularly volunteered to go first. I preferred to watch all of the other students before trying myself. Sometimes I volunteered to go second to impress Erik.

I was uncomfortable piloting a man overboard drill or heaving to even though I knew I would have to do that if Erik were ever thrown overboard on our hypothetical boat. The things I liked were going barefoot, working with the ropes, and steering toward a visible destination. *Barnaby* had a big round helm that made sense, like a giant car steering wheel. If I wanted to go right, I would turn the wheel to the right. Easy.

The Baths are probably one of the biggest tourist attractions in the British Virgin Islands. Cruise ships drop hundreds of passengers on the beaches daily. We arrived early to compete for a mooring ball. The travel magazines showed a secluded pool of water surrounded by smooth boulders illuminated by a shaft of sunlight dancing off the bronze shoulders of some gorgeous couple. I loved the Baths. The whole place is more playground than romantic hideaway. It's like a family reunion of granite boulders, half on land and half in the water. Erik and I saw the quintessential romantic spot and the line of tourists waiting to take their pictures in that shaft of light. A little boy in a lime-green lifejacket was holding his mom's hand. He had Down syndrome. I introduced myself. "Sure, we take precautions to keep him safe, but so far there hasn't been anything he can't do," his mom said. There was nothing he couldn't do, just like Lily.

We took our romantic picture and took off exploring. We used some fixed ropes and a few wooden steps, but mostly we scrambled over boulders and shuffled through hot sand. I set down my load of responsibilities and worries for a couple of hours to play in the waves with Erik. I couldn't remember the last time I had felt such unselfconscious curiosity.

"The kids would love it here," I said.

"We should bring them someday," Erik said. It didn't seem realistic—about as likely as our buy-a-boat plan. Learning to sail, that was a lot easier than purchasing a livable vessel. We were reaching for the moon and catching the stars.

By the end of the muggy week, which felt like a month, I sat next to Erik in the air-conditioned testing room. I got an A on my exam. Surprise! As expected, Erik did too. We both certified as bareboat charter captains.

UPPER MANHATTAN, NEW YORK

ERIK

Our table is square. One side is normally pushed against the wall to leave more space in the room, but to fit everyone at mealtimes, we pull it out and sit on all four sides. This is generally where we hash things out as a family. This was where Emily and I tossed around the idea of buying a Chilean island (asking price $8 million as I recall) and turning it into an eco-resort. I sent the agent a query for more info but never heard back. This was where we bandied about the idea of affixing solar panels to our minivan and driving to Patagonia (that was Emily's idea). I contacted a Chinese solar company about sponsorship but never heard back. This was where we discussed going to live with traveling Romani in Wales to make a documentary. That was a close one. We got passports for the kids and I'd arranged a leave of absence from work. But then our contact in Wales got in a bad car accident and our financial sponsor backed out.

There was no shortage of out-there ideas discussed around the Orton table. These big ideas and close shaves sometimes sent our kids on emotional roller coasters. They imagined leaving friends and familiarity behind. Karina got wise and told the younger kids, "Don't get all worked up. Mom and Dad just like to dream."

We continued to follow the Nortons, *Bumfuzzle*, *Totem*, *Galactic*, and several others.

Miss Tippy (the Nortons) had crossed the Atlantic when their dad accidentally cut his head deeply when some rigging broke loose. The twelve-year-old son took the helm and steered fifty miles as they made an unplanned stop in Puerto Rico. Mom was a nurse. She bandaged up Dad and stayed on the radio with the coast guard. The two daughters kept their dad company so he wouldn't go unconscious. Those kids grew up a lot that day.

Scary, painful experiences teach us. Nobody wants them to happen, but they do. In Puerto Rico the Norton children were comforted with pizza, ice cream, and sleep, but nobody could take away the growth. They knew things about life and its fragility. They knew how precious a family is. They'd faced a crisis with a clear priority. They had glimpsed a world where the only thing that mattered was a child's love for Dad and Mom and their love for their child. The whole family had some intangible, special thing after that. I wanted that thing for our family.

Emily and I started yet another breakfast-table conversation. Karina looked up from her pancakes and asked, "Do you have the guts to do it?" She had my attention. "I hear a lot of talk, but I don't see any action."

I took this personally. Karina had taken sailing lessons with us. She and all her siblings had sailed with us in the Long Island Sound. Emily and I had just gotten back from our sailing class in the Caribbean. We were taking action. I was also proud of Karina. She'd learned that doing what you say you're going to do matters. She continued, "You just keep talking about it. Why don't you just do it?"

Why didn't we? What was stopping us? Our credibility and integrity were on the line. We knew our kids were watching us.

In *How to Stop Worrying and Start Living*, Dale Carnegie asks, "What's the worst that could happen?" Then he asks, "If that happened, how would you deal with it?" Finally, he asks, "How likely is that to happen?" We figured the worst that could happen would be death, with financial ruin and/or embarrassment in close second. They seemed pretty unlikely, but if they happened, we felt we could handle them. And it would be worth the risk. That's when we came up with a question of our own: What could go right?

This question stumped me. The prospects were endless, but I

hardly spent any time contemplating them. I was good at bracing for failure, but not so good at allowing for success. In a best-case scenario, we would sail safely, enjoy our time, see some beautiful places, make some wonderful memories, and come home happy. I had a limited imagination. Was that the best I could do?

I think it's important to manage risk, but to not acknowledge the vast array of positive outcomes was to ignore half the reality of the situation. Positive possibilities are unlimited. In taking a risk, I want to acknowledge the worst-case scenarios, but I couldn't stop there. What were the potential best-case scenarios that I'd give up if I didn't go for it? What was the risk of *not* going? Looking at the full picture includes answering that question: What could go right?

EMILY

Two Years before *Fezywig*

"Can I show you some boats I've been looking at?" Erik asked.

"Sure, I'll take a look," I said. I sat next to Erik at his desk and he opened a world of boats for sale.

"I like that one with the Jet Skis loaded on the back," I said.

"I don't know," Erik smiled. "The one with the helipad looks pretty good to me. I'm a simple man. I just need one plain vanilla yacht and a basic helicopter."

After that, I got emails with the subject line "Boat of the Day." That was a misnomer. Sometimes there were three or four boats a day from exotic locations all over the world. Erik believed in *gathering information*. "It never hurts to ask," he would say. I knew gathering information usually led to opinions and decisions. Eventually, the Boat of the Day prices dropped below the millions and high six figures into a price range that felt more doable.

"What would you think about going to see a couple of boats for sale on our anniversary? We've never done that before," Erik asked. We have a tradition of celebrating our anniversary by doing something new. Being beginners makes us feel young and unified. We both feel a little uncomfortable, but we're in it together. This would be our sixteenth anniversary.

"In winter?" Rhetorical question. "Where are they?" I asked.

"One is in Connecticut and one is in Rhode Island."

"What about the kids?"

"They can come with us. It will be romantic," Erik winked.

As it turned out, boat shopping was like dating. It was good that all of the kids came along, because we needed a boat to match our whole family. In Connecticut, we met the broker in his office next to the marina. He was tall and slim, wearing pressed slacks and a tucked-in polo. He matched his office. It was the kind of place with wainscoting, brass desk lamps, and cut-glass candy dishes. The children helped themselves to toffee and sat bouncing on the tightly upholstered seating. Erik and I reviewed the boat specs in a glossy folder. The broker guided our little parade across the parking lot. It was the off-season, so boats were shrink-wrapped in thick white plastic and stacked in a multi-level storage facility. There were hundreds of boats. We only needed one.

The boat we had come to see was lifted onto blocks and steadied on stilts. The outside was covered in white shrink wrap, but we climbed a ladder to get a look inside. We had more children than the broker had eyeballs, so he kept turning to see where they were and what they were doing. Alison tested the helm. Eli and Lily wandered into the cabins. SJ and Karina sat on the cushions. It was an older boat, rough around the edges, but it was a boat. It was for sale. We were looking at it. We didn't know the process for buying a boat, but Erik figured the first step was to look at one. So, that's where we started. Erik and I thanked the broker for his time and for the glossy folder.

"What did you like about that boat?" I asked the kids at Subway twenty minutes later. They were deep into their sandwiches.

"I liked climbing the ladder," SJ said.

"It would be fun to have a boat like that," Ali said.

"Are we going to see another boat?" Karina asked. It had already been a long morning for the kids. Outside of the few minutes unnerving the broker, it had been a lot of boring sitting around.

"There is one more I'd like to see," Erik said. "But it's in Rhode Island. So it's far. It will be dark when we get there, and this boat is in the water, so it will be really cold. And way past bedtime when we get home. Are we up for that?" It wasn't much of a sales job, but I think we all appreciated the honesty. With a majority consensus, we went for it.

We found the marina and realized why the owner was willing to meet us on a holiday with short notice; he lived aboard. He was like Santa Claus on a sailboat. He had the white hair, beard, and bowl full of jelly. He welcomed us aboard and told the kids to explore wherever they wanted. That took my anxiety way down and gave this boat about a million points in my book. Then he invited us downstairs. It was so warm and cozy we felt like we'd been sledding all day and come home for a bowl of chili. "Santa" had heaters placed throughout the boat. Being warm matters to me. A lot.

Everything was in order, but nothing was too precious. The interior was flanked by dozens of drawers. Few things make a big family happy in a tiny home like lots of organized storage.

"What kind of wood is this?" I asked opening and closing various drawers.

"Ironwood," Santa said. That sounded sturdy and safe.

"What did you think?" I asked Erik as we buckled up for our late drive home.

"It needs some work. I took some pictures and I'll take some notes, but I liked it. It felt good," he said.

"I liked it too," I said. "I think we could make it work even though it only has two cabins. For sixty-five grand I'd be willing to put down the salon table at night and make up a bed for two kids there." We had a winner. This was happening fast. I was excited. Erik put in an offer.

"It's not you. It's the boat." The news from the loan officer broke our hearts. We knew we didn't have enough to buy a floating home outright, but we could make a down payment. We had excellent credit, so we assumed we'd be able to get a loan. But this boat, our boat, was too old to finance. Apparently, banks don't finance old, custom boats. They finance new, mass-produced boats with predictable resale values and a strong collateral position. They didn't care about our dream. We had the consolation that doing something for the first time makes it easier to do a second time. Back to the drawing board.

ERIK

1 Year before *Fezywig*

Emily and I didn't even know if the kids would be able to adjust to life on a boat. It seemed like a good idea to try before committing. That year the stars aligned. The winter holidays fell perfectly between two weekends. I used only three personal days to get eleven days off. Our big idea: drive to the Florida Keys and charter a boat. That was even cheaper than flying to the Caribbean. Of course, I haggled and nickel-and-dimed the charter company for weeks over the phone. I got them down to about $1,500 for three days.

We spent Christmas Day with my parents in Virginia. Then we drove ten hours to Georgia and spent that night with friends. The next morning, we were off. After three days of driving, we arrived in the Keys and tossed our duffle bags aboard our charter boat. We weren't allowed to sail after dark, so Emily and Karina raced to the grocery store and returned with dozens of shopping bags that we simply piled on the counters in the galley. We would unpack later. We were supposed to leave the slip by 2:00 p.m. to allow enough time to sale to our anchorage. It was 2:30 p.m.

I pulled out, turned to port, and then suddenly jerked back to starboard. I'd forgotten to release one of the docking lines. Rushing wasn't helping. We sorted that out without running into anything or anyone else and were off.

We weaved our way out of the marina and through the channel out to sea. We were in the Atlantic Ocean aboard a forty-two-foot Hunter monohull motoring north at six knots. We were all onboard and sailing as a family. Victory.

The kids were giddy. Eli opened and closed cupboards as quickly as he could find them and then ran above deck to open and close hatches. Lily tucked into a bookshelf, pretending it was her bed, and then jumped out and ran to find another bookshelf. From a seat in the corner of the cockpit, Jane surveyed the boat with the eye of a monarch, then scurried off to scout the rigging. Karina practiced rocking the oven that swung on a gimbal. Alison inspected the dinghy on deck, trying to figure out how to lower it into the water. Emily stowed provisions below deck in the galley.

"I think they like it," she called up.

"Yeah," was all I could manage. I was still getting acclimated. We had picked an anchorage twenty-two miles up the chain called Newfound Harbor. I did my best to read all the instruments and indicators. None of the boats we'd sailed in the Long Island Sound had had any electronics, and our BVI trip hadn't been long enough for me to get it all in my bones. I tried some speed and distance calculations in my head. We had the sails up and the engine was running, but we weren't making fast enough time to beat the sun. The moon rose over the horizon, directly in front of me, with the sunset directly behind. I was caught between trying to enjoy this celestial moment and gunning it so we weren't anchoring in the dark.

Eli screamed. He'd gotten an Indiana Jones-style fedora from my parents for Christmas. In all his excitement and jumping, the wind had blown it off his head and overboard. Giant tears rolled down his little round cheeks. I was alone in the cockpit with the sails up. I needed a hand.

"Hat overboard!" I called out into the wind. The family went into recovery mode. We'd practiced this dozens of times in daysailers. I assigned Eli and Alison as spotters. Their job was to continuously point at the hat so I would know where to steer. In the BVI, Matt had taught us to put the most worried person in charge of pointing. In this case, Eli. We would sail four or five boat lengths on our current course, do a one-eighty, sail a figure-eight course, and come up on the windward side of the hat. We would extend a boat hook to the overboard sailor— or in this case, hat—and bring it back aboard. We performed the maneuver correctly. SJ kept Lily safely out of the way while Emily and Karina looked for the boat hook, but there was no boat hook aboard. We drifted past the hat and watched it fade behind us.

"We're coming around again," I yelled over the wind.

I pointed the boat downwind and repeated the figure eight, but this time with a tool in hand. Eli's other Christmas gift was a Nerf sword. As we came alongside the hat, Karina reached down, snagged it with the hilt of the sword, and brought it safely aboard. Eli wiped the tears from his eyes and clutched the hat close. Despite all we did not know, we now knew we could recover a brown felt hat in the ocean with a Nerf sword. That was something.

I wasn't eager to navigate into a new harbor in the dark, let alone drop and set anchor. I was still getting used to the GPS. In the BVI our destinations had been hilly islands clearly visible in the distance. Matt knew the water like a local. Here we were new to town and on our own. The Keys were incredibly flat and deceptively shallow. To sail toward land—despite there being wide-open fields of water—it was crucial to find and navigate up grooves on the ocean floor. And beware running aground. The reason the Keys have not been eroded away is because they are essentially stone. The hard coral floor is not friendly to fiberglass hulls.

The sun was below the horizon and the moon continued rising beautifully. Daylight slipped away as we reached the mouth of the channel into Newfound Harbor. From the helm, I fixed my eyes outward, looking for markers and reflectors. Karina and Alison did the same at the bow. We worked our way slowly and gently up the channel and watched as the depth rose to just under our keel. It was now dark.

We found, essentially, a shoulder on the road, pulled off, and anchored. I killed the engine and took a deep breath.

During the sail, Emily prepared macaroni and cheese with hot dogs. Tomorrow there would be bacon. Her idea was that with enough comfort food, the kids would love living on a boat. I felt comforted.

We raised anchor the next morning and headed for a new destination. Halfway out the channel, we realized we were perfectly happy in Newfound Harbor. We didn't have to move for the sake of moving. We could stay and enjoy. We turned around, wound our way farther up into the channel, and tucked ourselves into a nice little cove. Our boat stood at anchor in turquoise water behind two flat islands, each no more than 200 or 300 feet long, with a shallowly submerged bed of bleached coral connecting them. We'd have to explore those. Eli walked around the deck taking in the scene. "I like wearing my pajamas outside," he said. City kids don't get to do that a lot.

We spent the rest of our charter there. Alison and I lowered the dinghy into the water and attached the outboard motor. She and Karina took turns driving laps around the boat as their younger siblings waved enviously from the deck; heady stuff for kids without driver's licenses. We ferried ourselves to the smaller of the two spits of sand—Picnic Island—a few hundred yards away. I dropped off Alison and Jane near a cluster of mangrove trees. They scampered to the top branches and waved with smiling eyes back to Emily and Karina on the big boat. I took Eli ashore and we found a swing set. This was clearly a party

We didn't have to move for the sake of moving. We could stay and enjoy.

spot. I went back, picked up Emily, Karina, and Lily, and brought them ashore. I put Lily in a tire swing, hung out on the beach, and generally chilled until the sun set. We learned one of the best parts of sailing was staying at anchor. This sailing as a family thing was going to be easy. I liked relaxing.

The next day, when it was time to go, Sarah Jane asked, "If we go live on a boat, will I still be able to go to go to girls' camp?" That was really thinking ahead. Every year our girls went upstate to one week of camp sponsored by our church. It was a big deal for them. Twelve years old was the minimum age to attend. Jane was then ten. She had vision. Karina and Alison looked at Emily and me for an answer. Emily looked at me with questioning eyebrows.

"*If* we ever live on a boat, I'm sure we can figure it out," I said as I winked at Emily. We pulled anchor and headed to the marina.

We could do this.

CHAPTER 3

BOAT OF THE DAY

UPPER MANHATTAN, NEW YORK

11 Months before *Fezywig*

ERIK

I continued to send Boat of the Day listings to Emily. In my downtime at work I browsed boats online, trying to figure out what all the listing details meant. I learned all kinds of new terms like *bimini* (which has no relation to *bikini*), *windlass* (which has more to do with raising anchors than Irish ladies), and *bow thruster* (which I thought sounded rather saucy). I'd do my research and email Emily a link to the listing with some commentary. Sometimes I commented about the boat itself, sometimes the location (I was looking all over the world), and sometimes the price and how I thought we could afford a particular boat.

The next Boat of the Day we toured was built by a major manufacturer within the past ten years. It was much more expensive than the Santa boat. I wasn't sure how we could afford it, but I didn't let that stop us from looking. I knew if we stared at the problem long enough, we'd figure out a way. I believe a lot of good can come from staring at a problem for a long time.

At work, I shared a big double desk with Mark. He always said, "Life is not a dress rehearsal." He wasn't talking about me or my Boat of the Day emails, but it encouraged me. If my life was a movie and I was the hero, the cameras were rolling. I had no time to waste. I started building spreadsheets, with everything from timelines to budgets to routes. I like to have all the details in front of me. Then I tweak my spreadsheets. Mark—without looking over at me—would ask, "What kind of bomb are you building?" I revised and refined and reviewed and revised and refined. I was homing in on what would work best for our family and our budget. But we still had a major decision to make: monohull or catamaran?

Maybe that should say: monohull *vs.* catamaran. Monohulls are traditional sailboats, with a single hull. Catamarans have two hulls connected by a deck and originate largely from France, so naturally they're suspect. If you are not a boater, I warn you: this is a serious debate, not to be taken lightly, just like the French. We engaged in the debate, and our house was divided. Emily wanted a monohull. She liked the centralized galley like we'd had in the Florida Keys and the BVI. From there she could keep an eye and ear on everyone at once. She was particularly nervous about safety for Lily.

I argued that a catamaran would be more comfortable for living and was equally safe. It wouldn't bob side to side while at anchor. Catamarans were faster, so we could outrun storms. They had a shallower draft, making more anchorages accessible. They had the redundancy of a second engine as a safety feature. It was nearly impossible to tip a catamaran. It would be a lot easier to sell when we were finished using it.

"Before we make a final decision, let's try out a catamaran," I said.

"You want to take the kids back to Florida?" Emily asked.

"No, let's go back to the BVI. We'll invite some friends and share the cost," I said.

Miraculously, three other couples agreed to join us. Emily and I decided not to renew our membership at NYSS so we could funnel that money into the BVI trip. I returned to the BVI wearing my own broad-brimmed straw hat, just like our instructor, Matt. I was getting serious.

It was nice to be somewhere familiar. Going somewhere new can be exhausting. It starts out invigorating but requires a lot of energy to take in so much newness. No wonder babies sleep so much. I had plenty of newness to worry about. This was my first time captaining a big boat in big water. I was pushing myself. Part of me wanted to take a nap.

We motored out of the marina, got the sails up, and pounded our way across the Drake Channel, the main basin of water between the islands. On the other side was the wreck of the RMS Rhone. One of the couples wanted to dive on the wreck. By the time we got there and tied up to a mooring ball, I was dog sick. Almost all of us got seasick—even on a catamaran, much to my chagrin—but we tried to look happy and reminded ourselves we'd paid for this.

That night we anchored in the flat cove of Peter Island. Most of us, including myself, dinghied to shore, lay on our backs on the beach, and discussed the causes of and cures for seasickness while letting our inner ears reestablish equilibrium. I was responsible for everyone having a good time, and we were off to a rocky start.

By the third morning, we all felt much better. We were exploring the Dog Islands and deciding whether to visit Anegada. Morale was high. I felt good as a captain. Because Anegada is extremely flat, it sits below the horizon until you are almost on it. I'd never sailed toward something I couldn't see, and I liked the idea of that challenge. But as with all things in life, choosing to go meant we wouldn't have time to visit other places that also looked interesting. There is always a trade-off. We sailed in the direction of Anegada with the caveat that we might detour to Virgin Gorda Sound.

It was a beautiful beam reach.[5] The trade winds came in from the east and the boat moved smoothly north toward the horizon. With perfect weather and conditions, I invited everyone to take a turn at the helm. They were tentative at first, so I stood alongside while they got the feel of things. It didn't take long before they were comfortable. I took a break and walked around the boat while each couple took a turn steering. There was something satisfying about giving up control.

Gradually little spikes appeared on the horizon. Those quickly turned into palm trees, and eventually we could see the island itself. There was almost nothing to do on Anegada except get a lobster dinner and take a cab to the beaches on the far end of the island. We'd had a nice sail but decided we'd rather spend our time in Gorda Sound. I'd done what I wanted to do. I'd sailed toward something unseen and watched it come into view. I knew I could sail us into port. I was satisfied. We turned the boat east.

People tell you all kinds of things. They tell you what's out in the world. They tell you how things are. Yet, you never know for yourself unless you venture out. I believed Matt when he told me Anegada was there. I even had a map that showed it. But heading out there on my own, pushing across the curve of the earth enough to see something that was previously out of reach, was important to me. If I could do that, what else could I do? What else could I discover? Something was starting to emerge for me. I was learning to trust myself more.

We flew home and picked up our five patient children from my parents, who had graciously cared for them.

"So . . . catamaran or a monohull?" Karina asked.

"I really liked the catamaran," I said.

---

5. Beam reach: point of sail where the wind comes from the side of the boat. Used in a sentence: If I died and went to sailor heaven, I'd sail all day on a beam reach.

"I still prefer a monohull, but maybe after you kids move out," Emily said. "You'll like the trampoline on a cat."

"There's a trampoline?" Jane beamed. She and Eli looked at each other with oval mouths.

"Not that kind of trampoline," I tried to clarify.

"And there is less heeling[6] on a cat," Emily tried to finish, but Jane, Eli, and Lily were jumping up and down as though they were already on a trampoline.

When we got back to New York City, Emily and I taped a picture of a catamaran to the inside of our bedroom door. We set our sights on something over the horizon.

A couple months later a friend of Emily's family called. He was looking for crew to help sail a big monohull from the Chesapeake Bay to Maine. They wanted to know if I'd be interested. I had already been to the Keys in January and the BVI in March. Now I wanted to take a week in August to sail to Maine. My workmates were getting jealous, and my supervisors were getting suspicious.

"I'm not sure I should take time off right now," I said to Emily. "We're trying to save money for our own family trip."

"True, but this could be a chance to get some experience sailing overnight," she said. "Neither of us has ever done that before." She was talking me into this. It would be a chance to sail overnight, offshore, and for multiple days at a stretch. She continued, "At least *one* of us should have experience with that, because we're going to have to do it when we go as a family."

"I *would* rather try it out on someone else's boat first," I said. I decided to take one for the team. Of course I wanted to go, but it would be a week on a new boat, in new circumstances, with new people. I'd need a nap.

---

6. Heeling: when a boat tips sideways because of wind or waves. Used in a sentence: "When I do yoga while sailing, I like to call it spiritual heeling."

Jim owned the boat with his son-in-law, Tom. They assembled their crew by midday. We motored out of the harbor and turned north up the bay. The sun set as we settled into a watch schedule. Night watches were important—I learned—because despite being in open water, lots could go wrong. Responsibilities include tracking other ships, keeping an eye on the weather, and monitoring the navigation. Safety is strict. The worst time to fall overboard is in the dark. Life jackets and jacklines are imperative.[7] Usually night watches were mellow, but when they went bad, you had to be on point. We would teach this to our kids later, but for now I was on with Jim for a couple hours and we had a chance to talk.

"Night sailing is the best," Jim said in his gentle South Carolina accent. "It's a perfect time to think." We talked about sailing and family and money and the world. Then I stepped in a turd.

"We're shopping around for a catamaran," I said.

Jim was nice about it, but he explained all the reasons catamarans were a bad idea and went on to extol the virtues of the best kind of boat money can buy: monohulls. I should have known better. We were in not just a monohull, but a sixty-five-foot monohull. We moved on to other topics and agreed to remain friends.

Three days later we pulled into Rockland Harbor, Maine. I'd sailed farther offshore than ever before in my life. I'd stood watch each night. We'd navigated two canals, thick fog, and a thousand lobster pots as we closed in on the Maine coast. I'd made some terrific friends. I was grateful for everything about the trip.

My work supervisors had good reason to be suspicious.

---

7. Jackline: a cord or strap that runs the length of the boat from bow to stern. Usually there is one jackline along each side of the boat. A crew member wears a chest harness with a tether that clips to the jackline. If the crew member accidentally falls overboard, he or she will still be connected. I think they're named after a guy named Jack who used to fall overboard a lot.

EMILY

6 Months before *Fezywig*

"Let's talk about money," Jane imitated Erik's bass voice at the breakfast table. Everyone smiled. Erik was in problem-solving mode. We had everything we needed to live on a boat—except a boat. We wanted a catamaran. We couldn't afford a catamaran. Money was the solution, but how to get the money was a puzzle. Erik approached it by separating all of the pieces and putting them in order.

"I know this is going to sound counterintuitive," he said. "Just hear me out." He's really good at preparing me to hear his big ideas. I knew he'd been staring at this problem for weeks. I overrode my automatic defenses and listened.

"I think we should buy a newer catamaran," he said.

"That's going to be a lot more expensive," I said. "How could we afford that?"

"Here is my reasoning," he said. I reminded myself we were only talking. "If we buy a more expensive, relatively current production-line catamaran, we could finance it, which would free up cash for our living expenses," he said.

"We can't get a loan on an older, cheaper boat, so we have to buy a more expensive boat so we can get a loan?" I tried to follow. The kids cleared the table as an excuse to exit this boring topic.

"Right. Banks only finance a boat if they can predict the resale value. So a newer, standard model makes more sense." He continued, "It would also improve our chances of selling the boat when we're done. The next buyer would also be able to get a loan. That's not going to happen if we're looking at boats made more than ten or fifteen years ago."

"Okay. That is weird, but it makes sense," I said.

"And . . ." he paused and smiled, "a newer model won't need as much maintenance, which will be safer for our family given our inexperience in boat maintenance." I agreed with his plan. The puzzle was coming together. We focused our search on ten-year-old catamarans and kept thinking about how to pay for one.

Financing a boat requires twenty percent down, about the same as buying a home. This would be the first home we'd ever purchased. Erik sent listings of the most reasonably priced catamarans he could find, and the down payments were still beyond our reach. There was a price tag between us and our dream, so we got creative.

"What if we split the cost between four families? We could each sail for one year and then sell the boat," Erik said. That didn't work out.

"What if we posted a swap on the Women Who Sail Facebook page?" I suggested. "We could trade one year in our New York City apartment for one year on someone's boat." We got some nibbles, but no bites.

"Maybe we could get a sponsorship from one of those outdoor companies," I said. "Like, be an ambassador for Patagonia." Erik loves our family, but he didn't think we were *that* adventurous or going anywhere *that* dangerous.

"What if we borrowed money from my parents?" Erik asked. He thought it was brilliant. I had reservations. We had both read *The Richest Man in Babylon*, which advises never loaning money—especially to relatives—unless there is a clear and likely plan for repayment. Of course, Erik had a clear and likely plan. He really did. In an earlier pinch, we had borrowed and returned with interest two thousand dollars from his parents, and it had been fine. Even so, we can be emotional about money.

"It changes the dynamic in our relationship," I said. "Right now we are independent. As soon as we borrow money, we become accountable to them. I don't mind being accountable to a bank, but in a family it can be complex."

"I don't think it has to be complex. We've done it before, and they've always earned a better rate from us than from the bank," Erik said.

"We haven't done anything at this scale," I said. "It puts both of us in a potentially uncomfortable situation. They would have a right to our financial records. They would be able to ask about ordinary unrelated purchases we make. When you borrow from family, it's all related. For them, they might want to say yes and feel bad if they need to say no. Suddenly they become an obstacle. Or they might want to say no, and how are we going to feel about that?"

"I know my parents," Erik said. "I'll let them know yes or no, it doesn't make a difference to us. It never hurts to ask." A classic Erik line. I yielded. He presented the plan to his parents.

At one point we had thought sailing was for rich people. Sailing for a year was almost unfathomable. If you sold a business, retired, won the lottery, or inherited your rich uncle's fortune, then you could go sailing. Average earners didn't do that sort of thing. Now we knew better. We were far from money-rich, at least by first-world standards. By any other standard, we were prosperous because we had a happy marriage, a happy family, good friends, strong faith, a roof over our heads, clean water, food in our cupboards, and we were literate. For us it was important to remember those luxuries.

Erik approached his parents with a spreadsheet. If they would lend us ten percent of the cost of the boat, we would cover everything else. We would make interest-only payments for the first eighteen months and then make payments at six-percent interest thereafter. By month thirty-six, we would make a balloon payment to pay off the balance and be done with the loan. Erik explained our rationale for buying a newer boat with a plan to resell it or keep it and simply pay off the loan upon our return. They agreed to the terms.

Erik found a boat: a Lagoon 380 for sale in the BVI. They were asking $180K. We made a low-ball offer of $100K. Earnest money for boats is ten percent, so it was still a chunk of change. It's tough to describe the feeling of wiring ten grand to an offshore island for a boat you've never actually seen before. You kind of hope you either get the boat or get your money back. We'd been suckered early in our marriage. The bad guy went to jail, but we were both tense about this deal. In this case, the offer was rejected and we got our money back. Honestly, we were relieved. We had made our first offer on a boat. The next time should be easier. Risk-taking requires emotional stamina.

There were more Boat of the Day emails. Our kids were bored of the conversation. Their general feeling was do something or don't, but stop talking about it. Unfortunately for them, in our marriage almost nothing happens without lots and lots of talking. At one point Erik looked into canal houseboats in Amsterdam. I'm not sure if that was desperation or distraction. Then he found *Longhi* in Saint Martin. I wasn't sure where Saint Martin was. I thought *Longhi* was a lame name for a boat, but that was the easiest thing to change. Erik contacted the broker. It was for sale through the Sunsail charter fleet.

People who live aboard boats call themselves cruisers, and a lot of cruisers said charter boats were a bad buy. Inexperienced users have hammered them, they've suffered from hasty maintenance—whatever it takes to get the boat back on the water for the next customer—and they had no soul. This one was priced to sell, so Erik forwarded me an article by Zero to Cruising, a blog by cruisers who had been sailing the world for years. They argued that charter boats were sailed only in good weather, and were lightly used at that. The base quickly resolved any issues, so the boats were generally in good shape. It made sense to both of us. As for soul, our family had more than enough personality to make up for a boat's pedigree.

Erik emailed Pat on *Bumfuzzle* for a second opinion. Pat wrote back from Mexico: "Great choice. Ali and I loved our boat, despite its issues, but always said if we had to get another cat it would be the Lagoon 380. Perfect size, and a respectable company." That cinched the deal for Erik. We discussed it at length, prayed about it, and slept on it.

"Hey, will you join me in here while I email this offer?" Erik called from our bedroom office. I sat next to him at his desk as he clicked send. This time our offer was accepted.

ERIK

3 Months before *Fezywig*

Oh, great. Now we *had* to buy this boat. Of course Emily and I had an out if we didn't like the survey results. But that would be us looking for an excuse. One by one, our fear-based excuses to not do this were falling away. I found that disconcerting.

We had to find a lender. I thought that would be easy. I should have known better. We had adequate savings, impeccable credit, and steady employment. Three gold stars! What we didn't have was a borrowing history. Like most New Yorkers, we rented. We'd been faithfully paying our rent for over a decade. The bank didn't care. They wanted a precedent.

The next strike against us was that Emily and I were debt-free. We'd paid our way through school with minimal loans, and we'd paid those off a week after the one-year grace period. I took great pride in the fact that we'd paid less than twenty dollars of interest for our college educations. Our mantra is, "Ortons don't pay interest, we earn it." Well, lah-dee-dah. Now no bank would lend us money to buy a boat.

Aha! Now I had one more reason to buy a boat: establish our borrowing history. If we ever wanted to buy something larger, like a home, buying this boat would help. That made both Emily and me laugh. But it's true! You can see for yourself the kind of logic we used to talk ourselves into why something would be a good idea. Our plan was: buy a sailboat with a loan, quit my job, and sail around the Caribbean for a year to build our credit. Nice.

So how did we do that when every lender in the country was turning us down? Google search. Up popped "Chesapeake Financial." That sounded good. I knew where the Chesapeake Bay was. It was the Friday of Thanksgiving weekend, but I called and left a voicemail. This was our window of opportunity. We were doing this now because, if we did it any later, Karina would be off to college. We would turn that corner where we start to launch our kids. They would come home between semesters or between jobs, but they would never really be home again. They would start to have lives of their own outside our home and family. That was good and what we wanted for our kids, but we didn't want to miss the chance. This time of having them with us would never come again.

We were at a gas station on the New Jersey Turnpike the Monday after Thanksgiving. My phone rang. Phil at Chesapeake Financial wanted to help get us the loan. Great. I told him I'd fill out the forms the moment I was home. Phil was our last shot. If he didn't get us the loan, I didn't know what we'd do.

I was so stressed about this whole "buying a sailboat" thing, our concerned neighbor, Tiffany, checked in on us. "How are you guys doing?" she asked, with sympathetic eyebrows. Emily and I shook our heads and gave her our sob story. "Would you guys like a massage?" she asked. She was a massage therapist, and who's going to say no to that? She arranged with another friend to give Emily and me a complimentary couple's massage. Emily and I now have a running joke, which of course we say with a snooty accent: "I'm so stressed buying my yacht. I need a massage." I felt like a spoiled brat, but I'm not gonna lie: the massage was great. And I think it helped.

Phil got us the loan. A Google search, a New Jersey parking lot, and scanning some forms to PDF. That's what a dream coming true looks like.

I'd hoped for a lower interest rate. Am I ungrateful or what? We want our dreams to come true, but when they do, we get picky. I was sweating again. I called Jim—from my trip to Maine—and asked his advice. Jim was a smart lawyer who had helped start several banks. His advice: "Erik, in the eternal scheme of things, it will be fine." Jim was wise. Emily agreed with Jim. We took the loan and signed the papers. Emily and I looked at each other with bugged-out eyes. Was this really happening?

We put down $20K out of savings.

My parents borrowed $10K against their house and loaned it to us. I was grateful they believed in us. We could have paid for the boat on our own, but this approach gave us a little cushion for the inevitable surprise expenses. We agreed to pay my parents enough to cover their costs plus a little, so it was a profitable investment for them.

We financed the other $120K, for a total of $150K. Again, we'd planned to buy a much less expensive boat, but this route gave us the best shot at selling it when we were done. Selling the boat was key to us not going broke down the line. We could afford to rent our apartment or pay the mortgage on this boat, but not both. The rest of the trip would be paid for from savings.

It was early December when I called out, "Family meeting," and everyone gathered in the living room. "Big news."

"We bought a boat?" guessed Karina, our child most likely to stick around for boring conversations about money.

"Merry Christmas," I said.

"Wait . . . what?" Sarah Jane asked. All the kids' eyebrows went up, except Eli's.

"That's so cool! Can I drive the dinghy?" Alison said.

"When are we going?" Eli asked. "I don't want to miss any sledding days."

"We will be the official owners in January, on our anniversary," I gestured toward Emily. "There are still a few steps. We need a survey and a sea trial. I'll get somebody in Saint Martin to do that for us. What we need now is a name for our boat." Emily taped a giant sheet of paper to the living room wall and held a marker at the ready.

Thinking of boat names had been a family pastime, but this was serious. We wanted no sailing puns and especially no cat puns. I love a good pun, but boat owners can take it too far, especially catamaran owners: *Catatonic, Catalyst, Cat Me if You Can.* Need I say more? Some of our suggestions included *Hoity-Toity* and *Higgledy-Piggledy.* Eli proposed *Luigi* from the Nintendo video game. If he had to go, he'd rather sail in a boat named *Luigi.*

Emily said, "If our boat name had a Z in it, we could say 'Zulu' every time we hail somebody on the radio." We started thinking of names with Z: *Zany, Crazy, Snazzy, Bowzer*—another Nintendo shout-out from Eli.

"*Fezziwig,*" Emily said, looking from face to face to make sure we'd heard her.

"What's that?" Alison asked.

"Like Mr. Fezziwig from *A Christmas Carol.* It's Scrooge's boss, the happy guy who throws a party." Emily found our copy on a bookshelf in the entryway and read aloud to us, her favorite thing to do.

> Scrooge cried in great excitement:
>
> "Why, it's old Fezziwig! Bless his heart; it's Fezziwig alive again!"
>
> Old Fezziwig laid down his pen, and looked up at the clock, which pointed to the hour of seven. He rubbed his hands; adjusted his capacious waistcoat; laughed all over himself, from his shoes to his organ of benevolence; and called out in a comfortable, oily, rich, fat, jovial voice: . . .
>
> "Yo ho, my boys!" said Fezziwig. "No more work to-night. Christmas Eve, Dick. Christmas, Ebenezer!

Let's have the shutters up," cried old Fezziwig, with a sharp clap of his hands. . . .

"Hilli-ho!" cried old Fezziwig, skipping down from the high desk, with wonderful agility. "Clear away, my lads, and let's have lots of room here!" . . .

Clear away! There was nothing they wouldn't have cleared away, or couldn't have cleared away, with old Fezziwig looking on. It was done in a minute. Every movable was packed off, as if it were dismissed from public life forevermore. . . . The warehouse was as snug, and warm, and dry, and bright a ball-room, as you would desire to see upon a winter's night.

In came a fiddler with a music-book. . . . In came Mrs. Fezziwig, one vast substantial smile. In came the three Miss Fezziwigs, beaming and lovable. . . . In came all the young men and women employed in the business. . . . In they all came.

"I don't know . . ." Karina said. The other kids looked doubtful too.

"I like it," I said. Emily smiled and nodded toward me. "He's a guy who works hard but knows when it's time to play. He put time and money into celebrating people and making memories. That's what we want to do."

"I like that," Alison said. It was growing on them—plus, it was nearly Christmas. We tweaked the spelling because we're Yankees, so when we got on the radio, we would say: *Foxtrot, Echo, Zulu, Yankee, Whiskey, India, Golf. Fezywig.*

We heard back from our surveyor in Saint Martin. His inspection turned up a list of things needing to be done. By now I knew words like *bimini, windlass,* and *transom.* I knew I didn't want a boat with bow thrusters. But I didn't understand the electric and engine mumbo jumbo. Thankfully, Sunsail agreed to fix everything except one item:

the fresh water gauge. But that was probably for show. They didn't want to look like pushovers. We were getting a great deal on a perfectly functional boat, our boat: *Fezywig.*

EMILY

1 Month before *Fezywig*

We had cleared away a lot of stuff to make room for a boat in our lives. I stowed tax papers, journals, photo albums, and other irreplaceables I didn't want to take with us in Erik's parents' basement. We painted our apartment for a series of subletters he had lined up. We'd seen our dentist and physicians and had a plan in case of a medical emergency. We packed everything we wanted to bring on our flight to Sint Maarten in our minivan. Then, just like the Fezziwig family in Dickens' story, we pushed back the furniture.

We didn't have to hire a band because, fortunately, we are a band. Erik plays piano, violin, guitar, drums, penny whistle, and any other instrument he picks up. Karina plays ukulele, mandolin, and piano. Alison plays ukulele, guitar, and a little piano. I jump in on egg shaker or tambourine as needed. We all sing. We play street fairs, organic farms, and Christmas concerts. Mainly, we host a live music night every couple of months. Everyone is invited to bring music and food. With everyone on holiday and our departure imminent, this would be our biggest live music night ever.

Our tiny apartment quickly filled up with friends of all ages and foods of every kind. One trumpeter pinned up a giant black Jolly Roger flag. The musical offerings tended toward nautical themes. Our goal for this sailing sabbatical was to make family memories, but we would dearly miss these friends. We knew we would meet people while on the move, but we didn't think we'd be anywhere long enough to make friends. Eventually, the stack of guests' coats piled on top of the bunk beds started to shrink. It was way past bedtime for the toddlers, and the party wound down.

We gathered our family to sing the traditional closing number one last time. It's a song Erik wrote called "Harvest Time."

> *We are here and they are there*
> *They've all moved on and this earth feels so bare*
> *What we know, we cannot see*
> *But we'll plant again, just you and me*
> *Seasons come and seasons go*
> *Things grow up and then they go*
> *Seeds and soil, sunshine and rain*
> *Giving thanks. It's harvest time.*

ERIK

A friend who worked for a magazine asked about our trip. In a brief phone interview I said, "A lot of times people feel like, 'Oh we have kids so we can't do that until the kids are out of the house.' The time to go is when you have your kids with you because you only have them for a short period. There will be plenty of time to make more money. There'll be plenty of time to take it easy in retirement when you're older, but the reason we're going now is because we want to go while our kids are with us. Let your kids be a reason rather than an excuse."

After I hung up, Emily said, "I think a lot of moms are gonna love you and a lot of dads are gonna hate you." Let your kids be a reason rather than an excuse. This inverted logic became a motivating mantra for us. Nobody is going to send me an invitation. There will never be enough money. There will never be a convenient time to go. Time only moves in one direction, and it keeps moving faster.

The checklist we'd created for our departure unfolded quickly.

Emily drove to my parents' with the kids and our last batch of storage items. I would meet them there. They cried their way down the New Jersey Turnpike.

I moved to a spare room in our neighbors' apartment. Our subletters moved in. We didn't own our boat yet, and we no longer had an apartment. Technically, we were homeless.

Every summer Alison complained about her thick, long, red hair. She knew it was going to be a hassle in the salty Caribbean wind, so she planned to crop it short before we arrived. Like us, she worried about how to earn money while living on a boat. She found one solution to both problems and decided to sell her hair. Our sweet neighbor, Tiffany (the one who gave us the couple's massage), had sold her own hair twice before and mentored Alison through the process. Alison found a buyer online who made hair extensions and cut a deal to the tune of $700, a chunk of change for a fourteen-year-old. Upon receipt, the buyer told her he'd gotten a bargain, but Alison was all smiles and no regrets. It was a bald stroke—I mean, bold stroke—and I was impressed.

I requested a year-long leave of absence at work. They turned me down. I had to decide what to do next. *Decide* comes from the same root as homicide, suicide, fratricide, pesticide. It's about killing. I don't like the idea of killing, but I do it every day. I decide; I kill one option so the other can live. Saying yes to something means I need to say no to something else. Sometimes I say yes to what is established. Sometimes I say yes to change. But I can't say yes to both at the same time.

Quitting my job would start the clock running. Based on our best budgeting, we'd saved enough money to sail for a year. After that we'd be broke. But Emily and I had *decided* a long time ago. We felt it was worth the risk. We believed I could find work again once we were back. I dropped the knife. I turned in my two-weeks' notice.

Two weeks later I got on a bus headed toward Emily and the kids. We hadn't stepped foot on our boat yet, but I already felt like we were casting off.

PART
TWO

Day 1

to

Day 30 aboard *Fezywig*

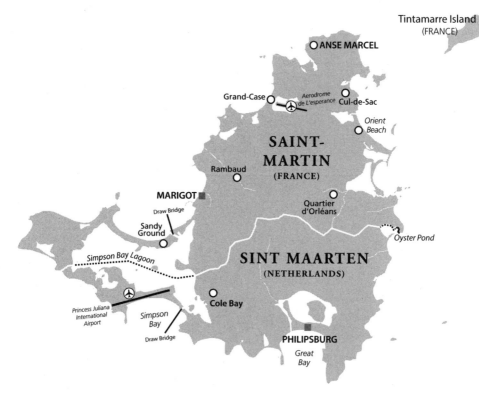

Tintamarre Island
(FRANCE)

○ **ANSE MARCEL**

Grand-Case ○ — ✈ — *Aerodrome de L'esperance* ○ Cul-de-Sac

Orient Beach ○

**SAINT-
MARTIN**
(FRANCE)

Rambaud ○

MARIGOT ■

Draw Bridge

Sandy
Ground ○

Quartier
d'Orléans ○

Simpson Bay Lagoon

SINT MAARTEN
(NETHERLANDS)

Oyster Pond

✈

Cole Bay ○

Princess Juliana
International
Airport

*Simpson
Bay*

Draw Bridge

PHILIPSBURG ■

*Great
Bay*

CHAPTER 4

DREAMER'S REMORSE

SINT MAARTEN, DUTCH ANTILLES, CARIBBEAN

Day 1 aboard *Fezywig*

EMILY

From the airplane all I could see of Sint Maarten was a cluster of lights. Erik said, "I never thought we'd make it this far." The first time we had sailed together, our family had made perfect stairsteps from baby to father. Now Karina and Alison were taller than I was. Sarah Jane was up to my eyebrows, Eli up to my chin, and Lily up to my chest. Our flight had been delayed four days due to a snowstorm in Chicago. When we arrived at the airport, our carefully packed Rubbermaid bins were deemed unacceptable luggage until we begged a supervisor to request an exception.

As the wheels lifted, Eli and Lily raised up both arms and she said, "We're flying like a bird."

"I can't wait to do this trip," Eli said, which surprised me until he added, "so we can go home to New York." I had a lot on my mind as well. I was sure I'd make lots of mistakes. I would feel stupid and unprepared, but we were doing it. We touched down at Princess Juliana International Airport. For about an hour everything went according to plan. Our luggage arrived looking much sturdier than we felt. We were relieved and grateful, but wobbly. The shuttle driver stood waiting and ready. Erik took the first dolly full of bins to the van. My stomach growled. We were all hungry. I sat with Eli and Lily on the airport floor while Karina watched the carousel for our straggler bags. SJ and Alison explored the airport, discovering all the shops and restaurants closed for the evening. I was fresh out of goldfish crackers and granola bars, but all of our luggage had arrived, so we started for the taxi van Erik had prearranged. Seventy-five thousand people lived on this island and ate every day. I'd figure out dinner after we got to the boat.

As we made our way to the exit, a woman's voice called, "Are you the Ortons?" I turned to see a woman and a man in their sixties. He was slim with white hair, a white button-up shirt, and dark slacks. She was barely over five feet with short, intensely red hair. They held a handmade paper sign that read, "Welcome Ortons!!" Who were these people? I noticed the small black rectangular name tags and recognized them as missionaries.

"How did they know we were coming?" Karina asked. I didn't know, especially since we'd had a four-hour delay with our connecting flight. "Yes. We're the Ortons," I said shaking their hands and introducing each of the children.

"We came to welcome you," said the man whose nametag read Elder Thompson. "We came earlier today and learned that your flight was delayed, so here we are." Erik returned for more luggage and greeted our unexpected welcome committee.

"If you're planning to come, church is at eight tomorrow," Sister Thompson said. "And you better hurry if you're hungry. The grocery stores close early on Saturdays and are closed on Sunday." Grateful for the generous greeting of friendly faces and the timely local wisdom, I waved goodbye. I hoped we'd have food before Monday. In the taxi, Erik reminded me that he had contacted the local congregation weeks earlier looking to hire a ride from the airport to the marina. Nobody was interested. But that's how they knew we were coming.

Our driver idled while I ran into the Market Garden grocery store. Any store with the word *garden* in the name is probably expensive. I returned with bread, peanut butter, jelly, pasta, marinara, a gallon of water, and the sinking feeling this was going to be a short trip. Those few staples cost sixty dollars.

"How did it go?" Erik asked. My response was pressed lips, slightly flaring nostrils and a sideways glance. In the dark, we shifted through hills, twists, and turns until we arrived at Captain Oliver's marina on the central east side of the island. Erik paid the driver and gave me the pressed lips look.

"It was a hundred bucks to get the seven of us ten miles across the island," Erik said. "I've already arranged for him to take us back to the other side of the island for church tomorrow. That's another hundred for eight miles. We need a better plan." We'd eat, sleep, and figure it out in the morning.

Gwen was our point of contact at Sunsail. Since the office was closed when we arrived, she left instructions on where *Fezywig* was docked. All the other sailors were settled in for the night, so all the dock carts, parked next to the main office, were at our disposal. I filled one with duffle bags and Rubbermaid bins and followed Erik and his cart across a narrow plank bridge onto the maze of permanent wooden docks. SJ kept a firm grasp on Lily, who wanted to swim—in the dark. Almost home.

"Welcome aboard," Erik said, coming to a stop. He hopped across the starboard steps into the cockpit, opened the sliding glass door, and found the light switch. That night our housewarming party involved getting our gear from the dock to the deck. There was a gap I navigated carefully. I didn't want to drop anything or anyone into the water in the dark. Lily sat at the oval table in the salon while the rest of us, even eight-year-old Eli, hefted our carefully selected belongings onboard. I'd planned a quick, salty, high-carb meal of spaghetti and marinara, something simple before dropping off to sleep. Bare cushions waited with clean folded sheets. The kids made their beds. No towels. No pillows. No blankets. It didn't take long to spread their sheets and pull on their pajamas, T-shirts and shorts. By the time they were ready for dinner, I still hadn't coaxed a flame from the stovetop. I checked the propane tank and connections and flipped the propane switch several times, but I couldn't get a flicker. Erik checked as well. It was one more thing that would have to wait until tomorrow.

"Hey, Mom," Sarah Jane called from her cabin, "Will you come take a picture of me?" I stepped down to find her eyes red with giant tears rolling down her cheeks. "I want to remember how sad I am about missing my friends and my bed at home." I took the picture, gave her a hug and a kiss on the forehead, and hopped back up to the galley. I slapped together seven peanut butter and jelly sandwiches and we said our prayers. We had a lot to be grateful for. Mostly, we were grateful we could finally go to sleep.

The next morning was our first chance to really see *Fezywig*. She was thirty-eight feet long and twenty-two feet, ten inches wide. The keel sunk four and a half feet into the water, and the mast extended fifty-six feet into the sky. There was no mainsail. Surely, Gwen would explain later. *Fezywig* was all washable white fiberglass—perfect for a passel of kids. The stern included a helm station and a cockpit with built-in L-shaped benches and a stationary white plastic table. Above that, faded blue canvas covered a metal frame. That was the bimini. Its purpose was to shade the helm and cockpit. I considered it a jungle gym. A wide side deck ran up both sides of the boat to the front deck. There, divided by a rigid walkway, was a net trampoline. That was the feature most anticipated by our children. In their Sunday dresses, the girls were face down on the netting watching the water roll by. Inside were four double-berth cabins and two heads—double the number of bedrooms and bathrooms in our apartment. The galley, salon, and navigation desk all shared an elevated space between the two pontoons inside. Nobody wanted to be inside that morning.

Our Sunday ride to church was also our first chance to see Saint Martin. We took a good look because we knew we'd be leaving in a week or two. From our taxi the island felt like an amusement park, a roller coaster ride of steep hills and hairpin turns. One moment the road hugged a lush green mountain; the next it swung us out overlooking turquoise waters lapping tan beachfronts filled with boats. Classic.

"I love the pinkish-purplish flowers everywhere," Sarah Jane said.

"Fuschia," Karina said.

"What are those islands?" Alison asked from the back seat.

"That one is St. Barts, and the one way off is Saba," the taxi driver said.

We knew three people on the island—the two missionaries we had met at the airport and our hundred-dollar taxi driver. By the end of church, we'd made several new friends.

"I had a good time," Eli said after Sunday school. "Can we go back to the boat?"

"Not New York?" I asked.

"Living on a boat is fun," Eli said. Morale was up. I wondered if it would last.

"It was so great to have Ocean with us today," a dark-haired woman smiled when I picked up Lily from class.

"Ocean?" I asked as the teacher handed me a scribbled drawing with the name 'Ocean' on it. "You mean Lily? Her middle name is Ocean."

"Well, she introduced herself as Ocean to us, so that's what we called her."

"Come on, Ocean," I said, taking Lily's hand. SJ had stayed with me for class, so I gathered Karina and Alison. They had met a handful of other teenagers.

"Why didn't you come to class?" Alison asked SJ. "The kids were nice." SJ shrugged.

"Hey, I want you to meet Mitch and Arielle," Erik said, joining us. "I asked them about the local buses and they offered to give us a ride home. It's going to take two cars to fit all of us, so another guy, Monte, is taking his family home first."

"Thank you so much," I said, shaking hands with the tall, slim, attractive pair of Canadians. Lily shook their hands too.

It sounded like she said "Enchanté," but she had really said, "I'm Ocean Orton." Erik's eyes narrowed.

"She's calling herself Ocean these days," I said. I held up the picture. He smiled. He had always wanted her first name to be Ocean.

Monte returned with fruit and homemade brownies from his wife, Claire. You may not know you're homesick until somebody shows up with brownies. Bless Claire! We gave our new friends the nickel tour of *Fezywig*. Arielle volunteered to come back the next day and take us provisioning (grocery shopping for two to eight weeks) for our imminent trip to the British Virgin Islands. Before they left, we sang for them. Singing helped us feel like ourselves in this new place.

That afternoon we met our Sunsail team: Gwen, who facilitated the sale, and Joachim, who supervised repairs for the sale. Gwen was the first to stop by. Her white polo and broad smile stood out against her olive skin and mass of black curls.

"Welcome aboard!" she said in her French accent. "How is everything?"

"It's great! We love it. Everything is good," Erik said. "We were wondering about the mainsail?"

"Oh, yes. You are getting a new one. It will be installed in a couple of days. Not a problem."

"Great!" Erik agreed. "That's fine. We have errands to run, so we won't be ready to leave for a couple of days anyway."

"Good. Good," said Gwen. "Is there anything else?"

"Yes," Erik admitted. "We're having trouble getting our oven and stovetop turned on."

"Okay. Yes, very good," Gwen smiled. "Joachim will be by shortly and answer any questions you have about the boat. Have a good day!" We shook her hand and waved goodbye even though she was only going to the office a few hundred yards away.

Joachim arrived. He was a transplant from Germany, but his English was clear.

"Hello," he said. "You have a problem with the oven?"

"Yes," Erik explained. "My wife couldn't get the oven started last night." Together they looked at the propane tanks inside the cockpit benches. Then Joachim came inside the galley and flipped open the fuel line. So far, so good. Finally, he pushed in the knob for the stove before turning it.

"Oh! That's it. We have to push the button *in* first and then turn it," Erik noted.

"Yes. Push in," Joachim confirmed. I needed to get comfortable feeling foolish. We were rookies. The advantage of being a rookie was that people expected us to be ignorant. But we had to humbly acknowledge our ignorance and focus our energy on learning. We couldn't let pride get in the way if we wanted to succeed.

Joachim reviewed the switches and dials above the navigation desk with Erik. Then he advised, "I will tell you about the heads. When you flush, you must keep the switch on wet and pump fifteen times. Every flush. Fifteen times. Not ten times. Then you dry pump. You will have no troubles." Just to be on the safe side, we told the kids to pump the head twenty times.

Monday morning, while the kids unpacked, Erik and I went provisioning. We met Arielle and her tiny car in the marina parking lot.

She was prepared with designer jeans, a mustard-colored cardigan, and a Diet Coke.

"Aren't you hot?" I asked.

"No," she replied. "I'm used to it now." I was prepared with Tevas, a backpack, and a massive grocery list including everything from pickles to pillows. Arielle knew where to go: Cost-U-Less. I liked the sound of that.

Think Caribbean Costco. You could buy "Iguana Gone" by the gallon. Two hours later, Erik and I walked out, each pushing a heaping grocery cart. Our receipt was four feet long, and it had nearly given Erik a heart attack. All the prices on the shelf were listed in three different currencies. He had tried to keep a general tally but was completely unprepared for the massive total. What could we return? Pillows, beans, or flip-flops? I had kept the list lean. We needed everything. The cashier saw Erik's flushed face and the beads of sweat on his brow. Better than a paramedic, she said, "That's in guilders." It was about half that number in dollars. We survived our first provisioning trip.

"Mom and Dad are back!" Sarah Jane called out. "And they have a lot of food!" By the time we reached our slip with two dock carts piled high, all the kids had gathered.

We survived our first provisioning trip.

"There's more in front of the office," Erik said. "Karina, Alison, after we unload, I want you two to take these carts back and get the rest of it." Then he looked at me. "Emily, where do you want this stuff?"

"I'm not sure," I said. "Let's start by getting it into the cockpit, and I'll figure it out from there."

Since October, this adventure had been a series of sorting, shopping, packing, unpacking, cleaning, and reorganizing. I donated bags of books, clothing, toys, and home goods. I drove hundreds of miles back and forth storing irreplaceable journals, photo albums, and the kids' old schoolwork in my in-laws' basement. I weighed and packed everything for the flight to Sint Maarten. I painted our apartment. I scrubbed every surface and washed every pillowcase. I wanted preparing for boat life to end and the living to start. We began the loading process again.

I got really efficient at this over time, but that first day was slow as I decided where to stow everything. Every. Thing. A bag of onions split, and two rolled into the water. Erik grabbed our net, leaped onto the dock, and snagged them just as they floated past the other side of the dock. This was my new normal.

Valentine's Day marked the end of our first week. I walked with all of the children to the small local market to buy frozen raspberries and heavy cream to go on our celebratory pancakes. I was still learning how to cook in the stainless steel pans that had come with *Fezywig*, so I knew our pancakes would need some special help. I don't speak French, and I accidentally bought sour cherries. C'est la vié.

I got the right cream, but I'd never whipped it by hand. I'd seen enough British period dramas to know people ate whipped cream before electricity was invented. I wondered how long it would take to whip cream by hand, so I did an experiment.

"I can take a turn," Karina said. She noticed I had switched arms three times in two minutes. I passed the bowl to Karina. Rather than stirring normally, she held the whisk handle between both hands and rolled it. Her method was more effective. "Hey, Ali, you wanna take a turn?" she asked when her muscles burned. Alison eventually passed it to Jane. We went around and around again until the drippy cream held a peak. It took us thirty minutes. That may seem like a lot of life to trade for some whipped cream, but we talked and laughed working side by side. I believe in labor-saving devices, but those were the most precious thirty minutes of my week. We stuck to it and created something delicious together. Good memories are the best investment because their value always goes up over time. And the pancakes were good, too.

After the mainsail was installed and before we sailed to the British Virgin Islands, Erik wanted to make some other improvements. Sint Maarten has all the shops and experts a cruiser could ever need, but not where we were, on the French side. This tiny island is jointly owned by France and the Netherlands. The folk story is that the dividing line was decided by two speedwalkers. The French walker and the Dutch walker started back to back. That was one end of the border line. They walked the perimeter of the island in opposite directions. Where they met up marked the other end of the border dividing their two nations. The French claimed their walker was faster because he carried lightweight wine for refreshment rather than heavy Dutch gin. The Dutch accused the Frenchman of running. Either way, the two sides are different. As Erik says, "The French side is where you go if you want a baguette. The Dutch side is where you go to get things done." I put homeschool on hold to shop for solar panels, wind generators, and water makers. We also needed a dinghy, an outboard motor, and a Wi-Fi booster. If confidence came in packages, Erik and I would have stocked up. We were fresh out.

A film montage of this period would include an establishing shot of all the kids sleeping in their berths. It would show one of their tiny fans running and zoom in on their sleeping faces, sweet but sweaty. Then the focus would shift to Erik and me in our berth with both lights on. We'd be leaning against the back wall of our cabin, a legal pad in Erik's hand, our brows furrowed. Closing in on the legal pad, you'd see the words "solar panels" across the top and then a long list of pros and cons running down from there. Some words would be scratched out and other notes scribbled in.

You'd see the kids in their pajamas around the breakfast table waving goodbye to us. We'd be fully dressed with VHF radios in hand and backpacks on. The focus would zoom in on Lily crying at the closed glass door because we were leaving—again. It would show us in our tiny rental car with that legal pad and our furrowed brows. You'd see us crossing the island up and down hills to the Dutch side. You'd see us in various chandleries looking at oddly shaped items, our brow furrows deepening as the prices were revealed. You'd see us speaking with various tanned salesmen in polo shirts, all gesticulating for clarity. The camera would show Erik's eyes concentrating as he took more notes on the legal pad. You would see my eyes glaze over as I wandered into the life vest section of the store—something I understood. The camera would show me in a shop loft smiling next to a giant spool of safety netting as a shop assistant measured our many, many yards of it.

To indicate a passage of time, you would notice our hair getting lighter and lighter. You would notice the legal pad running out of pages. The focus would turn to Erik, in another shop, showing pictures of *Fezywig* to a man holding steel tubing. Then it would cut to Erik in the driver's seat of our rental car, cupping his forehead in one hand, legal pad on his lap. The camera would zoom in on the legal pad where three giant Sharpie dollar signs were underlined. You would see no solar panels on *Fezywig*. You would see no wind generator on *Fezywig*. You would see no water maker on *Fezywig*. Sometimes the result of all our effort and research is the decision not to change anything. The montage would close with Karina saying, "We miss you guys. Didn't we come out here to be together? You're gone all day, every day."

"Why don't we sail out to Tintamarre?" Erik suggested. Ile Tintamarre was part of the Saint Martin Nature Reserve, about three miles east from our protected marina in Oyster Pond. There would be no shops, no restaurants, and no garbage cans. Just lizards and fish. It sounded perfect.

This was gonna be good. Finally a chance to relax and do what we had come for. We all went to the deck to enjoy the ride and help raise the sails. To be on the safe side, we tethered Eli and Lily in to the jacklines. Erik sat at the helm with his big straw hat and sunglasses. The engines grumbled and sputtered as we made our way to the channel opening. What a relief to part ways with the dock, even for just a few hours. We would be back before dark.

We rounded the steep rock outcropping that stood between us and the ocean. To our left a jagged hill climbed high and pinched the water into a narrow cut. The ocean swell started to bounce the boat. Erik revved the engines, and their sound rose into a rapid, loud clacking. The whole boat pitched forward steeply, and everyone's feet came up off the trampoline.

"Holy crap!" Erik said from the helm. Everything not strapped down inside the boat started to crash. Books slid across and off the table. Dishes clanged to the floor. The iMac we'd brought for school tipped over onto its face and threatened to tumble to the floor. The printer slid sideways across the shelf.

"Emily, can you pin all that stuff down?" Erik shouted over the engine noise, his voice pitched higher than usual.

"Eli and Lily, let's get inside," I said. The boat angled backward as it rode the next wave, throwing Alison and Karina tight against the mast where they waited to raise the mainsail. I cautiously shuffled sideways back toward the cockpit, keeping both hands on the chrome bars in front of me and Lily trapped between me and the boat so she didn't go flying. Jane did the same on the other side with Eli. Once inside, I sent Eli and Lily below deck so nothing would accidentally fall on them.

"You okay?" I heard Erik call out.

I looked through the salon windows to see Alison and Karina

bear-hugging the mast. At least they were wearing life jackets. This was supposed to be a quick, peaceful jaunt.

"Hold on and be careful," Erik told them as they made their way back into the cockpit, the mainsail successfully aloft.

We made it to Tintamarre and back safely that evening. We later learned the channel in and out of Oyster Pond was one of the most dangerous in the entire Caribbean.

We were out of our depth, above our pay grade, and so tired. We hadn't known how long days could be until we entered this learning curve. It seemed to catch up with Erik the following morning when he wrote this letter home:

ERIK

Dear Dad,

Good morning. 5:30 a.m., Oyster Pond, Saint Martin. I hope you guys are faring well through this next snowstorm. We're doing okay here. Had a rough day yesterday.

Remember the phone call I made to you from the DMV after buying that old brown VW Rabbit? This is that call. If you don't remember it very well, it went something like this: I bought the Rabbit with all the money I had in savings. It was a 1974 stick shift with one headlight, no windshield wipers, no padding in the front two seats, and worst of all, no radio. I didn't know how to drive stick shift. But I had to drive it from Chad's house to the DMV, past the mall, during rush hour, a few days before Christmas. I stalled in a few intersections and sweat many, many bullets. By the time I got to the DMV I was pretty rattled. I called you and told you I thought buying the car was a bad idea and that I should take it back. I don't remember exactly what you told me, but it was something to the effect of, "Just go ahead and register the car. You'll learn how to drive it. You'll be fine. I love you." Something like that.

The learning curve is steep here, and everything is expensive at every turn. I'm feeling a bit hemmed in. We seem to be going through eighty gallons of water every day, and I just can't figure out why. Is there a leak in the tanks? Some drainage valve left open? Are we mega-water hogs? I don't know. The 220V inverter that runs our fridge has started to switch off on its own, but then comes on again. Is that us? Or the power supply here on the dock? The wind indicator at the top of the mast was supposed to be fixed. That's not working. The fuel gauges don't work. We'll use the hour indicators to know our level. The brackets to mount our solar panels are likely going to be massively expensive. I'm still awaiting quotes, but that's the word from the friendly electrician working on the boat next door. I'm trying to muster my courage to take a do-it-yourself approach. I could go on and on about all the stuff swirling through my head. Why else would I be up at 5:30 a.m.?!

Speaking of swirling, we finally took the boat out for a short sail yesterday. We'd waited several days while they rigged the new mainsail. Then we could take her out. We went to an island called Tintamarre about four miles north of where we're staying. A nice easy jaunt to try things out. We all promptly got seasick. No one puked . . . yet. We were sailing perpendicular to the wind, so were rolling right-to-left with every passing wave. Awful. Emily and the kids were real troopers.

We were not expecting things to be nearly that "rolly," so stuff was flying everywhere inside the boat. We got to the island and it took us three tries to get the anchor properly set. (Everyone is still learning their posts.) And then we all lay there for a few minutes before doing anything else. There were a bunch of other boats already anchored off this amazing beach, so we were pretty far out. But the kids still really wanted to head in. We only had a couple hours of daylight left, and the idea was to get back to Oyster Pond, and not stay overnight at Tintamarre.

As soon as we landed our dinghy on the beach, the kids were in the water. We taught them how to use snorkel masks, and then they added fins. They kept coming to show us every shell, rock, and piece of coral they found. They were in heaven. I broke up the party and told them we needed to head back. Alison even asked, "Can we come here first thing tomorrow so we can spend all day?" It was a beautiful spot. But back in the dinghy, back to the boat, pull up the anchor, and head out. The sun was low in the sky.

The entrance to our harbor is sketchy in daylight, treacherous in the dark. We motored the whole way just to make sure we didn't get caught out in the ocean in the dark. Seasickness returned almost immediately. Everyone was passed out like sloths slumped over whatever spot provided the most comfort. (Except Alison, who lay down on the bow of the boat and enjoyed the waves, unaware of the misery going on behind her.) I stayed at the helm, but was green and gaunt. I always get seasick the first few days of sailing. This was no exception. I did pretty well until SJ came above deck and did her best to reach the back of the boat before puking. She got most of the way. I immediately set the boat on autopilot and jumped down from the helm, got out the deck shower hose, and started to rinse the puke off the back of the boat. The last thing we needed was the smell of puke wafting around. Once that was clear, I went back to the helm, but the whole thing already got me. I began tossing everything in my stomach. I lost count: five, six, seven times?

I was able to get myself back together in time to make the entrance to the harbor. The sun was now way behind the island mountains. But I found the markers in the undulating water, stayed as close to them as I could, and steered us in. Once inside, the waves immediately subsided. We'd never been so grateful for a safe harbor. What a real thing it is, to be protected on all sides, to not be tossed every which way, to have a place where you can rest and recover. We all need that, in so many ways in our lives.

Alison was great and helped me pull the boat up dockside and tie it down. We only put one small scuff on the port bow. Alison apologized, and I said, "It's just a boat." In retrospect, I think that's the smartest thing I said all day. Except for telling Emily and each of the kids that I loved them. Safe harbors.

I drank most of a ginger ale, took off all my wet clothes, and promptly fell asleep for several hours. I woke up as the kids were going to bed. Happy Valentine's Day.

So that's it. That's the wonderful and awful account of our Friday. We all agreed that we would much rather have been on our couch in NYC, sitting through a blizzard, watching movie after movie on Netflix. But we chose this instead.

So basically, I feel like I did that day when I was sixteen and stalled out my new-to-me-but-still-a-junker-of-a-car in the middle of the intersection by the mall two days before Christmas. I wanted to run away. I wanted to give it back. I wanted you to just come and pick me up so we could return the car. But you encouraged me to stick with it. In the end, I came to love that car. I fixed it up and it ran beautifully. (And you gave me a radio and some speakers for Christmas.) I made so many happy memories with that car. Of course it's not about the car, or the boat, but where they take you, and who you're with when you go.

The happiest moment of the day was on that beach watching our kids discover the world through a snorkel mask. I told Emily, "No one can ever take this back. We're here and it can't be undone." What I meant was, however this all plays out, this memory has been made. My kids have had this experience. We've had it. That can't be undone. So while it's hard today—and I believe there will be hard and probably expensive days ahead—I'm confident we'll pull through. I finished my can of ginger ale. I took a shower. I slept in a safe harbor. We'll sail out again tomorrow. I love you, Dad.

—Erik

We took one day to regroup, return our rental car, and borrow a dinghy from Sunsail. The following morning the sun rose over Oyster Pond and I called out, "All hands on deck." Everyone buckled into their personal flotation devices. Karina cued up a playlist. Music always helped distract us and prevent seasickness. Alison untied the dock lines, threw them to Jane, and gave us a shove as she jumped aboard.

All we wanted to do was get to the BVI. But first we needed to get ourselves sorted out. We weren't going to do that from Oyster Pond on the French side. We needed to move to Simpson Bay Lagoon on the Dutch side.

As we motored toward the channel, we cleared all the tables of dishes and books and stowed the ridiculous iMac and printer we'd brought. Lily and Eli stayed below deck and Karina and Alison clipped into the jacklines. Emily and Jane stood in the cockpit, ready to release the jib sheets. The engine clanked loudly as we pounded our way back out of the channel for the second time in three days, but instead of turning left toward Tintamarre, I turned right toward Simpson Bay.

CHAPTER 5

WHOSE DUMB IDEA WAS THIS?

SIMPSON BAY LAGOON, SINT MAARTEN, CARIBBEAN

7 Days aboard Fezywig

ERIK

Shrimpy was a retired diver-for-hire who ran a laundromat and consignment shop on the edge of the Simpson Bay Lagoon. His radio net was basically a daily VHF town hall meeting for all the local cruisers. He gave the latest on weather and safety. Activities like group hikes and card games were announced. New arrivals introduced themselves, and those sailing to other islands said goodbye. Lastly, anyone could advertise goods or services, and others could chime in with what they needed. We needed goods, services, and, ideally, mentors.

Early the next morning while the kids slept, Emily and I quietly slid into the bench seats in the salon and turned the VHF to channel 7. We didn't hear anything.

We were anchored a few hundred yards from the end of the airport runway. An early flight took off and passed over head. "We could be home in six hours, door to door," Emily said. I nodded but stayed focused on the task at hand. I double checked the guidebook. I was on the right channel at the right time, but still nothing.

I scrolled through the channels and stopped when I heard, "Anyone have items to buy or sell? Buy or sell?" It was Shrimpy.

I pushed the VHF talk button and said, "We're *Fezywig*. We're brand new cruisers and have a lot to learn. If anyone is willing to talk to us about solar panels or Wi-Fi, please let us know." I released the button. In response, I got a public tongue lashing from Shrimpy on radio etiquette. There was an appropriate time for introductions, and we'd missed it. I didn't let the hand slap slow me down. I was too happy to finally connect with other cruisers to be embarrassed. Back to Shrimpy's next point of order: vessels started chiming in with goods to sell. Emily handed me a fresh legal pad and I took notes. A boat called *Pyxis* was selling an inflatable dinghy. Someone else was selling foldable bikes and partially used scuba tanks. We wanted all of them, but we really needed our own dinghy. We hailed *Pyxis* and made an appointment for that afternoon. I gave Emily a high five. We knew what we were going to do that day.

"*Fezywig, Fezywig*. This is *Silverheels*," we heard a man's voice crackling in our VHF.

"*Silverheels*, this is *Fezywig*," I responded. "Let's switch down to channel six." Emily and I looked at each other with question-mark eyebrows.

"*Fezywig*, we're happy to talk about cruising and answer any questions we can," said *Silverheels*. We agreed to meet after breakfast. We were going to leave the kids again. But hopefully this time we'd come back with more answers than questions.

Emily and I dinghied over to *Silverheels*—a forest green monohull—and our training began. "Not there. Tie up here," Ken directed. Because his name wasn't *Silverheels*, it was Ken. For cruisers, their boat name serves as their last name in the community. So Ken and his wife Lynn were *Silverheels* collectively, just as we were *Fezywig*. "Now, hold tight to

the railing here. That's it. And step up through here. Step down here."
And before we knew it, we were sitting and drinking cold water—which
was already a treat—in the shaded, cushioned cockpit of *Silverheels*.

Ken and Lynn are Canadians, but their love of warm weather had
led them to the Caribbean for the past eleven years. It didn't matter
what they did before that. They were cruisers now. Talking to Ken,
you might never notice his gray hair. His open, patient kindness made
everything about him seem youthful. Ken told us about Wi-Fi, solar
panels, outboards, dinghies, and dinghy security in local waters. He
gave us a tour of the boat.

Then Lynn returned. If Ken seemed youthful, Lynn was ageless
with her tall, muscular build and broad smile. She gave Emily a fail-
proof bread recipe and explained how baking rolls in cupcake tins required less time and propane than cooking a loaf of bread. She told us
which laundromats were most accessible by dinghy and named the best
stores for provisionsing. She showed us all the improvements she had
personally made to the boat: foot-pumped water in the sink, a deep
freezer. She even did the fiberglass. "We don't believe in blue jobs and
pink jobs," Lynn said. I was seriously impressed by their rock-hard ice
cream. These two were pros.

We returned to *Fezywig* bearing gifts from *Silverheels*: a gigantic
silver mixing bowl that belonged to Lynn's mother, a silicone cupcake
pan, and the grand relief of friendship.

We stopped at our boat for lunch. SJ had filled a Rubbermaid bin
with seawater as an on-deck pool for Lily. Eli was playing with his favorite stuffed Luigi doll. Alison was playing ukulele in her cabin and
Karina volunteered to wash the dishes. Emily and I left again.

Pyxis was a gorgeous monohull with a highly polished teak deck
docked at the Simpson Bay Yacht Club. Captain Brian, a Brit, invited
us to sit in his shaded, cushioned cockpit. We had cold drinks for the
second time that day. *Pyxis* was having a custom brass bimini installed
before heading back to England. While he waited, Brian was cleaning

out his storage compartments and had found a spare five-seat inflatable dinghy he'd never used. We had seven in our crew, but two of them were small, so I was interested. Like *Pyxis,* we were heading out soon and couldn't do it without a dinghy. If a boat was a cruiser's house, a dinghy was a cruiser's car. We agreed to the $300 price right away. As we were leaving, I noticed Brian's beautiful Wi-Fi setup.

"I just installed that," he said. "I had another one that worked great, but it didn't look right. Too modern for my boat."

As we tucked in to sleep that night, we were the proud new owners of a used inflatable dinghy and a modern-looking Wi-Fi booster. Now we needed an outboard motor and a chain to lock it all up. And we needed to figure out how to install the Wi-Fi booster. They were all clear objectives. I went to sleep content that we had some idea what we would be doing the next day.

On the third day, Ken and Lynn visited *Fezywig,* and our whole crew crowded in the cockpit to meet them. Sarah Jane showed Lynn her cabin and told Lynn that Lily sometimes stole her training bra. They dinghied Emily ashore for a foot tour of their recommended grocery stores. As they motored away, I asked SJ why she had told Lynn that story. She said, "She's one of the coolest people I've ever met. I wanted her to think I was funny."

The seven of us split four cabins just like this.

"You are funny," I said, not meaning ha-ha funny.

While Emily was gone, I started on the Wi-Fi booster. The instructions said, "Attach it to a power source." I looked but there was no plug, just two dead-end wires. I radioed *Pyxis.* "Brian, how does this thing connect to a power source?"

"Oh, sure. You just solder it to an open circuit on your electrical panel."

Right. How silly of me.

I dinghied to shore and bought a soldering kit. I radioed *Pyxis*. "Any chance you'd have some time to show me how to solder?"

After a couple days of scrounging parts, trial and error, and trouble-shooting, all the lights on the booster lit up green. "Yes!" I said as I pulled a fist in toward my bicep.

"It's so beautiful," Eli said. I agreed.

The booster was attached to a bimini pole in the cockpit, and the antenna inside broadcast the signal to every device on the boat. A few days later it rained. Too bad I had installed the booster upside down. It filled with rainwater and shorted out. There were no lights at all. *Trial and error, works every time.*

I'm not sure when I first made up this phrase, but it was funny enough to stick. I think it's the ironic juxtaposition of bumbling and certainty that we Ortons love. We expect boondoggles, but we trust that—if we're tenacious enough—something will work out.

I looked up how to order new parts for the Wi-Fi router, but I wasn't sure where to have them sent because we were leaving for the BVI in a couple days. I'd have to figure that one out later.

Our final errand was to return the dinghy we had borrowed from Sunsail in Oyster Pond. Then we would be off. As we motored around to the other side of the island, the portside engine started smoking. Then it failed completely. I started to sweat. I called ahead and said we were coming in with only one engine—that same scary channel, but with only half the horsepower and half the control. I felt like a WWII bomber pilot calling the tower after being all shot up over the drop zone. We were limping home, and I wasn't sure we'd make the runway. We made it past the rocks, through the channel, and into protected waters. Emily, Karina, and Alison stood ready with fenders. Jane kept Eli and Lily below. I didn't know how to dock a catamaran with one engine. A pilot boat dinghied out to meet us and a dockhand hopped aboard. I gladly turned over the helm.

"What happened?" he asked.

"The engine was putting out a lot of extra smoke, then it sputtered out." I made a few sound effects. It was the classic dropping-the-car-off-at-the-mechanics conversation. I worried I'd done something wrong but, if so, didn't know what it was.

"What's that in the water?" Emily asked, leaning over the port-side. A charcoal-like powder was floating below the exhaust spout. The dockhand and I peered over the lifelines.

"That doesn't look good," I said.

"No. Not good," he agreed. "Someone should take a look at that."

After a few tries, he got the engine started. He checked the oil. It was low, so he topped it off and said we were good to go. I had my suspicions. All that smoke had come from burnt oil. I wasn't sure they'd gotten to the root of the problem. I saw Gwen on the dock and mentioned this and a couple other miscellaneous items. She was polite but also in a hurry. A big regatta was kicking off next week, and lots of boats with paying customers were arriving. We needed to move off the dock to a mooring ball. I spoke to the mechanic's boss, Nicholas. He wanted us gone, and we wanted to get moving. I proposed a solution, "Can the Sunsail base in the BVI take a look at all this?"

"That's a good idea," he said. "I'll set it up."

We returned the borrowed dinghy, moved to a mooring ball, and started rigging our own dinghy to the stern. It was immediately clear our new spot on the mooring ball was a hot and stuffy with no breeze.

"Shall we get out of here?" I asked Emily. I was fed up. "We can spend the night at Tintamarre, sail around to the lagoon tomorrow, go to church the next day, and leave for the BVI right after that. We have to leave from that side of the island anyway."

"Sounds good to me," she said.

We'd figure this all out in the BVI.

I pointed *Fezywig* out of the channel. This was our third time sailing out this channel. I officially hated it. But we knew what we were doing: music cranked, jacklines clipped, tables and counters cleared. "Hang on," I called out as I revved our one engine and headed into the oncoming waves. Nausea crept in. I didn't care. I wanted out of that stuffy marina, I wanted off this island, and I wanted to get our trip started.

We motored to Tintamarre. No sails this time. When we arrived we saw several boats already moored off the beach. There was one mooring ball close to shore, so we headed straight at it.

We inched up to the mooring ball, Karina and Alison on the bow, ready to grab the line and tie us off. But they missed it.

"Ali, take the helm!" I shouted to the bow. As she came to the helm, I stepped down to the stern and—as we floated past—grabbed the mooring ball line with my hands. Our boat weighed twenty-eight tons and was being pushed by fifteen-knot trade winds. The mooring line was cemented to the ocean floor. I was trying to hold the two together and was clearly the weak link.

"Bring me a docking line!" I shouted to everyone. One appeared. I laced it through the mooring line and tied it off to one side of the stern.

"Bring me another one!" Another one appeared. I laced it through the mooring line, tied it down to the other side of the stern, and balanced out the two docking lines into an even Y. We were now anchored, but backward. I proceeded to shout and bark orders until we had pivoted the boat 180 degrees and it was pointing into the wind. I didn't know if I was mad at my family or myself. Probably both. Why was everything going wrong? Why couldn't Karina and Alison get the line on the first try? Why didn't the engine work? Why did I have to be seasick? Why, why, why?

We all slumped around the salon table, each of us looking off at nothing in particular.

"Whose dumb idea was this?" I asked out loud.

A couple heads lifted up from the table. All eyes turned to me.

"It was *your* idea!" they all said, and they busted up laughing.

I held my grumpy face as long as I could, and then I a let a smile slip through.

"Hey, that's not entirely true," Emily said. "We've *all* been planning this for years. We decided together."

The kids knew she was right. I knew the kids were right. It had been my idea in the beginning, but now we all owned it. We sipped our broth and chuckled quietly. Nobody had the energy for any big moves.

I stumbled below deck to sleep in my cabin. Alison made it to her cabin. Karina and SJ wrapped up in beach towels and slept on the trampoline until they got too cold. Emily "slept" on the salon floor with Eli and Lily curled up on either side.

The next morning I was happy to get up early. I couldn't wait to get to land and hold still. Emily and each of the kids all had the same idea. We piled in the dinghy and motored to shore. We were the only ones there. I was strung out. This was not what I'd bargained for. I wanted quality time with my family in a beautiful setting, not an emotional, physical, and financial suffer-fest. We needed this quiet place where the only sounds were crashing waves and wind rustling the tall grass. Lizards silently warmed in the sun. They didn't judge us. Emily and I sat at a shaded picnic table and decided not to feel sorry for ourselves. I know that sounds ridiculous. We were in the Caribbean living the dream we'd been planning for the previous six years. If there was such a thing as dreamer's remorse, we were feeling it, but we knew the cure: gratitude.

I pulled out my smartphone to record this low moment. I went around the circle asking everyone, "What was awesome about today?" Sarah Jane liked the breeze. Emily liked Karina's cheery board shorts and the patterns that lizards left in the soft dirt with their tails. Lily liked the water and being together. Karina and Alison liked having pancakes for breakfast and keeping them down. Eli liked the bandage Emily had made for his newly scraped toe. I was grateful for the breeze, the shade, and that no one had vomited so far that day.

Mostly, we liked being together experiencing this journey. We spent the whole day doing things that couldn't be undone. We looked in each other's eyes, rested in a hammock, stared at the sky, picked up shells, marched through the brush, watched birds nesting, held hands, and smiled.

The sun got low in the sky. We wanted to be at anchor in the lagoon before dark.

I tried to start our good engine. I turned the key and got nothing. I stopped smiling. I was able to get our smoky port engine going, but that didn't fill me with confidence. I hailed the catamaran next to us, and the gents sitting down to dinner with their wives agreed to put their meal on hold to help us troubleshoot. One of the more experienced sailors explained Yanmar engines sometimes have a "dead spot" on the starter motor. He showed me how to manually rotate past it. I turned the key and the engine started right up. I thanked them both, cast off from the mooring ball, and headed to Simpson Bay Lagoon.

"Maybe that's what was wrong with the other engine," I said to Emily as we motored along.

"Maybe," she said. But neither of us sounded convinced.

By nightfall we were anchored back in the lagoon. The next day we'd finally leave for the BVI.

At church, we hugged our friends goodbye. I happened to mention our little engine situation to Yuanita. Yuanita was from the Netherlands and had lived on this Dutch island for decades. "My husband, Robert, will come take a look," she said. "I insist." Yuanita was a formidable woman, not to be trifled with. "He ran a boat yard for years." I wasn't opposed to getting a final signoff before making my first ocean crossing with my wife and five kids.

Robert came to check the engine. Like a surgeon preparing to deliver bad news, he said, "Come with me." He drove me straight to the diesel engine shop on shore and walked me in. Within minutes I had a referral for a follow-up appointment. At eight the next morning a guy named Nick showed up at our boat with a cigarette and a toolbox. He checked the compression. All good there. He removed the fuel injectors and took them back to his shop for tests. I wish he'd taken my blood pressure. The fuel injectors all failed their bench test. I was starting to feel dizzy. Couldn't someone get me some juice and cookies? *I wanted to get out of here. I wanted to get to the BVI. Was that so much to ask?*

I emailed Gwen and Sunsail with the update. It appeared they had *not* gotten to the root of the engine's problem. Her response: if I could pick him up, Joachim—the Head Physician of Boat Phase-Outs—would come to look at our boat in person. I liked Joachim. He had given us our first tour of *Fezywig* and showed us how to turn on our stove that first day aboard. Even so, our whole trip was unraveling. We'd already been on Saint Martin a month. Were we doomed to remain stuck on this gorgeous, Caribbean island forever? Oh, how I suffered! I agreed to pick him up, rested my head on the cockpit table, and the *Fezywigs* settled in for yet another night in the lagoon.

CHAPTER 6

THE ESSENTIALS

DUTCH SIDE, SIMPSON BAY LAGOON, SINT MAARTEN

30 Days aboard *Fezywig*

EMILY

"We can't live in crisis mode," I told Erik. "I feel like we've been running since Halloween. I'm exhausted."

"I'm exhausted too," Erik said. "But we still need solar panels and a water maker. I want to get a monitor for the batteries so we know if they're charging. We might need a bigger inverter."

That first month felt all new every day. Our rhythm was to wake up sweating and run all day through a thick jungle of new information and then fall asleep bone-tired with our clothes sticking to our bodies at night. We were running on emotional fumes. It was unsustainable.

"You're right. It's all important," I agreed. "We knew it would be like this. Everyone says the boat list is endless. They're right. But that means it's always going to be there. Maybe we could spend some hours every day working on the boat and then put a cap on it and do other things. I'd love a routine, so we have time for the boat, school, and fun."

"And sex?" Erik suggested.

"Yes," I laughed. "If we weren't dead tired." I went on, "What needs to happen for you to consider your day a success?"

"I like food three times a day," Erik said. "I like to write in my journal or work on my novel. I like to take care of business for the boat or our apartment. I like to spend time as a family. I like to play music and maybe read. I like to get seven to eight hours of sleep."

"That sounds like a good day," I said.

"How about you?" he asked.

"I feel good about my day if I practice yoga, journal, and read my scriptures. And just read in general. Those are the things I need for me, so I don't feel like I'm completely out of control," I said. "For school, I make sure each kid does reading, writing, and math, but I really like reading aloud to the kids. Food is important . . . and I would definitely feel more adventurous if I got enough sleep every day."

"Wait—you like reading aloud to the kids?" Erik teased.

"The point is . . . " I said, "we came out here to be together. I don't know how long we have to wait for our engine to be fixed, but we don't have to wait to be together." The British Virgin Islands were our destination, but our goal was making memories as a family. The question was whether our goal could override our destination. Finally, our destination fever broke.

Thanks to Joachim, Nick paid us a visit. Nick traveled the lagoon on his pontoon boat fixing the boats assigned to him by Gordy, who ran the Yanmar diesel engine shop. Nick cleated his boat off our stern and inspected our portside engine. He was young but leathery and didn't talk much. He said we needed a new part and ordered it. A few days later he returned to install the part and test the engine. It didn't work. He smoked a cigarette, packed up the useless part, and dinghied back to the island. The ritual started over again. And again.

Each attempted fix added three to seven days to our wait. Thank goodness we'd let go of our timeline. Nick became another friendly face in our routine instead of a nagging reminder that we were stuck in Sint Maarten.

I practiced yoga before the Cruiser's Net. I listened to the Net while setting out breakfast. Most days, I served dry rolled oats with lukewarm boxed UHT milk, walnuts, craisins, and honey. What I prepared is irrelevant. The point was, I didn't have to decide what we would eat every day. Making it routine conserved decision-making energy for more important things. After breakfast, I didn't have to assign dishes because I had made a chore chart. Karina, Alison, and Sarah Jane were trained in water conservation techniques: rinse everything in saltwater, scrub everything, rinse everything in freshwater. After breakfast, I read scriptures and wrote in my journal. Then I supervised the older kids and did school with the younger kids. Lunch marked the end of our academic work.

I supervised the older kids and did school with the younger kids.

In the afternoons, meal preparation was a shared event. The kids used their leisure time to accompany Dad on errands, read, play on deck, or help with chores. Karina tied flat sheets to the rope trampolines and they filled like windsocks, making shady tents for playing, reading, or napping. The marinas had trading shelves where we found interesting books. Eli tried setting up rows of game tiles one day, but they fell down every few seconds when *Fezywig* shifted. Dang Caribbean breezes.

Once a week, I did laundry in a large plastic garbage bin with a plunger set apart for washing. I filled the bin with laundry, covered it with water and added a little soap. All the kids helped. Even Lily took a turn agitating the wash with the plunger. After several rinses and twisting out as much water as possible, we each got a handful of wooden clothes pins to help hang the laundry to dry, including Lily. Her occupational therapist would have been proud. The laundry didn't always *look* cleaner, but it smelled cleaner. Hanging laundry to dry in the sun felt satisfyingly wholesome.

We ate dinner together every night. We told each other about our days—the highs and the lows. Just because you share a thirty-eight by twenty-two-foot space doesn't mean you know what is going on in each other's lives. We looked in each other's eyes. We cleaned up together afterwards. Many nights Erik read aloud, in various accents, from *Kon Tiki,* about a group of scientists sailing their re-creation of an ancient raft from Peru to Polynesia. The kids loved it. We shared favorite passages from books. One of our favorites was from Robert K. Massie's *Catherine the Great: Portrait of a Woman*: "Gradually, guided by her own curiosity, she was acquiring a superior education." We don't want our kids to grow to be despots, even enlightened ones, but we loved this sentiment and still quote it to each other from memory. Whatever we shared became a common point of reference connecting us as a family.

Maybe we were a little *too* connected on the boat. One afternoon, the girls and I were doing schoolwork at the salon table when we heard Eli in the portside head counting slowly and with great effort, "Seventeen, eighteen, nineteen, twenty." A moment later he appeared.

"Did you flush?" Sarah Jane asked.

"I pumped it twenty times," Eli said.

"That's not the same thing," Alison said. She went to check and shouted, "Eli, you're not done in here!"

"Look, it wasn't my idea to live on this stupid boat," Eli said. He stomped away—as far as he could get on a sailboat. Hopefully, away enough that he didn't hear us laughing.

I shouldn't laugh. I wasn't a savvy sailor either. One night, the Tidmarshes, a family from church, invited us to dinner. We were lucky to have friends on land. It was always a treat when one of them invited us over and a little bit of a trick to get there. All five kids were already in the dinghy with their life vests buckled on. I stood on *Fezywig's* bottom starboard step, checking with my hands to make sure I hadn't forgotten anything.

"Backpack, purse with iPhone and local phone, VHF clipped on, Tevas. Okay, I'm ready," I said to myself and I stepped toward the dinghy where all the kids were already waiting. Erik was in the salon grabbing the outboard key off the navigation desk. As I stepped my right foot to the dinghy, I heard a splash. The VHF had fallen into the water. It was waterproof, and I could still see it. If I didn't dive after it now, we might never find it again. *Fezywig* was always shifting directions with the wind, and the bottom of this lagoon was murky and covered with plants. I knew Erik would be

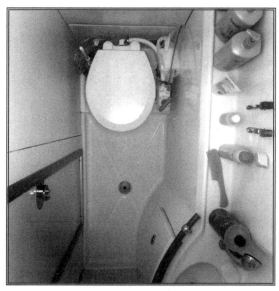

"I pumped it twenty times," Eli said.

upset if I lost the VHF. I was fully dressed, but I dove for it. I could almost reach it. I pulled myself down into the water with both arms, but I wasn't making much progress. I'm not a great diver, so I knew I had to grab it before it got deep. I kept struggling to get down as the VHF easily sank out of reach and out of sight.

I resurfaced disappointed but certain I had made my best effort and that Erik would understand. I sat on the lower steps of *Fezywig* to catch my breath and wonder how the VHF had dropped. The clip was still on my purse. Maybe my knee bumped it out of the clip when I stepped toward the dinghy. Oh, no. My purse. I had dived in with everything on. I unzipped my tiny black polyester purse to find two wet phones—mine and the local one I had borrowed from the Claire Sala.

Erik was on deck now, and I immediately owned my mistake.

"The VHF fell in, so I dove after it, but I was still wearing my purse and backpack, so both phones are wet now."

Erik was stony. "Of course you couldn't get it. Your backpack was like a flotation device. Why would you jump into saltwater with phones?! Now we've lost two phones and the VHF." He grabbed two snorkel masks and threw one to me. We slipped into the lagoon to hunt for the VHF. It was essential for communication.

After fifteen minutes, we gave up. *Fezywig* had already shifted, and now we were late for dinner, too.

"I wish we could *call* our friends to let them know we'll be late," Erik said. "But we don't have a VHF, or a local phone, or your iPhone." Erik rolled his eyes my way before revving the motor. In trying to be a hero, I had effectively broken all forms of communication in one dramatic swoop.

The kids were smart enough not to complain about saltwater spray on our way to our friends'. Of course we were all smiles, even though we were late and Erik and I were still damp. He explained our delay as if it were already a joke to him. I was relieved to have someone to talk to. We ate delicious food made in a full-size oven. We swam in their freshwater pool. I playfully tossed Lily into the shallow end where Erik was waiting. I expected her to surface with confidence in her personal buoyancy. That's how Erik was taught to swim. She surfaced, but stopped trusting me in the water and clung to the pool sides and stairs after that. I wasn't sure if that was good or bad. I wanted her to trust me. I also didn't want her jumping off *Fezywig* when nobody was looking. That's why we had netting, tethers, and a life vest for her. That's why she slept in the room right across from me.

Our friends let us use their washer and dryer. I'm sure our boat lifestyle seemed peculiar to them. I doubt any of their land friends washed their clothes in their host's machines during a dinner party, but they were good sports, and we were grateful. On the way home, Erik flipped on his headlamp so other dinghies could see us as we splashed across the dark lagoon with a dinghy full of sleepy children and warm laundry. We bought a floating VHF a few days later.

We had never expected to be in Sint Maarten long enough to build a community. But now we had land friends who sometimes let us swim in their pools and do our laundry during dinner. Our lagoon friends were always changing. While *Silverheels* prepared to sail to Grenada, *Copper Penny* showed up in Hawaiian shirts and became our new sailing aunt and uncle. Larry was a silver-haired career cop with a Southern accent and a heart of gold. Penny had a grandmother's heart, a mother's smile, and a teenager's sense of adventure. Their trawler was docked at the luscious Simpson Bay Marina. They gave us chilled orange juice and let Lily pet their dog. We visited their slip whenever we went ashore . . . until they sailed to the BVI. We hadn't met any other boat families with kids. That didn't matter when we thought we were leaving. When we were leaving, we were in a frenzy to get everything ready. We were desperate for a routine that brought us together as a family. Now that we were staying, the lagoon had become a giant waiting room.

"Since we're not going anywhere, can we invite friends to visit?" Alison asked. That was a good question. We, the kids especially, spent most of our time at anchor, surrounded by unswimmable water with limited electricity, limited internet, and *un*limited humidity. Those dang Caribbean breezes helped. I had no idea how long it would last.

ERIK

"What would you say about moving to the French side of the lagoon?" I asked Emily one morning. She had plenty of complaints about the French side: gross water, sketchy, rusting boats, triple the distance to the chandleries, and we didn't know anyone on the French side. "Good points," I agreed. "But it would be quieter. We wouldn't get jostled every morning by boats going out the drawbridge and tourists on Jet Skis." I kept thinking out loud: "We aren't going to shore as much these days, and we don't really know anybody on the Dutch side anymore either." This was all true, but also, I was getting lazy. It didn't seem worth all of the trouble to re-anchor until I added, "It's only five bucks to anchor on the French side. That's a flat rate, not a weekly rate." The Dutch side charged twenty dollars each week. The engine repair was taking a lot longer than we had expected. We kept returning to the Dutch office and paying to extend our stay. At this point, we preferred to extend our money.

"That'd be fine with me," Emily said. We pulled anchor and re-dropped it west of the Causeway Bridge on the French side of the lagoon.

"Now we can stay forever," I said.

"That sounds nice," she said.

"Really?"

"I'm coming around. I'm focusing on the good stuff, like being rocked to sleep, having a jungle gym onboard, and Eli asking about iguanas. I still like to watch the planes take off. But I don't want to be on them anymore." That was something. The kids were doing pretty well too, but they were still adjusting.

"I wish there were some kid boats here," SJ said as we sat around the salon. I didn't blame her. I was with my best friend—Emily. But SJ wanted a friend who understood what she was going through, someone besides her family. We were unexpectedly creating a new life in this place. We'd never intended to stay so long.

Once our destination fever broke, I accepted that our engine would be ready when it was ready. I stopped wishing we were somewhere else and started exploring where we were.

Our boat faced a hill that rose steeply up out of the lagoon. It was the tallest point in Simpson Bay and was called the Witch's Tit.

"That's a sucky name," SJ laughed at her own pun.

Alison rolled her eyes. "I'll call it The Witch's *Hat*. It looks like a pointy hat more than that . . . other thing."

"Who wants to climb the Witch's . . . Hat later?" I asked.

Sarah Jane pulled her hair into two aggressive pigtails and said, "I do!"

Jane and I took a VHF, got dropped off at the base, and started up the cliff face. It was steep but not steep enough to need ropes. We scaled the volcanic rock, passing goat scat and nodding to the goats that silently watched as we moved upward.

At the top everything fell into place. I could see the whole lagoon, the two bridge entrances, the airport runway, the beaches outside the lagoon. I saw Marigot to the west and Philipsburg to the east. All over the lagoon and bays sat tiny white specks that all swung in unison as the wind shifted. Directly below us, in a field of green and turquoise, was our tiny white speck.

Our boat was *our* whole world. But it wasn't *the* whole world. I had my own ideas and expectations. Emily, Karina, Alison, Jane, Eli, and Lily each had their own too. But there were other ideas and expectations out there. Beyond the edge of the island, the ocean spread far into the distance. St. Barts and Saba and Sint Eustatius broke the horizon. I saw how small I was, how small we all were. We were all part of a beautiful picture. There was plenty to see. We would wait.

PART

THREE

40 Days

to

4 Months, 9 Days aboard *Fezywig*

Dog Island

Prickly
Pear Cays

ISLAND HARBOUR ■

ANGUILLA
(UNITED KINGDOM)

SAINT-MARTIN
(FRANCE)
■ MARIGOT

SINT MAARTEN
(NETHERLANDS)
■ PHILIPSBURG

Île
Fourchue

**SAINT
BARTHÉLEMY**
(FRANCE)

GUSTAVIA ■

L E E W A R D   I S L A N D S

SABA
(NETHERLANDS)
THE BOTTOM ■

ST. EUSTATIUS
(NETHERLANDS)

ORANJESTAD ■

**ST. KITTS
& NEVIS**
(NETHERLANDS)

CHAPTER 7

DISCOVERY, DISCOVERY, THIS IS *FEZYWIG*

FRENCH SIDE, SIMPSON BAY LAGOON, SAINT MARTIN

40 Days aboard *Fezywig*

EMILY

On the first day of spring, we celebrated Erik's fortieth birthday with *Silverheels,* cinnamon rolls, and boat fenders as balloons. One month later, on Easter Sunday, we celebrated my fortieth birthday with sunrise singing, colored eggs, and cardamom cake. Between those two holidays, everything changed. We had visits from two different New York City friends, we met two kid boats, and we fell in love with them so quickly that we moved *Fezywig* to anchor near them.

Our first NYC visitor was Ty, a photographer who arrived with origami paper, dark-chocolate-covered almonds, and no return ticket. Erik and Sarah Jane had taken the dinghy to pick him up at the airport. The rest of us crowded around the salon table coloring welcome signs when we heard two kid boats, *Discovery* and *Day Dreamer,* hailing each other on the VHF.

"Karina, jump in," I nudged.

"I'm not doing it," she said. Her eyebrows rose at the suggestion.

"Okay. Let's practice first," I said, "Pretend you're calling: '*Discovery, Discovery*, this is *Fezywig*,'" I said. Karina picked up the VHF, her thumb hovering over the button to open communication. She held the radio up to her mouth and inhaled through her nose. The rest of us gathered around her. She set the radio down. It was a no-go. Alison opened her palm in a willingness to try. We repeated the practice, but she also chickened out. The radio sat quiet on the navigation desk.

Discovery and *Day Dreamer* stopped talking. The channel went quiet.

"I'm sick of this!" Eli said.

He picked up the radio. He pressed the button with his thumb and said, "*Discovery, Discovery*, this is *Fezywig*," He repeated himself once more. Then we waited.

"*Fuzzy-Wing*. This is *Discovery*. Let's move to channel six," the girl's voice said.

"Wahoo! Yay!!!!" Cheers broke out aboard *Fezywig*. Eli was a hero. He had made contact with another kid boat. Alison helped him switch channels.

"Who are you?" the girl's voice asked. Each of the *Fezywig* kids shouted their own version of the appropriate response. Foxtrot. Echo. Zulu. Yankee. Whiskey. India. Golf.

"We're *Fezywig*. We're a kid boat. We want to meet you," Eli said, but between our shouting and his thumb losing grip on the button, the girl was confused.

"What?" she asked.

Karina held her hand out and Eli gave her the radio.

Thumb firmly pressing the channel open, she said, "We have five kids. We want to play."

"Ooooooh! Do you want to meet today or tomorrow? We finish school after 1:00 p.m. We're at the Boca Marina."

It was Friday. We had Ty with us, a playdate Saturday, and church on Sunday. Our social calendar was filling up. First, all of our kids played at *Discovery* with most of their family. Next, we combined for a beach day with most of *Day Dreamer* and most of *Discovery*. Eli broke all his personal records for distance swimming, buoyed by a life vest. Then all of our kids played at *Day Dreamer*, where Sarah Jane discovered boat swings, a bosun's chair at the end of a long rope attached to the top of the mast. "I don't want to go back to the city now. The boat is better," she said. "Can we get a swing?" Erik set one up the next day. Finally, we got everyone from all three boats together.

We met aboard *Discovery* for their youngest daughter's birthday party. Other families were there, but the ones that stayed in our life were *Discovery* and *Day Dreamer*. *Discovery* included John and Michelle, who jointly ran a tech company that allowed them to be digital nomads with their four children: Kate, fourteen, who was eager to learn and nearly always cheerful; Jaci, ten, a competitive equestrian; Genna, seven, I'd only ever seen her dancing to the music on her iPad; and Jack, four, a zombie killer and Minecraft expert. Eli was happy to have another boy around. They also had two dogs and a cat.

Day Dreamer included Peter, who worked remotely managing websites and loved to cook; and Lisa, who scuba dived, was the main teacher on their boat, and did not love to cook.[8] Lisa would've been easily mistaken for one of her three daughters except her hair was cut into a bob and she always carried a backpack. Their daughters were Emma, a precocious fourteen, with long white-blonde hair, and a natural leader; Anna, about twelve, who had dark blonde hair with brassy highlights and loved to draw; Sara, ten, who was blonde with freckles and always moving. *Day Dreamer* also had a lively black rescue dog.

Erik played his guitar. Karina and Alison joined in on their

---

8. These awesome folks blog at thenonconformist.com, a wealth of information, experiences, and long-pondered thoughts about the live-aboard lifestyle.

ukuleles. Emma brought her electric keyboard, and Kate tap danced on the deck. As the party wound down, the kids and the adults naturally separated. The kids had already divided themselves into the "Bigs," Karina, Alison, Emma, and Kate; the "Middles," Anna, SJ, and Jaci; and the "Littles," Eli, Genna, Jack, and Lily. They all played on the front deck of *Discovery* while the adults claimed the seats on the back deck talking.

"It took us four days to check into the French side because it was either a lunch break or a holiday," Erik said.

"Another day in paradise," John said. Even before moving his family onto a boat, he'd been unconventional. He'd won science awards in high school and studied computers in college. He told us how his boss had asked him to stay on after his freshman-year internship. "I told him I had to go back to school. He asked, 'Why?' I told him I wanted to get a good job and make a lot of money. He said he'd pay me a lot of money. So, I dropped out of school."

"Makes perfect sense to me," Erik said.

"I still think college is a good idea," Michelle said. "Not just because employers are looking for it, but because it can be a great way to learn."

"The internet is a game-changer in traditional education," I said. This was one of my favorite topics.

"My girls have learned so much living on a boat: history, geography, languages. A lot is built into this lifestyle," Lisa said.

"That's what I'm hoping," I said.

"You guys are blending right in," Peter said. "It usually takes new cruisers about six months to really *slow* down."

"Our busted engine kind of forced that on us," Erik said. "We're not going anywhere. And I'm okay with that for now."

Ty got a gig and, after twelve wonderful days, had to return to New York City. Even though Eli was the hero that had hailed the other kid boat, he was more homesick for his old life than he was happy about his new buddies, especially since six of them were girls. The day of Ty's return flight, Eli stood on deck with his backpack, ready to go. He had packed all his plushies and one pair of underwear.

"I'm going back with Ty," he said.

"I'll be at work," Ty said. "What will you do all day?"

"I'll sit in your air-conditioned apartment and play video games," Eli said.

"Good plan, sweetheart," I admitted. "Except I would miss you too much." I wrapped my arms around Eli, backpack and all. Tears slid down his face as Erik drove Ty to the airport in the dinghy and we waved goodbye. Eli resigned himself to make the best of his circumstances. With new friends so near, that was getting easier.

Our second visitor was Karina's best friend, Ruth. She stayed for a week catching up on her sleep, learning to drive a dinghy, and hanging out with the other boat kids. After she left, we hoped Erik's parents would visit. They wouldn't want to stay on the boat, but we were only one hundred feet from the Le Flamboyant Hotel. It couldn't hurt to ask. In a short time we'd made our own little neighborhood on the French side of the lagoon—*Fezywig* and *Day Dreamer* on the southwest and *Discovery* on the southeast. We weren't in a hurry, but we wouldn't be in one place forever, either. Nick always said the next part would solve the engine problem. Once we had two working engines it would be tricky to predict where we might be.

Up to now, we had called our boat *Fezywig,* but the hull and bow said *Longhi.* Erik ordered weather-resistant decals in a Dickensian font to reflect our namesake, Mr. Fezziwig. Ever so carefully, Erik aligned the "Y" decal on the boat's hull and made sure the center of the "Y" was split symmetrically. Then he evenly spread the "FEZ" and "WIG" on either side. Finally he added "NEW YORK, NY," our homeport, on the stern. Now everyone would know we were officially the *Fezywig*s.

Discovery decided to leave the steady flow of shore power, water, and internet to anchor near us and *Day Dreamer* on the northwest side of the Simpson Bay Lagoon. Our kids were thrilled. They stood at the stern cheering as John circled for an anchorage. When he shut the engines off, Alison and Sarah Jane swam over to greet them. This trifecta of kid catamarans clustered together marked the unofficial beginning of the honeymoon phase of our sailing sabbatical.

Now that the kids had friends nearby, they were more attentive during school. They wanted to finish so they could play. Karina and Alison gave Kate and Emma ukulele lessons and started having jam sessions, filled with cover tunes and originals. The *Fezywig* kids taught the others how to bake bread, cinnamon rolls, and pumpkin bars. Emma taught Karina and Alison to make Swedish pancakes. Kate and Emma choreographed diving routines including the Middles and Littles. The Middles staked out *Day Dreamer's* boat swing and turned it from a human tetherball game into an aerial art, though they would still pass the Littles back and forth like a tetherball. The Littles painted, built Legos, and built worlds in Minecraft. The older girls made origami, jewelry, and handwritten film scripts. All of the kids were in the movies. Some of these projects took several days. And there was always the beach, snorkeling, and kayaks or sunfish to paddle around. They never ran out of ideas. "It's way more fun than hanging out watching a movie," Alison said, recalling her land friendships. But every now and then even these boat kids would pile onto *Discovery* and watch a movie.

As our kids' social lives expanded, I had less and less help at home. I was floundering as an educator. In my conventional life, I had leaned heavily on online resources and a printer for our homeschool. On the boat, the printer blew up the first time Erik plugged it into the European outlets and the internet was rarely accessible. I scrambled for a new plan. Michelle and Lisa shared their personal libraries with me, but where would I find the time? Hours I would ordinarily spend preparing for school were gobbled up with hand-washing laundry, collecting water, and preparing three daily meals from scratch.

"Do what only you can do," Erik suggested. "The older kids can handle meals. It will be good for them."

Erik told the kids about it at lunchtime.

"I'm not sure what we have or what needs to be used first," Karina said.

"I can guide you there," I said. "That's actually a good skill. It's not just following a recipe; it's managing ingredients."

"I like cooking," Alison said. "Can I make Swedish pancakes for dinner?"

"What if I'm responsible for lunch, but I'm at another boat?" SJ wondered.

"Come home ahead of time so lunch is ready," Erik said. "Not ready in a pot, ready on the table with the table set." Karina, Alison, and SJ took over all the weekday cooking.

A few days after the new meal prep rotations Erik found me sitting on our bed surrounded by books, binders, and spiral notepads.

"How is lesson planning?" he asked.

"I feel guilty reading and taking notes while the kids are working." Lily came in for a hug and a kiss.

"You are working," Erik said.

"I'm the best cook onboard."

"They'll get better," Erik said.

"It's not about food. It's about nurturing relationships. I want to take care of my family," I said. Eli came in to show me a drawing.

"You need to be an executive," Erik said, not for the first time. "Being a mom doesn't mean you have to cook and clean. It can, but it doesn't have to. Let the kids grow by taking on responsibilities. Take that time to do the things you want to do and only you can do." SJ poked her face in our overhead hatch, inviting me to watch her latest trick on the bimini. I stood up on our bed and rested my arms on the hatch, ready to be impressed.

"Where is the cumin?" Alison asked from the galley. I answered.

Karina popped out of her hatch directly across the stern to share a well-phrased paragraph from *Atlas Shrugged*. I sat back down on our bed.

"I came in here to run some ideas past you," Erik said. "But maybe now is not a good time."

"Everybody wants a piece of me," I said. Peeling back a layer of domestic responsibilities brought into focus what only I do in our family. As a wife and mother, I am the emotional touchstone. The mechanism can be anything; cooking, reading aloud, laundry; but the relationship is the goal. Every person in our family wants me to see them, listen to them, and encourage them. The main thing they wanted was my attention.

Well, they wanted my attention when they were around. Being near so many friends still felt like a special event. The kids from all three boats spent as many hours together as possible, so Sarah Jane was surprised when she hailed *Discovery* and Kate said, "Our mom says we can't play. We're having *Discovery* day: no friends and no electronics." Michelle was a pro. She had cycled through traveling friendships before. She realized that if this friendship was going to carry on—and who knew when our engine would be fixed—she needed to set some boundaries. I appreciated her example. Jaci sat on the bow of *Discovery* and SJ sat on the stern of *Fezywig*, looking at each other across the water, wishing they could play together.

Family relationships are like doing yoga on a boat, trying to stay balanced while the floor is constantly shifting beneath your feet. This may come as a surprise, but as a newlywed, Erik—Mr. "Our family of seven on a boat is enough universe for me"—was reluctant to even discuss having children. He assumed it would require sitting at home every night staring at the baby. He didn't want to be tethered to a tiny theoretical tyrant.

"We are the nucleus," I said. "Any children we invite into our family will be the protons and electrons. We are the center, and they'll join us. If we want to do something, they can come with us." That must have resonated with Erik, because before long we had a handful of children and he was sharing *his* parenting philosophies with me. I had subscribed to the idea that parents sacrifice to give their children a better life. Erik had other ideas about what we as parents could give our children.

"Marriage and parenthood include plenty of sacrifice," he said. "But the best thing I can give my kids is for me to live the fullest, richest, most productive, generous life I know how, and bring them along for the ride. My job is not to tell them how to live. My job is to show them." Together we were cultivating a lifestyle of family-centered experiences.

Erik and I were figuring out how to claim our space as a couple, too. We tried sitting in the dinghy and letting the line out so far the kids couldn't hear our conversation, but Lily stood on deck crying the whole time. The relationship equation was always changing. Our first month in Saint Martin had been all urgency and high-stakes decisions. We were together constantly, but under a lot of pressure. As those pressures eased, we divided the various life responsibilities between us. That lightened the load but kept us apart much of the day. If we were together, there were usually children around so no real privacy. And we'd added all these great friends. This was too important to put on autopilot; only manual steering would do. We tinkered with the balance of work, play, time together, and time apart. We shifted between kids, friends, and each other. We tried to balance commonalities and divergent interests. For now, Erik and I followed Lisa and Peter's example and started taking evening walks along the beachfronts at the Flamboyant Hotel, taking turns talking and listening.

On our boat my older kids did most of the cooking, but I was still the buyer. I joined Michelle and Lisa for grocery runs. *Discovery* inherited a local mid-size car from a Swedish family that had sailed back to Sweden. The trunk was permanently locked. While we drove we made up stories about what might be in there. We never found out. We did figure out how to fit a two-week supply of groceries for three families—eighteen people—inside that beater.

Between them, Michelle and Lisa had nearly two years of local shopping experience. They initiated me into their routine of hitting three or four different grocery stores and taught me what to look for at each spot. They'd go in with three separate carts and stay together through the produce aisle, comparing deals.

"This is a decent price on strawberries, but they might be cheaper at Simples," Lisa might say. Some of the money we saved on produce we spent on chocolate. We ate our chocolate and talked as we rode with giant packages of toilet paper or heavy bags of rice on our laps, my cruiser version of a Girls' Night Out.

Our new neighbors helped us with food and water. I used to wonder what cruisers did all day. Now, I knew. A lot of time was spent buying groceries and ferrying them to the boat. Lots of time was spent making three meals a day from scratch. Our boat didn't have a microwave or refrigerator, though most did. And twice a week we spent a few hours getting water.

ERIK

I'd always taken water for granted. Turn on the faucet and there it was. Not so on a boat. On the boat I would say it became a preoccupation. My kids would say it became an obsession. Let me explain.

To be at anchor meant we had 160 gallons of water available at a time. The average shower in America uses seventeen gallons for a single shower. There were seven of us. Those 160 gallons had to be used for drinking, cooking, cleaning, and bathing. Thank goodness the toilets used seawater. Unless we were mindful, we'd go through our water in a day. If we were mindful, we found we could stretch it to three days. I helped the kids become mindful.

After one of Nick's recurring engine visits, he asked if he could wash his hands. "Sure," I said. He then stepped into the kitchen, turned on the water, and proceeded to let the water flow unabated while he washed and talked, talked and washed. The kids stood around silently shifting their eyes from the faucet to my face and back. What was Dad gonna do? What was Dad gonna say? If it had been one of them, it would have been, "Have you freaking lost your mind?! You don't need a gallon of water to wash your hands!" But this wasn't the kids. I let Nick finish, thanked him, and bid him farewell. Next time he could wash up at his shop.

Each water day we pulled anchor, motored to a dock, sometimes ran aground in the mud on our way, tied on the bumpers, tied up to the dock, put a hose into our tanks, filled up, untied from the dock, put the bumpers away, motored back to our spot, and re-anchored. I know moving a boat every three days may not seem like a big deal, but with one engine, it was a pain.

Discovery and *Day Dreamer* helped us establish a simpler routine. When *Discovery* was on the dock, John and Michelle let us raft up to buy water from their dock. At anchor, they used a water maker.[9] I wished we had a water maker, but that would be a $7,000 project that included drilling holes in our hull. Emily and I weren't ready to commit. *Day Dreamer* didn't like to pull anchor either. They had perfected their water collection system so they could gather rainwater off their large, hardtop bimini—which we didn't have and couldn't get—and also had large containers they used to ferry water from a dock to their boat.

They lent us their containers: several jerry cans and a large two-foot-by-five-foot flexible bladder. Originally *Discovery* let us use their

---

9. Water maker: if you want to get technical, it's a reverse osmosis contraption. A series of pumps pull in seawater, push it through increasingly refined filters at massively high levels of pressure, and output clean water.

dock water. When *Discovery* anchored near us we found another source, but in either case, every three days we would spend five hours moving 160 gallons of water from a dock to our tanks using *Day Dreamer's* containers.

So when my kids saw the profligate Nick blithely letting water run down the drain, they read my mind and knew I was doing the math. He was wasting my time.

On the flip side, after a particularly soaking rain, Emily collected one cupful of pure water in a metal bowl set under the drippy edge of our cockpit table. Each of us got a sip. It was delicious. Karina and Alison were discussing elaborate plans for catching more when the *Day Dreamer* girls pulled up in their dinghy and surprised us with four full jerry cans of rainwater. It wasn't quite chopping wood and smoking meat for the winter, but boat life was taking on a *Little House on the Prairie* feeling. *Little Boat on the Lagoon,* shall we say?

EMILY

Each boat added something to the community that made life better for all of us. *Fezywig* could bake, make music, and fold origami, but we needed help when it came to electrical wiring. Erik had learned to solder for the Wi-Fi booster, but now he was installing a battery monitor—a digital readout that would show how full our batteries were. We'd accidentally drained them and been in the dark a couple of times. It was a lot more complicated than setting up the Wi-Fi booster, so John, who had built robots, came to guide Erik's efforts.

Erik cut the hole on the navigation desk for the digital readout. They mapped out the wiring together and John left Erik to run the cables between the nav desk and the battery bank under Karina and SJ's bed. He would come back once Erik had everything ready to wire.

Erik pulled up all the cushions and boards to access the space underneath.

I got out of the way with Eli and Lily. Lisa and I talked homeschooling on *Day Dreamer* while the kids played on the swing. When Karina hailed my VHF to coordinate a dinghy ride home to make lunch, I returned to a full report of Erik's project.

"John took like half-a-dozen electrical shocks for us today," Erik said. John was packing up his toolbox.

"That's a true friend," I said.

"Twelve volts is no big deal," John said. "It's the 110/220V that hurt."

After John left, Erik kept talking, using all the science terms John had just reviewed earlier that afternoon: ohms, amps, resistance. I had learned those words in high school physics. But what I heard was, *I love you guys and I've been stressing out about how to keep you safe. It's lonely, but now this other dad has showed up. Just having someone who feels the same pressure helps, and he also has really good ideas. Now, I feel better.* Erik spelled out the next steps for the project.

"What do you think?" he asked.

"It sounds great, love," I said. "Let's do that."

Our rhythm accelerated. Every couple of weeks we gathered for Taco Night on one of the bigger boats. *Discovery* was forty-five feet and *Day Dreamer* was forty-seven feet On *Discovery* all twelve kids watched movies, danced, and drank water with ice. On *Day Dreamer* they took turns swinging or playing with Pippin. In either place, Lily roamed from group to group with a full plate and the parents told stories.

Sailors have always told stories. Epic storms. Strange customs. Dodgy bureaucracies. Drunken sailors. We got to know each other and we got glimpses of dozens of lives all over the world. Peter regaled us with tales of Grenada, an island about 300 miles south down the Caribbean chain. If Sint Maarten was the repair shop for cruisers, Grenada was the amusement park. Peter said every day the net buzzed with information about game nights, tours inland, grocery shopping trips, beach volleyball, and yoga. Peter told us about a drink stand where he bought exotic syrups for his famous smoothies.

"You'd love it there!" Peter said. Then, leaning back, he asked, "Would you consider heading south?" John, Michelle, and Lisa sat silent for a moment, like they were waiting to hear our answer. I had never considered heading south. But Erik and I had also never considered staying in Saint Martin for three months, yet here we were. We felt less rushed or rigid than ever. It was becoming obvious there are many templates for a happy life, not just the ones we imagined. I was more open to the beauty, adventure, and challenges of each day. I was flexible.

"Maybe. We'll have to think about it," Erik said, looking at me. The others leaned back, seemingly happy it was on the table. "One thing I definitely want to do is play Lagoonies' open mic night this week. Anyone interested?" *Discovery* was up for it.

And John had an invite of his own: "What would you guys say to a day sail out to Philipsburg Bay for Carnival? Traffic will be bad, but we could motor over on *Discovery* and walk in."

"I think that sounds fun," Michelle said. One of the Bigs overheard our conversation, and soon all of the kids were in the cockpit begging to go to Lagoonies and Carnival.

That weekend *Discovery* joined us at Lagoonies and kept our plates full of nacho chips until our set. Eli sat right next to the platter. They clapped for us while we played a few songs. We didn't know it was a competition, but the crowd cheered us to victory—first place out of two. We won an old-fashioned orange life preserver ring. Lily worked the crowd and kept checking in at the bar to grab mints from the candy dish. When the nachos ran out we took the kids home for a late bedtime.

"Aw, man!" SJ said, "It's just getting good." The retiree crowd at the bar put shiny fish hats over their bald or graying heads and were dancing around like teenagers.

A few days later was Carnival. John was right about traffic. The streets were in absolute gridlock. I was thankful to arrive by boat. There were semi-trucks full of blaring speakers preceding flocks of women famously clad in high heels and thousands of colorful feathers. I don't know how they managed. I was dying in sandals. It was so hot. Erik made a rope harness for Lily so I wouldn't lose her in the crowd. She tended to wander off. Even Lily was ready to escape, so we all left to get gelato.

I collapsed into shaded seating under thick striped umbrellas. I was too tired to make decisions, even about ice cream flavors. I asked the Bigs from each boat to sort out the orders.

"So," John said, stirring his vanilla shake, "Once your port engine is sorted out, are you heading south to Grenada or north to the BVI?" Was he reading our minds? Had he planted some tech hacker device on our boat under the guise of helping Erik install our battery monitor? No. We'd been thinking about it ever since Peter had asked at Taco Night. It was an obvious question. We used to have an obvious answer. We used to have a plan.

Our financial hourglass was emptying. Every month on *Fezywig* moved us closer to $0. Erik thought he might find a way to make money remotely. *Discovery* and *Day Dreamer* both had mobile jobs, but we hadn't cracked that code.

Yet we were attached to these cruisers. We wanted to stay with them. I don't think we realized maybe they wanted to stay with us, too. Maybe they were hanging around because they were waiting for our answer. *Day Dreamer* was definitely going to Grenada, but would love to go together. *Discovery* was planning on Grenada, but would consider heading north to the BVI if that's where we were going. When you're not alone in the world, people care about what you choose. We felt the pressure to make a decision.

"We're not sure," Erik said. "My parents are coming to visit next week for Alison's birthday, so we won't go anywhere until they leave."

"They're not coming until next week?" John asked. "What if all three of us get out of the lagoon and go to Anguilla for the weekend? You'll be back before your parents get here."

CHAPTER 8

EVERYTHING BUT THE ENGINE

SIMPSON BAY LAGOON, FRENCH SIDE, SAINT MARTIN

82 Days aboard *Fezywig*

ERIK

Fezywig hadn't pulled anchor in over a month. Anguilla, a British territory, sat a few miles north of us. It was visible from Saint Martin, but it wouldn't be a day sail. It would mean leaving the lagoon for a few days. All three crews, the other two captains, and Emily were thrilled with the idea, but I needed some convincing. I was most worried about getting through the bridges on one engine. Catamarans are not meant to be maneuvered in tight spaces with one engine. They're designed to be symmetrical. John did a good job winning me over. "You only really need your engine for the drawbridge and anchoring. We'll sail the rest of the way. If anything happens, we'll be there." Knowing I'd have backup made the difference.

All three boats pulled anchor and queued up for the drawbridge. Having one engine is a problem only if you lose your momentum. With enough momentum it's possible to keep the boat straight regardless.

Michelle drove their dinghy in the canal, ready to help in case we had any problems. We did. There was a long queue at the bridge, so we came to a dead stop. The water shallowed quickly around us. As we sat still in line, we started to drift toward the shallow mud. Michelle motored around and nudged our bow to keep us in the channel. Once it was our turn to proceed, she gave our bow a solid shove as we got up to speed. Then she zipped back to *Discovery*, tied off their dinghy, and climbed aboard. All three boats were on our way.

It was a gorgeous day and a beautiful sail. It was like the day sails we used to do in Long Island, but on a much bigger boat and with a stereo system. Everything was on full blast: the sun, the wind, and the music. This was definitely feeling like a good idea. We arrived in Anguilla in time for lunch and anchored near each other.

That afternoon, we took Lily ashore to stretch her legs. She was immediately attracted to live music playing at a cafe. When she realized the cafe was full of people, she wanted to stay. Emily and I spotted John and Michelle and sat with them. Within five minutes Lily started walking from table to table saying hello to perfect strangers. She snuck a sip of wine before any of us could stop her. We spent the rest of the time trying to prevent her from charming and beguiling well-meaning tourists with her cuteness. Lily is slow in some ways, but in others she is wicked fast.

The next day, we established a protocol we would come to follow for visiting a new island. Once the boat and the kids were settled post-journey, the adults would dinghy to shore to clear-in at the customs office. Then we would scout the town. We would circle around—on foot, in our dinghy, or in a rented vehicle—to see what was available. We looked for amenities: groceries, water, fuel. We kept an eye out for items of local interest. Peter and Lisa always packed spoons in their shore bag in case ice cream was a possibility. We thought this showed wise foresight and came to adopt this practice. Once we had a general idea of the territory, we'd return to our boat, discuss with the kids, and make plans.

In Anguilla, all the parents went ashore together. After a quick exploration and shopping run—which did, in fact, include ice cream—we decided the real gems of Anguilla were the outsider islands.

We piled into *Discovery*, since she was a motor yacht, and zipped out toward the Prickly Pear Cays and Dog Island. It was a full boat: twelve kids, six adults, two dogs, and a cat. Two captains would have the day off. Peter and I high-fived, and John was more than happy to give his mostly-at-anchor engines a workout. Everyone—dads, moms, and kids—was stoked. It was the first time any of us had been to these places. We would be discovering them together.

John fired up his engines and we set out for Dog Island. When we arrived, I was immediately glad he'd talked me into getting out of the lagoon. There was nobody else on this island. The water was perfectly clear. We could see tiny ridge patterns in the sand below as we set anchor in twenty feet of water. Nothing larger than a small bush grew on Dog Island. There were no fish and no shells to collect. It was barren and bleak in a way, but beautiful. After snorkeling, kayaking, swimming, and burying each other in the sand, we were ready to return to Anguilla. The kids from each boat brought homemade bread they'd all baked together. They made grilled cheese sandwiches. Then the Bigs, with some help from the Middles, created a distribution system to feed everyone as *Discovery* pushed through the exquisitely aqua and blue water back to Anguilla.

It was a fun eight-hour vacation from captain responsibilities. But now I was back on duty. *Fezywig* was nearly tapped out of water. We were only in Anguilla a few days, and I didn't want to spend half a day shuttling water into our tanks. Emily and I continued studying our water maker options but had yet to pull the trigger. It was an expensive and—for my skillset—complicated project. This little excursion was teaching us we couldn't safely sail for any real length of time without the threat of running out of water. We could live without solar panels. We could live without a wind generator. But we would always need water. What to do in the meantime?

John and I put our heads together. John filled his water tanks any time he ran his engine, so he was already full. In the end, our solution was a combination of *Discovery* design and *Fezywig* ingenuity.

John and I ran a hose from their boat to our water tanks. Now we had a hundred-foot hose floating below the surface in an anchorage with people coming and going by dinghy. Hoses don't take kindly to outboard propellers. We enlisted the kids to swim out and attach floaties and life jackets to the hose about every ten feet. Any lifeguard would be proud of our consideration for safety. John started up his engines and, over the next couple hours, 160 gallons of water miraculously transferred to our tanks. It sure beat hauling jerry cans from shore. I was starting to see how this was all going to work out, and I liked it.

EMILY

Back in Saint Martin, Grandma and Grandpa arrived to a flurry of hugs, stories, and questions. Karina, Alison, and SJ thumped luggage up the cement stairs to the second-floor room. Eli chased Lily down hotel corridors, corralling her back to the room. Their room was a basic space with a bathroom, two beds, and a dresser. Sadly, the shower held only three minutes' worth of hot water. Happily, there was a small outdoor balcony overlooking the pool, and it had a dinette set, a refrigerator, a sink, a toaster, and a burner.

Grandma produced a bright yellow bag of peanut M&M's and a DVD from her tote bag. The kids immediately tucked in, relishing a normal bed. Erik and I sat with his parents at the dinette, taking in the balmy evening, palm trees, and the lagoon.

"That's us over there," Erik pointed out *Fezywig*.

"I'm sorry you're stuck here," Grandpa said. He wasn't being ironic. "They've kept you two and half months behind schedule."

Schedule? I remembered schedules. They sound like a foreign concept in this new life.

"We don't feel stuck," Erik said. He meant it. I could've kissed him.

Unusually heavy rains poured down for the next few days, soaking us on our commutes from *Fezywig* to the hotel. But we had enough sunshine that week to take Grandma and Grandpa for a day sail. Grandpa diplomatically pronounced *Fezywig* "snug." We showed them a few beaches, Grandma snorkeled for the first time, they joined us for church on land and a Taco Night on *Day Dreamer*—the deluxe tour of our new life.

If not the highlight of their visit, Alison's birthday was the most memorable event. That morning the boat-kid girls joined us on *Fezywig* to celebrate her with thoughtful, homemade gifts. We spent the rest of the day with grandparents. I prepared a pasta salad while the kids swam in the pool below. I noticed Lily walking away from the pool pulling at the crotch of her swimsuit.

"What do you need, Lily?" I called down.

"I gotta poop!" she shouted.

"Alison! Hey, Ali. Will you bring Lily up here to use the bathroom?" Alison was in a good mood with all this birthday attention, and she hopped right out of the pool.

"Mom! She's already pooped in her swimsuit. It's just hanging there," Alison called up.

"Oh, dear. Let me throw you some wipes or paper towels. Hang on," I called back. I tossed her a package of baby wipes. They landed on the ground and she picked them up. Alison deftly grabbed the poop out of Lily's swimsuit without ever touching it with her hands.

"What should I do with this?" She shouted. With the poop in her hand, I was starting to wonder what the other tenants were thinking of this conversation.

"Just throw it in a garbage can." I advised. Alison shook her head and started looking for a garbage can—this is where it goes wrong—but she slipped on the wet tile surrounding the pool, falling to her hands and knees. The poop package went flying into the air. None of us saw where it went.

"Now what?!" Alison cried, eager to be relieved of these duties (I cannot help myself). After all, it was her birthday.

"Find it," I said. Alison started crawling on her hands and knees looking under tables and chairs and in the bushes.

"I found it!!" She shouted as if it were a good thing, which it was, but you wouldn't ordinarily imagine shouting with that much enthusiasm when you'd just found a package of poop.

Apprised of the situation, Erik had only one question: "Was it in the *turd* place you looked?" Alison's best birthday present was a story that never gets old.

ERIK

During my parents' visit, Sunsail proposed a compromise: they would rebuild our port engine if we would return to Oyster Pond. I wasn't excited about passing through that channel again, but after my parents left, Emily and I agreed to go. Then we had to break the sad news to our kids and the other boats.

"I have bad news, John," I said as we hung out in *Discovery's* cockpit. "They're gonna rebuild our engine."

"Are you kidding? That's great news."

"But we have to go to Oyster Pond. They say it's gonna take two weeks."

"So?"

"I know you all need to get going. Hurricane season isn't going to wait for our engine. You guys need to get south."

"Yeah, but listen: Michelle is heading back to the States for some work. It's easier for me to solo-parent on the dock. We'll just come with you."

"Really?"

"Yeah. It'll be fun," he laughed. John's laugh always reminded me I didn't have to make everything a big deal.

Word must have gotten around, because next thing I knew, Peter told me, "Yeah, we need to do some deep cleaning on our boat. I think we'll head to Oyster Pond and pick up a mooring ball." I couldn't believe it. The band was not breaking up.

Once again, we all set sail together, like the Niña, Pinta, and Santa María. After we docked in Oyster Pond, I ran into Joachim, our reliable Phase-Out Director.

"I told them from the beginning they needed to rebuild that engine for you," he said. "It would have saved everyone a lot of time and money if they'd done it then, but I'm glad it's finally happening."

I was new to this boat ownership thing, so I was insecure throughout the whole process. I appreciated Joachim helping me feel like I wasn't crazy. We'd stayed the course, and I trusted everything would get resolved.

With two weeks on the dock, I doubled down. We bit the bullet and ordered a water maker ($5,500), a generator to run the water maker ($1,000), and the replacement parts ($120) to fix the Wi-Fi booster I'd soaked, plus shipping for everything ($400). It was hard to spend that money because it was a lot of sand out of our hourglass, but Emily and I agreed it was the best way to keep us safe, and the dock was going to be the best place to install it.

Emily took advantage of the dock to get the kids' end-of-school-year online tests done, even though most of what they were learning wouldn't be on those kinds of tests. We were cleaning house, too. The kids' only goal was to spend as much time together as possible. Once school tests were done, the kids had lots of outdoor options: play in the windward hills overlooking the ocean, swim in the marina pool, or chase iguanas.

Emily or I swam with Lily every day, gradually regaining her trust. She increased her solo distance daily but stayed close to the perimeter for a quick escape. Eli asked if he could bake cookies for another boat in the marina he wanted to befriend. It turned out to be the ferry to St. Barts, which brought in dozens of people a couple times a day. We ate the cookies ourselves.

Everyone had somewhere to go, and I was thrilled to have an empty boat while I planned the water maker install. It would require drilling a hole into the underside of the hull. This made me nervous. In truth, it all made me nervous. I was now dealing with "big juice"— 220V power, the kind that hurt when you touched it. I would be drilling holes in bulkheads, running water through parts of the boat I really wanted to keep dry, and connecting high-pressure filters to remove biocontaminants. In essence, if I didn't do this right, I was looking at electrocution, a leaking hull, and drinking water that could make us sick. As I always tell my kids, "Don't mess up."

I laid it all out, ran it past John and Peter, who gave me their advice and ultimately their thumbs up, and then I started drilling. Like the Wi-Fi router, nothing came with a plug. I had to buy wires and connectors, fixtures and adhesive. I had to solder, jigsaw, and plumb my way through our floating home. This cheap, do-it-yourself approach still tapped out about thirty percent of the total budget for our trip. If this didn't work, it'd be tough to afford another approach.

It was a sweet victory when I ran the kitchen faucet and out came delicious, clean water made from our own water maker. I felt as though I'd discovered some mystical alchemy, like we had a money-printing machine in our basement or something. We could go anywhere and have unlimited clean water. Everything was open to us. We could go anywhere in the world and have a drink.

The Wi-Fi router was a quick fix once I had the right parts. The

Sunsail IT guy even came out to our boat and asked about it. "Your signal is very strong. I am picking up your boat from way over at our office. What system are you using?" I have to admit I was feeling pretty pleased with myself.

All we needed was an engine.

CHAPTER 9

SHAKEDOWN

OYSTER POND, SAINT MARTIN

117 Days aboard *Fezywig*

EMILY

The day had finally come when the rebuilt engine would be installed. Erik motored *Fezywig* to a slip closer to shore so a crane could lift the massive engine into place. We all gathered to watch. The mechanics weren't used to having a crowd cheer for their work, but they liked it. We all smiled and took photographs with the mechanic, with his assistants, and with our perfect, practically new, port engine. I left Erik to enjoy the whole process. Michelle, Lisa, and I went on one last provisioning run before the shakedown tour.

When I returned with food, Erik said, "Listen to this." He turned on the port engine and it purred to life.

"Are you coming on to me?" I asked.

"Mom! Geesh," Karina said. "He's been doing that all afternoon."

"It's so beautiful," Erik said as he turned off the engine. Then he switched it on again and smiled.

ERIK

"You'll want to take a shakedown cruise," John and Peter said. This was sailor common sense. After having such significant work done on the boat, we should take it for a spin and make sure it was working properly before heading off on our own. We could go anywhere in the world. We had everything we needed. That's a heady feeling. We talked about the Panama Canal, the Pacific Ocean, and circumnavigation. Emily topped up our provisions. We had a water maker. We had Wi-Fi. We had a trustworthy engine. But we decided to start by moving in slowly expanding circles.

When Michelle returned from business in Florida, we'd head southeast to St. Barts; then sail almost directly south to Sint Eustatius. From there we'd sail northwest to Saba. It was a little triangle of the three southern islands closest to Sint Maarten, but who knew where that might lead? We were feeling confident. This would be the shakedown sail of a lifetime. From Saba, *Day Dreamer* would continue on to Grenada or maybe loop back to Sint Maarten. *Discovery* would definitely return to Sint Maarten to wrap up some business ashore. *Fezywig* would wait and see.

"Last time in this stupid channel!" I called as we pounded our way out of Oyster Pond. Both engines were purring. *Day Dreamer* had left earlier in the day. They planned to sail the entire way and had plenty of tacking[10] ahead of them. *Discovery* was enjoying a leisurely morning. As a motor vessel, they could travel much faster—one, because of their speed, and two, they didn't have to tack.

---

10. Tacking: sailing the hard way. The easy way is to have the wind behind you. Sailing toward the wind is tricky. You can't sail straight at it, so you zig and zag (tack) across it to make headway. Peter liked to do things the hard way whenever possible, just for fun.

"Next stop: Philipsburg Bay!" I said. We were in full party mode. School tests were done. The engines worked. We were hitting the seas with friends. Music was blaring, and we started our no-seasickness dance party. In the interest of time, our plan was to motor to fuel dock in Philipsburg Bay, fill up the fuel tanks there, and then sail to Ile Fourchue, a small outer island of St. Barts, where we'd meet up with the other two boats.

We weren't more than fifteen minutes out of the channel when the port engine sputtered and died. All of the party went right out of us. I turned off the music. Everyone stopped dancing, and we stared at each other. We were deflated balloons.

"Should we go back?" Emily asked. I didn't say anything. I looked out to sea. None of us wanted to pass through that rocky channel ever again, especially on one engine.

"Let's get to the fuel dock. We'll figure it out from there."

While *Fezywig* was refueling, I opened up the port engine locker to take a look.

"Hey, mon," the dockhand said. "We close in an hour."

"It's the middle of the day," I said.

"Holiday. We close in one hour," he repeated. I pulled myself out of the engine locker and grabbed a VHF.

"Hey, John, they close in an hour. You may want to get here ASAP."

"Copy that."

"By the way, the port engine conked out."

No response.

"Maybe you can take a quick look with me when you get here?" I added weakly.

"Sure thing. We're casting off."

I told the dockhand, "We have some friends coming. They'll be here in thirty minutes to fuel up."

"We close—" the dockhand began.

"I know. You close in an hour."

"What are you thinking about the engine?" Emily asked. By this time the kids were groaning because it was hot on the concrete dock and they worried we were about to get left behind.

"I'm not going back to Oyster Pond," I said. "Let's see what we can figure out once John gets here."

John and I took a quick look and couldn't figure it out. It was nothing obvious. We'd all heard it running fine the other day. The sun was lowering and none of us wanted to arrive at Ile Fourchue in the dark. We decided to cast off and take a closer look there. *Discovery* motored off and we did our best to keep up.

Ile Fourchue, the Fork, is a little crescent island with nothing on it except super steep ridgelines and rocks. It's roughly the halfway point between Sint Maarten and St. Barts. The only hospitality we hoped for there was a calm anchorage. The sky darkened and we imagined *Day Dreamer* and *Discovery* tucked inside, preparing their evening meals. We didn't want to eat. We all felt seasick. We expected that for the first couple of days. We simply wanted to arrive, anchor, and sleep.

I set my eagle eyes on Ile Fourchue. We closed in none too quickly in our race against the sun. We pounded headlong into the trade winds and the oncoming seas. With only one engine, it was slow going. We were still a couple miles out when what to our wondering eyes should appear but John Alonso catching air in his super speedy dinghy, zooming straight for us. Ordinarily, I wouldn't recommend taking a dinghy that far out into open, choppy water. But John was our friend. Indeed, the other two boats had anchored and eaten dinner. They had their eye on the sun as well. We couldn't reach each other on VHF because the anchorage was surrounded by steep cliffs. Every minute they didn't see *Fezywig*, they worried. John, who loves to sit around and enjoy the sunset just as much as the next guy, decided to get up and come find us. We could hardly believe he was out there with us, screaming with a high-pitched girl voice every time the boat hopped a wave. We love John.

He called to us to see how we were doing. He said he would guide us in. It was dusk. They had the perfect mooring ball all picked out for us. John's daring-do lifted our spirits. I followed him into the cove and he floated in his dinghy off our bow, helping us get our lines through the mooring ball. The crews on *Day Dreamer* and *Discovery* came out on deck to wave and cheer for us. We were the last runner in the marathon, but we had crossed the finish line.

While we were grateful to have slept, everyone wanted to move on the next morning. The seas had stayed choppy all night, even in the anchorage. Ile Fourchue was no place to look at a faulty engine. We were off to St. Barts.

EMILY

I imagined St. Barts as upscale and manicured. Colombier was nothing like that. We were almost completely encircled by the craggy island reaching out into the ocean. The crescent beach was a full mile walk from anywhere else on the island, making it too remote for crowds. There was plenty of room for all three boats among the half dozen already anchored. Rugged terrain; calm, clear waters; and friends surrounded us. A ribbon of steep mountainside trail laced through dramatic pitted rock formations. I couldn't wait to hike it.

First we wanted to check in and buy some Wi-Fi access. John volunteered to host a check-in party to the main town of Gustavia. It was a group date for the parents. Erik and I brought spoons.

Gustavia was more like I had expected St. Barts to be—a lush, green, hilly island with stunning views; quaint, colorful homes; and luxury boutiques. But it was unexpectedly quiet.

"French holiday," Erik said.

"What holiday?" I asked.

"Who knows?" he said. He was guessing, but he was right.

Fortunately, the check-in office was open. It boasted vaulted ceilings, multiple digital check-in screens, and lots of glossy pamphlets touting local attractions. The concierges sat behind a polished counter in matching navy polos tucked into ironed shorts and fastened with shiny belts. Erik bought a week's worth of Wi-Fi. After seeing Colombier, we definitely wanted to stay a few days.

We walked up and down the quiet streets of Gustavia, peeking in closed shop windows. Erik had started a photo collection of Caribbean doors. He added a few brightly painted hand-carved doors. He liked the craftsmanship, the unknown story behind each one, and the metaphor of possibilities.

"Who wants gelato?" Michelle asked, spotting the only open shop we'd seen.

"Peter brought spoons," Lisa said.

"We have spoons too," Erik said. Having spoons meant we were prepared for things to go right.

I was as eager as everyone else to explore remote and rugged Colombier. Nobody wanted to hear about this secondhand, so we launched our own mini-invasion of Colombier beach. This was an all-ashore affair. Everyone came. All the dads. All the moms. All the kids. Nobody was left behind. We were an army of rash guards, sunhats, and sturdy rubber sandals. We pulled the dinghies ashore. Where did that ribbon of trail lead? What was on the other side of those craggy hills?

The trail started narrow, so we walked single file. The Bigs and Middles got ahead. Jack stayed with Michelle, and Erik stayed close to Eli. I couldn't see the girls, but I heard them talking and laughing ahead. I stayed with Lily, which meant I was the end of the line. Ahead, a sharp right turn took everyone past my field of view. Lily and I were alone. Again. I pressed on slowly.

"Look at these leaves," I said.

"Let's go smell that flower."

"Oh! Lily, do you see the butterfly?" We passed under a canopy of tall bushes where butterflies darted in and out. How did this wild, arid, steep, volcanic island also have this shady, cool, green butterfly haven? We didn't get much past the butterflies when Lily lost interest. Her eyebrows knit together over rosy red cheeks. She tugged at the chinstrap on her hat.

"Get this off. Off," she said pulling through the Velcro and tossing the hat aside. She sat down on the path, her legs extended out like a V. She wasn't going anywhere.

"I'm hungry," Lily said.

"We just ate," I said. "We'll have lunch when we get back to the boat." She noticed little stones on the path. She picked one up and threw it down the steep hillside. It bounced along until I couldn't see it anymore. The ocean constantly foamed and crashed into the island beneath us, too far away to hear. Lily picked up another stone and threw it.

I coaxed, "Come on, Lily. Get up. We're walking. Do you want to be with Jenna and Jack?" She picked up another stone and threw it down the mountain. I tried again.

"Let's stay together with our group. Can you see Daddy?" Lily picked up another stone and threw it down the mountain. She was completely covered in dust now. Her sweaty face was dusty. Her pink and white rash guard was dusty. I stood behind her, hooked my elbows under her arms, and heaved upward. Lily didn't help. She let her dead weight hang and took advantage of her freakishly flexible shoulders. She started to slip from my grasp. I caught her butt with the top of my foot and clasped my fingers together in front of her chest. I heaved her up again.

"Put your feet down, Lily. Stand up! Stand up!" She stood up.

I couldn't see anyone from our group ahead on the twisting trail. *Why am I* always *the one who stays behind with Lily? Why am I risking my spine lifting her and carrying her? Why aren't Karina and Alison helping me? Why doesn't SJ care?* I understood why the kids walked ahead.

They helped a lot at home. *Why did Erik skip ahead as if he hadn't a responsibility in the world, without a moment's concern for me?* I had a lot of time to ruminate while I coaxed Lily down the trail.

Eventually I met up with the Bigs and Middles under a shady overhang.

"Hey guys," I said. "How was it?"

"Awesome," SJ said, climbing the overhang wall. "There's a really cool lagoon down there, so we all went swimming. It was really fun. You should've been there."

"Is it all right if Lily sits here with you so I can check it out?" I asked. The Middles looked at each other sideways. They didn't want to be responsible.

"Of course," Alison said.

I marched ahead to see what I had missed as Erik and the rest of the parents and Littles approached the overhang. Erik had the gall to smile.

"Hi," he kept smiling. I did not smile.

"Lily decided she didn't want to hike."

"Oh," he said, noticing I was *not* smiling. "Do you want to see the lagoon?"

"I'm on my way," I said still walking.

"I'll come with you," he offered. He walked the remainder of the trail again—with me in tow. I'm sure it was a lot less pleasant for him the second time.

"You guys left me back there all by myself with Lily," I complained once we were out of earshot. "She wouldn't move. Why do I always have to stay behind?" Erik mostly listened. He tried to point out the beautiful features of the island, but I was too bitter to enjoy it. It all sounded like descriptions of a party I didn't get to attend. I took one look at the shallow turquoise lagoon and marched back up the trail to the beach. But I saw it, damn it.

Back on the beach, Karina's face was completely flushed.

"Are you okay?" I asked. My maternal instincts overrode my personal frustration.

"I'm nauseous," she said. "My head aches. I don't want to move."

"Did you drink any water today?" I asked, quickly diagnosing her with heatstroke. I'd read so many medical books and articles on basic illnesses, as a mom, not just for this trip.

"Yes. I've been drinking water all morning," she said. "I threw up on my way to the beach."

"Let's get you into the shade," I said.

I put her arm over my shoulder and helped her step around the puddles full of black, spiny sea urchins to the dinghy.

Once back in her cabin, I closed all the blinds and put a towel over her face. The first aid guide recommended visiting a hospital, but also suggested sips of saltwater over time. For a nauseous cruiser who lived in saltwater full-time, the remedy was almost worse than the sickness. Every few minutes I checked in and gave her another small sip of saltwater. I could get to Gustavia if she needed a doctor, but I wanted to give the home remedy a chance. After an hour of horizontal rest and small servings of saltwater, Karina felt better. As a mother, my biggest concern was that my family might get sick or injured. That was true no matter where we lived. On *Fezywig*, I knew how little it would take to break an ankle, crush a thumb, or get jacked up in the ropes. I loved being on this journey, but the trade-off was constant vulnerability. I was grateful for every day that ended with my family whole and healthy.

"How's she doing?" Erik asked when I came to bed.

"Karina's fine."

"How are you doing?" He's a brave man. I was still upset about the hike.

"I feel really stupid, but I'm still angry," I said. "I feel like I always get stuck with Lily. I love her, but I feel like I miss out on a lot of things because of her."

"Maybe the kids could pitch in more."

"She's *our* kid. We are the ones responsible for her. The bulk of the burden should not be on them. I don't want it to always be me. We're out here in these beautiful places and I want to see them too. I don't always want to go at Lily's speed or be held hostage by her mood. She is getting too big for me to carry. And I'm stuck. I don't want to resent her, but sometimes I do." I went on and Erik listened. This was not his first rodeo. He let me spew the poison first. He heard me. That helped me let go a little more. Once I was all cried out and heard, we started seeking solutions.

"I know you love Lily," Erik said, opening his arms to me. Exhausted, I fell in and let him hold me.

"You are with Lily a lot," Erik said. "I want to be aware of that and take turns. I want you to be able to enjoy this trip too."

"I can do better at recognizing when I'm losing it," I said. "I could give you some warning and ask for help." Those conversations are never fun, and I always feel like a ridiculous baby afterwards. But our communication does improve.

I needn't have worried about missing the hike. Lisa, Michelle, and I hiked it every morning that week. The world over, women meet in the mornings to get some endorphins and some emotional support from their friends. I was doing it in Tevas on a volcanic island overlooking the Caribbean Sea. Same idea. Same structure. Same sanity. A little bit of morning time spent taking care of myself made me a much better wife and mother all day long. Erik didn't mind the quiet early morning writing session. We were both getting what we needed.

ERIK

The definition of cruising is repairing your boat in exotic locations. We'd done our check-in trip and hiked Colombier, so we three dads were ready to tackle the sputtering port engine. Peter, John, and I had all seen the completely rebuilt engine installed days earlier. With our own eyes and ears we'd witnessed its beauty and sublimity. Unless there was some dark voodoo magic at work, we figured the trouble was elsewhere. Emily returned from her morning hike to two dinghies attached to our stern but didn't see anyone aboard.

"Hello?" she called out.

"Down here," I said from the aft port cabin. That was usually where she found us when there was a problem. She craned her head around the staircase to see what was going on. John, Peter, and I were crammed into a space the size of a doormat. The mattresses and floor panels were pulled up to reveal the battery bank and fuel tank below. Peter leaned over the fuel tank. John and I shared the remaining space and looked over Peter's shoulder. We all had a sheen of sweat and grease on our faces to prove we'd been working. I smiled up at Emily, "It seems to be a fuel issue."

"Okay," she said a bit blankly.

I expounded: "The boat had been sitting still for so long at the dock that some kind of fuel algae had grown inside our tank—not unusual in a tropical climate—but it all settled to the bottom. As long as it stayed on the bottom, the engine pulled in clean fuel. That's why the engine ran smooth for hours while we were testing it on the dock. But as soon as we went out into open water, the fuel tank got stirred up. The algae mixed into the fuel and clogged up the fuel line. When the engine ran out of fuel, it just died." All three of us dads smiled up at Emily.

"That's great. How did you figure that out?"

"Funny you should ask," I said, clearly giddy about the fact that this problem had been solved. "John and Peter both suspected it was a fuel supply issue, so we tested the fuel line to make sure gas was flowing. When John sucked on the fuel line, nothing came through. Then we went to the tank, found the clog, and cleaned it up. When John sucked the fuel line again, he got a mouth full of diesel."

"Gross. Thanks, John," Emily said.

"No problem," John said, bobbing his head like it was no big deal.

Emily and I later decided "sucking diesel" was the new high bar for true friendship. Our port engine ran perfectly again.

It was a sweet moment in Colombier when we made our first batch of at-anchor water. I was nervous about turning it on properly. I didn't want to break it. There were a lot of steps that had to be done in the right sequence, but it worked beautifully. The water maker gave us a sense of competence and confidence. With enough provisions, we could travel anywhere. Once again we found ourselves around the dinner table.

"What do you think about the Mediterranean?" I asked Emily.

"Could be fun. Or if we cross the Atlantic in summer, we could visit your family in Finland," she said.

"I like that."

Karina rolled her eyes. She'd heard us talk big before. We'd successfully sailed our boat fourteen miles, and all of a sudden we thought we were Jacques Cousteau. She didn't have to say it. All the kids knew: don't get emotionally involved until it's real. It was a game for the older kids. They liked to guess what step we might take next.

"Are we going to Grenada with *Discovery* and *Day Dreamer*?" Sarah Jane asked. We wanted to live with the possibilities for a while. Now our own kids were asking for a plan. Didn't they already know *we* didn't know?

"What's your preference, SJ?" I asked.

"Grenada. I want to stay with our friends. There are lots of other cruisers there, too." SJ knew what she wanted.

Alison said, "Yeah, it sounds like a lot of fun. They have group game nights and the teenagers all get together."

Then Karina said, "Yeah, and there will probably be more boys in Grenada." The three young PR reps from *Day Dreamer* were doing their job.

As much as we wanted to dream about Scandinavia and the Mediterranean, staying with friends and meeting more cruisers sounded awesome.

"I'm really interested in Dominica," Emily said. "I've heard it has so many waterfalls and the most delicious water."

If we were going to have this conversation about reality, then I was going to ground it in reality: "How would we make money?" I asked. I'd hoped to trade stocks online to extend our savings, but we hadn't had enough Wi-Fi before now to make that work, plus I was completely new to it. I knew we only had a certain amount of time before our money ran out. We had a water maker, but money was a kind of water too. I hadn't figured out how to make money from the boat. So we couldn't sail forever. Our route would have to factor in getting us home while we had money enough to get us there. We'd sublet our apartment, rented out our van, and done everything we could think of to cut costs, but it was still not enough.

"We could go to Grenada and try to get jobs on the island," I said. "Living on this boat costs less than living in our apartment. So we can afford to earn less."

"We wouldn't need winter clothes," Jane said.

"We could write and record songs here on the boat and sell them online," Karina said.

"We could bake for other sailors and clean the barnacles off their boats," Alison suggested.

"It could pay pretty well except most cruisers are hardcore DIY people," Emily said. "It's hard to be an entrepreneur when everyone wants to do it themselves."

Eli and Lily stayed out of this one.

We filled numerous legal pads with the pros and cons of north vs. south. This conversation was getting old. A decision would be a relief.

CHAPTER 10

FAREWELL FLOTILLA

SINT EUSTATIUS, DUTCH ANTILLES

4 Months, 9 Days aboard *Fezywig*

ERIK

Our next island was Sint Eustatius, affectionately called Statia. Since it was a short hop, Emily and I decided to motor sail. We were halfway to Statia when the sound of the port engine changed. I couldn't believe it. This was becoming a running gag. I opened the engine compartment and looked inside.

"The alternator has literally fallen off," I said to Emily. I was proud of myself. I didn't growl or curse. I didn't even break a sweat. We laughed and continued on to our anchorage, where I confirmed what I had seen previously. With all the jostling of being at sea, the bolt had simply snapped and the alternator had fallen off. The engine ran fine. It didn't charge our batteries, which was important but not crucial. This was, after all, a shakedown cruise. After conferring with my fellow captains, Emily and I decided to get replacement hardware in Saint Martin and fix it there. But first, Statia.

"The alternator has literally fallen off," I said to Emily.

I was surprised to learn Sint Eustasius was the first country to acknowledge the United States of America as a sovereign nation. During the Revolutionary War, it was a hub of trading activity. A naval vessel pulled into port flying a U.S. flag. That boat received the proper salute from the Statian cannons, and the rest is history. That day is still celebrated every year on Statia, and I'd never heard of this place before. I realized I had a lot to learn.

Everyone wanted to hike the Quill, the 2000-foot tall dormant volcano that formed the island. It involved a dinghy ride to shore, a 300-yard hike up the steep road ramp to town, a walk through town out to the base of the volcano, and then the hike itself started up. It was a tough proposition for Lily.

"What if we take turns?" Emily proposed. "You go on this one and I'll stay behind with Lily."

"But you hiked with her last time."

"I know. But just having a plan in place helps me feel better. I want you to go on this one."

Once at the top, I have to admit, it was cool to see a cloud pouring over the rim of the volcano into the tropical jungle inside. I took lots of pictures to share. On the way down an afternoon squall soaked us, and the kids splashed down the roadside gutters as we walked past cows back into town. It was a good outing but probably a good idea Lily had

146

sat this one out. I would stay with Lily on the next one. Emily and I were learning better balance.

EMILY

I didn't want Eli to miss out. I persuaded him to leave the iPad and come snorkeling. We were anchored forty feet from the best snorkeling I'd seen. Erik and I swam it that morning. The older girls had snorkeled with their friends and were all playing on one of the other boats. Lily played in her "pool," a large storage bin full of water, on the back deck, and Erik was clacking away on the laptop nearby. "I'll tow you over in a float. You don't even have to swim. Just put your face in the water," I said. "Please."

"Fine, I'll go," he said, setting the iPad down.

He slipped into the water behind me.

"Do you want me to tow you over there?" I asked. I already had the floatie attached to a line tied around my waist.

"Nah. I'll swim," he said. I put my face in the water and he followed. Immediately, a large sea turtle swam ahead of us. I looked back at Eli pointing toward the turtle. He gave me an underwater thumbs up. He'd seen it. We both swam after it. We swam against the current all the way to the reef. He was a much stronger swimmer than he had been when we first arrived. He was also more experienced with the mask and snorkel tube. We explored the reef up and down. Besides colored fish, sea snakes, coral, and colorful marine plants there were old cannons, anchors, and various parts of sunken ships. Eventually, Eli gave me the thumbs up that he was ready to head back. We both surfaced.

"That was fantastic!" he said. "Can we do this every day?" Oh, honey. Welcome to the Caribbean. He climbed into the inner tube I had tied to a rope around my waist and I towed him home.

I met a local at Fort Oranje who embodies how friendly and

peaceful the island is. This slim, dark gentleman stopped his bicycle next to me and said, "Guess how old I am?" He was spry but appeared to have no upper teeth. I was stumped. "I was a police officer for thirty years and I've never been in a fight," he said. He was seventy-six. His retirement job was to sound the fort bell morning, noon, and night. This timekeeper didn't wear a watch. He showed us around the fort, asking every few minutes, "What time is it?"

Statia also holds the distinction of providing our first access to a library in the Caribbean. We hadn't seen the inside of a library since January, six months earlier. At home we knew all the librarians by name, went up to three times a week, and sometimes maxed out multiple library cards carrying our books home in a rolling cart. We had made do with marina book swap shelves. In Statia, I walked in like Alice in Wonderland. I felt the cool blast of air conditioning. The World Cup was playing in a room to the right. On the left, two beautiful, smiling women greeted us from behind a low desk. I waved. Behind them were bookshelves, tables, and local schoolchildren reading. Lily and Eli sat at a low table in the children's room with a green basket full of crayons and a stack of paper. Eli picked out a crayon and started drawing. Lily flipped through a picture book. Sarah Jane, Alison, and Karina were already respectively thumbing through books, perusing titles, and sitting on the tile floor reading. Getting inside a library was a respite from intellectual cabin fever. I was in heaven. After finding the library, all the boat kids went at least once a day.

By the time we left Statia for the last island in our tour, we knew we liked our traveling home. We didn't know if we would head north or south. Racing sailors use the weight of the bodies of crewmembers as ballast by leaning far out on the weather side of the boat to reduce heeling. It's called hiking out. Our hearts were hiking out on the south side of that decision, and our brains were hiking out on the north side. We weren't getting anywhere.

That's not entirely true. We were getting to Saba.

From a distance, Saba looks like a giant volcano rising straight up out of the ocean. The island itself is only about five square miles, but it boasts the highest point in all of the Netherlands: 2,910 feet, more than 1,000 feet taller than the Quill on Statia. Other Caribbean islands were hilly, but nothing like this. The water along its coastline was sixty feet deep, way too deep for our anchors. We hoped to nab one of the few mooring ball in Wells Bay on the west side of the island. We followed *Discovery* and *Day Dreamer* to the mooring field, but our necks craned upward. As we rounded the perimeter, we saw a massive rockslide. Unsettling. The Dutch check-in official did not alleviate our concern. He informed us the rockslide was forty-eight hours old. Sometimes you think things will stay a certain way forever, and then they change.

That night at our mooring ball we saw no lights from the local population, no beachfront restaurants, no beachfront. Above us rose a steep, forbidding rock face. Below us, the cliff continued down to the ocean floor. Our anchorage was a stopover for migrating humpback whales. They were long gone this time of year, but knowing large sea creatures could fit below our hulls didn't reassure us. All around us was the pitch-black expanse of the Caribbean Sea. A sliver of waning moon was the only light in the sky. The darkness felt darker than usual. Karina stood on the deck seat, steadying her hands against the bimini. None of us wanted to get too close to the dark and deep. She looked outward.

"Hey!" She shouted, "Look!" We all stepped in closer and looked too. "Nothing," she said. She was right. We could see absolutely nothing.

It was dark, but we weren't alone. We constantly radioed back and forth with the other two boats. We joked. We wondered what they were having for dinner. We stayed in touch about the smallest things. It helped us feel better. In the morning, we made our plans for Saba.

Sabans seemed even scrappier than the inhabitants of the other three islands we'd visited. They had the longest, steepest roads we have ever had the white-knuckled privilege of driving on. Erik did the driving. We both preferred it that way. He cruised down the forty-five-degree-angled roads of serpentine switchbacks. We've never taken our kids to ride a roller-coaster. Saba more than made up for that.

Imagine building those roads. The Sabans wanted roads, but nobody was willing to build them. So, one determined local signed up for a correspondence course in engineering. Once he completed it, he designed the roads and the Sabans built them. It's kind of like doing your own electrical work at home: slightly frightening, but impressive. I wouldn't have been eager for the task, but I admired the Saban spirit and felt encouraged to be more tenacious.

It was my turn to explore while Erik cared for Lily. The pamphlet said I'd be hiking through five different biomes. It all looked like overgrown, giant-leaf, dark-soil jungle to me. The muddy trail was veined with gnarly tree roots.

"Just be careful," the park ranger had told us. "A couple of people have died on this hike." I didn't know exactly what I was getting into, but with five adults on board I was sure we could handle it. I knew I wouldn't be held back or slowed down. I saw wild banana bushes, deep green vegetation, huge leaves and vines. The Middles painted their faces with the deep red mud, and one hiked barefoot because her flip-flops broke.

"Have any of you guys ever read *Lord of the Flies*?" I asked.

"No," Jaci and Anna said together. It was just as well. The trail ended unexpectedly at the entrance to a white five-star hotel. We walked right into the outdoor restaurant—all sixteen of us. While we were waiting for our small order, one of the muddy Middles slouched back on the white wraparound couch and began cleaning her fingernails with a toothpick meant for appetizers.

"This is a fancy place," she explained. I wished Erik could've been there, but I was grateful he had shared it with me by not being there. I love that guy.

The next day I stayed in with Lily while he took the kids snorkeling. We were working the plan, and the plan was working.

ERIK

Saba was our last stop. In a couple of days, we'd return to Saint Martin, fix our alternator, and decide which way to point *Fezywig*. *Discovery* would wrap up their business and consider their next move. *Day Dreamer* would circle back to Sint Maarten to wait out the north vs. south decision because it was safer and more fun to travel with friends. Emily and I, with the kids, considered every idea we could think of to make this last. Our friends suggested ideas and proposals. We'd thrown out and shot down multiple business ideas. But so far, we hadn't cracked the code.

This trip was our Intermission. Emily and I had both turned forty. We assumed while on this trip, we would figure out what we wanted the second act of our lives to look like. We couldn't even decide whether to go north or south.

We had anchored in Marigot Bay on the French side of Saint Martin when I received an email. I told Emily, "The Andersons want to lease *Fezywig* later this year."

"Really?" she asked.

The Andersons were a family we'd met online. They'd hoped to cruise with their kids the same time as us, but the timing hadn't worked out. We knew what a pain it was to buy a boat, so we'd previously proposed the idea of them leasing our boat when we were done instead.

We couldn't keep *Fezywig* unless we found a mobile source of income. Our savings hourglass was steadily draining as we fixed up the boat and paid for internet, fuel, and groceries.

"That would buy us some time," I said. "We can sail back to New York, lease out the boat, and figure out what we want to do."

"Maybe come back out?" Emily asked. "At least we don't have to decide about selling her. I'm feeling sentimental. This is the only home we've ever owned."

"Maybe. Or something else. They want to know where to wire the deposit."

"So, we're going north." Emily said.

"I guess so. What do you think?"

It doesn't sound dramatic. We got an email. We got a bite. But it affected everything. Emily and I made a plan. We knew where we were going. We would head north. We knew what would happen to *Fezywig*. She'd stay at sea while we went back on land and considered how to keep or sell her. But that was still months away. We'd already spent five amazing months aboard. We couldn't think about the end of our trip now. It was too emotional. *Fezywig* was our home. Two days later we would pull anchor.

Fortunately, the kids didn't need to pack. All they needed to do was say goodbye. Emily and I had plenty on our plates. We filled our fuel tanks and our extra fuel jugs. We filled water tanks and our extra water jugs. I spent a couple of uncomfortable hours at the top of the mast installing a new VHF antenna and running a cable through the mast to the new radio I'd installed. Peter helped me run the cable. I was gonna miss that guy.

We double-checked everything onboard. We provisioned. At the last minute, Emily and I decided to tear out the old refrigerator and install a new one. John convinced me a 12V fridge would be easier to power than the 220V power hog we had aboard. It would probably make the boat easier to sell. I hated thinking about that possibility.

Tearing out a fridge is a hot, messy business. Peter knew how to help. He lent me his Dremel saw, left me alone for a couple hours, and dinghied back over with a pineapple smoothie. He'd been treating all the kids to a smoothie party on his boat, but would never forget a fellow dad. I gratefully drank it down and returned the cup, and he left. Together, Emily and I maneuvered the new refrigerator into place.

"That will do for now," I said. We'd add the finishing touches along the way.

Emily and I took Eli and dinghied to shore for a few last-minute items at the chandlery. Joachim from Sunsail walked into the shop. He looked at me as if he were seeing a ghost.

"Don't worry," I laughed.

"I thought you were gone," he said.

"We just got back from Saba. Don't worry. Everything's fine. We leave for the BVI tonight."

He smiled, I smiled, and we shook hands. "I wish you well," he said. I believed him.

Emily and I walked outside and found Eli kicking a soccer ball back and forth with the cashier's son. He didn't speak a word of English, and Eli didn't speak a word of French, but they were having a great time together. It struck me as beautiful. We sat and watched them play for a few minutes. I was postponing the inevitable. It was time to go. Some people were happy to see us leave. Some people wished we could stay. We were both of those people.

We finally went to *Discovery* to collect our children and give our final hugs goodbye. It was a slow, gentle process. There were a lot of tears. Lisa knew we were proud of our Finnish heritage. My mother is from Finland and the kids and I are all dual citizens, so she made us a Finnish flag to hang with our colors. Those guys really knew what they were doing, making smoothies and sewing things at sea. We felt ready for this trip, but we still had a lot to learn.

With our whole crew finally in our dinghy, we motored back to *Fezywig*. I checked the weather for the fifth time that day. Everything looked good. The kids cut up the refrigerator box and made a house out of it. John was now wearing the house like a box-troll. He had his arms through both windows and his face at the door. We were going to miss that guy. He was our Fairy Godfather. We were going to miss them all: Michelle. Lisa. Peter. Emma. Kate. Anna. Jaci. Sara. Jenna. Jack. Even the dogs. I was glad we had somewhere to go right away, because leaving was really hard.

The sun was setting. We'd decided to cross at night so the kids could mostly sleep. The western sky provided a stellar display of orange and pink. As we pointed our bow into the sunset, we noticed *Discovery* getting into their dinghy. Life moved on, and they had other things to do. We continued waving. Alison and SJ sobbed. *Day Dreamer* got into their dinghy too. Both dinghies full of what now felt like family were silhouetted against the sky. They turned their dinghies, following us out to sea as far as they could. It was a tiny farewell flotilla. They floated, watched, and waved until we couldn't see them anymore.

PART
FOUR

4 Months, 25 Days

to

5 Months, 25 Days aboard *Fezywig*

BRITISH VIRGIN
ISLANDS

Anegada

Virgin Gorda

Jost Van Dyke

Tortola

St. John

St. Thomas

Culebra

St. Croix

Vieques

UNITED STATES
VIRGIN ISLANDS

FAJARDO

PUERTO
RICO
(U.S.)

ANGUILLA

SAINT MARTIN/
SINT MAARTEN

SAINT
BARTHÉLEMY

ST. EUSTATIUS

SABA

SAINT KITTS
AND NEVIS

ANTIGUA AND
BARBUDA

MONTSERRAT

CHAPTER 11

SOME THINGS CAN WAIT

MARIGOT BAY, SAINT MARTIN, FRENCH ANTILLES

4 Months, 25 Days aboard *Fezywig*

ERIK

We'd hoped for an uneventful crossing. That's not what we got.

We left Saint Martin under beautiful skies, calm winds, and a clear forecast. Emily made a simple stir-fry with peppers, onions, and black beans. We ate while looking at the stars. The Milky Way lit up the sky. The kids settled into a movie on the laptop, and Karina and I took the first watch. Eli pulled himself away from the movie, sat down in the cockpit, tilted his head back, and looked at the clear night sky.

"Whoa. That kind of looks like outer space," he said.

"Yeah. It *is* outer space," I replied.

He sat there for a while and got quiet. "Thousands . . ." he said, and his voice trailed off. Yes, son, there are thousands of stars.

As we pulled away from Saint Martin, the wind and seas picked up. I started to feel nauseous, so I lay down on the salon floor.

Karina's place of choice when she wasn't feeling well was at the helm. So that worked out. She took the wheel. Eli fell asleep in the cockpit. Lily fell asleep in the main salon, but she woke up a little before midnight. I helped her below to her bed. Going below made me seasick. When I came back up, I had time to pull out the large stainless-steel bowl. I threw up, dumped it down the drain, and rinsed the bowl. I went back to the salon floor and stayed there until the end of our watch.

12:00 a.m. We turned over to Emily and SJ. I stumbled below with my bowl in hand. I'd put on a scopolamine patch by now, but it was doing me no good. We hadn't tidied up too much before casting off, so our bed was covered with dirty clothes, books, and a dry bag.[11] I pushed it aside, flopped down, and promptly decided I needed to use the bowl again. My bowl of puke lay beside me as I dozed off. I felt like I'd just fallen asleep when Emily called for me, a sense of urgency in her voice. "We're spinning in a circle," she said.

I stuck my head up through the hatch. "I'll be right there," I said, and I was at the helm in seconds. As best I could figure, the autopilot had disengaged. Weird. There was another vessel within site off our starboard stern, but other than that nothing else was visible. The lights of Saint Martin were long gone. Within half an hour, the other boat passed and disappeared ahead of us into the darkness. The sky above alternated between star fields and shrouds of blackness. Clouds. With the boat back on course, I went back to bed. Going below felt like a tumble into a large, dark, undulating, creaking pit. This time I didn't need to throw up. I was too tired.

3:00 a.m. My alarm went off. Time to be back on shift.

The night had cooled. I pulled my windbreaker from the back of

---

11. Dry bag: a rubber bag with an opening that rolls over itself and clips shut to keep out water. Used in a sentence: "Hey, Emily, I need to transport the original Declaration of Independence to shore. Just to be safe, can I use your dry bag?"

my closet, stumbled above with my puke bowl, dumped out, and went to the helm. The boat pitched in the waves as we headed downwind on a broad reach. We originally left using just the head sail. We were making four knots[12] but I wanted to make six, so we turned upwind and raised the mainsail. I put on a preventer to be on the safe side.[13] Emily and SJ went below. They woke up Alison and sent her up on deck.

Alison and I lay down on the cockpit bench, head to head, our feet at opposite ends. We shared a set of headphones and listened to tunes from my iPhone. I'm grateful my fifteen-year-old daughter and I can enjoy the same music. I finally got over my nausea and checked our course. We were headed in the right direction.

Moving made me feel sick again, so I went to the rail. All the spaghetti dinner was gone from my previous watch, so this time it was just bile. The ocean hissed and the water teemed in the white glow of our stern light. We were moving fast, about seven or eight knots. I lay back down. I felt the wind pick up and the temperature drop. I went to the helm and looked at the wind indicator. I lay back down and said, "Alison, this is what thirty-one knots of wind feels like."

Then the wind shifted to the south and the boom threw over from port to starboard, pulling the preventer taut. The boom creaked. I moved quickly to the helm. The wind built and the rigging groaned. Then the rain started. Torrents, all in blackness. Wind at thirty knots,

---

12. Knot: I mostly say "knots" to sound nautical, and that's what our speedometer showed. Sailors used to measure speed by tying a rope with knots at even intervals. They would drop it in the water and see how many knots they passed within a certain time interval. That was their speed in knots. One knot is actually 1.15 mph, so they're almost the same thing. But if I said we were going 4.6 mph, it just wouldn't sound as cool.
13. Preventer: a line that prevents the boom from being thrown from one side of the boat to the other in case the wind shifts. I used a spare line, wrapped it twice around the boom, and tied it off to a deck cleat amidships.

thirty-five knots, then forty knots. I turned on the engines. "Alison, I'm going to point us into the wind to take the strain off the sails." The rain was inundating. I couldn't see anything. I was soaked. I took off my glasses and held them in my left hand while I gripped the wheel with both hands. The iPad we used to navigate fell into the cockpit. After the second fall I handed it to Alison. "I'm not going to use this," I said. I was going straight into the wind, pure and simple. Alison prayed out loud. We are a praying family. We know God doesn't always calm the storm, but He can calm us in the storm. We needed some inner calm.

The rigging and sails rattled like pent-up prisoners. I kept my eyes fixed on the wind indicator and the sails. No pressure on the sails. Keep them slack. That was the plan.

The rain kept coming. I was cold and started to shake. There was no time to put on more layers, so I was in track pants and a T-shirt, no socks. Motoring upwind took the strain off the sails but also moved us toward the back of the squall.

"What time is it?" I asked Alison.

"Almost 4:30."

The sky would lighten eventually and we could take the sails down, but I wasn't about to do that in the dark. Not in these seas. I was now heading east back toward Saint Martin. I saw its lights glowing over the horizon, but the light continued to widen. I was seeing the divide between the sea and the clouds overhead. Like a narrow strip of torn paper, a band of light started to open.

The winds gradually settled down. Once we were into a steady seventeen to eighteen knots, I started to trust the wind wasn't going to gust up and change directions again. I eased us north and let the sails fill again. The waves were now coming at the boat from behind instead of dead on. The waves carried us forward instead of us bucking against them head-on. With that one turn, the whole world seemed to calm down. The rain came with cold slabs of air, but now the air blew warm again. The squall passed.

My teeth chattered and my right leg shook as I propped it against the bulkhead. "Alison, I'm cold," I said. "Can you hand me the blanket?"

"It's wet," she said.

"That's okay, so am I." She handed me a pale blue blanket and I wrapped myself in it. My teeth chattered less. I wiped the saltwater off my glasses and put them back on. My nausea returned. My leg shook less. I prayed a little too—a prayer of gratitude.

The wind moved back to its original direction. I eased the boat west again, but needed to reset the sails before we could get fully back on course.

"Alison, we need to jibe,[14] and I'm feeling awful. Can you do the deck work?" She was wet and a little rattled, but she nodded her head. I talked her through all the steps to make sure we were on the same page. "Sound good?" I asked. She nodded. We went to work.

5:30 a.m. The sky was bright enough to see. Back on course, we slumped into the cockpit. At 6:00 a.m, I knocked on Karina's hatch and called her up for her watch. The sky was fully bright. We could see Virgin Gorda in the distance. We were going to make it. We'd made it through the night. Emily woke up to join Karina as I flopped into bed.

9:00 a.m. I woke up. The whole boat was full of laughter and happy shouting. I still felt nauseous but made my way to the bow and lay down on the trampoline. I watched as seven dolphins swam along below our hull, darting forward and up, playing with us and each other, racing ahead and jumping into a flip that landed them on their

---

14. Jibe: shift sails from one side of the boat to the other when the wind is coming from behind the boat. Not to be confused with a dance move. This was no time for dancing.

Anegada

**BRITISH
VIRGIN ISLANDS**

Virgin Gorda Sound

Jost Van Dyke

Tortola

Trellis Bay

O Spanish Town

The Baths

Virgin Gorda

British Virgin Islands

U.S. Virgin Islands

*L I T T L E
S I S T E R S*

St. Thomas

St. John

Peter Island

**UNITED STATES
VIRGIN ISLANDS**

St. Crioux

back. Eli and Lily squealed. The dolphins swam with us for almost an hour and then disappeared as quickly as the squall had.

By midday we'd reached Spanish Town, Virgin Gorda, British Virgin Islands. For better or for worse, it was done.

Our first crossing. Eighty miles down. Only 2,420 to go.

It felt good to be somewhere familiar. A year and a half earlier, Emily and I had been here trying a catamaran for the first time. Two and a half years before that, we'd done our sailing class with Matt. Now we were here with our kids. We took SJ, Eli, and Lily in the dinghy and headed for shore. We pulled up, tied off the dinghy, and stepped onto solid ground. It felt so good. We walked around to a grassy spot with shade, lay down on our backs, and felt the beautiful sensation of stability. Nothing moved beneath us. In our heads we continued to roll back and forth with the rhythm of the sea, but we knew it was an illusion. We were safe.

We got an email off to *Day Dreamer* and *Discovery.* They had been worried about us. A fifty-foot catamaran heading the opposite direction was hit by the same squall that hit us. It had ripped off their mast. They'd had to cut it loose and drop it into the sea to save the boat. They showed up in Saint Martin rattled and worn, but safe. We hugged our kids extra tight that night.

EMILY

"You guys are going to love the Baths!" I said. "It's this massive playground of boulders with hidden caves and tide pools and . . ."

"It's cool to finally be here," Karina said. "This is the one place we said we would go that we've actually gone to."

"We're doing it," I said.

"Are we going to have to swim in?" Jane asked.

"We'll take the dinghy in part way and swim in from there," Erik said. "Mom and I will tow Eli and Lily in the inner tubes." We woke up super early that morning to get one of the few daytime mooring balls. We would make good on our promise.

"Wear your rash guards and hats," I said. "Does everyone have sunglasses?" We made quite the water parade swimming to shore from *Fezywig* with our team of seven, including two inner tubes. This was one of my favorite places on the planet. By the time I got Lily ashore and stowed our flippers and tubes, the older kids were dying to race off into the maze of boulders. We arranged a meet-up and persuaded them to hold still long enough for a photo. Then they were off. That's exactly how I had felt the first time I'd come to the Baths.

Erik and I both stayed with Lily. We wanted the older kids to feel completely untethered. I held Lily's hand and remembered the little boy with Down syndrome I had met in that same spot years earlier. As I waded into the famous cove of water, Lily said, "Hold me," and wrapped around me like a koala. She was still learning to swim. Is it better to be scared and safe or fearless and reckless? We each have to decide for ourselves. I passed her to Erik, and he spun her around in the light streaming through the granite boulders. I was so in love with Erik in that moment.

We all made our own way toward Devil's Bay on the other side of the rocks.

"I can see why you like it here," Alison said, letting the coming tide spin her around in a tiny cove. "Thanks for bringing us." Even Eli climbed, jumped, and swam. This had to be better than a video game. My children's eyes sparkled with increased alertness and curiosity. They were fully engaged.

Of course we can all live and die and have a meaningful life without ever visiting the Baths, but it was special to Erik and me. It was a luxurious privilege to share this pristine natural landscape with our children. It was one more thing in their lives that could not be undone.

▲ Sailing as a family in open-cockpit boats in Long Island Sound.

▲ Eli and Lily crashing in their cabin after a day in the sun.

◀ Emily learning to read charts in the British Virgin Islands.

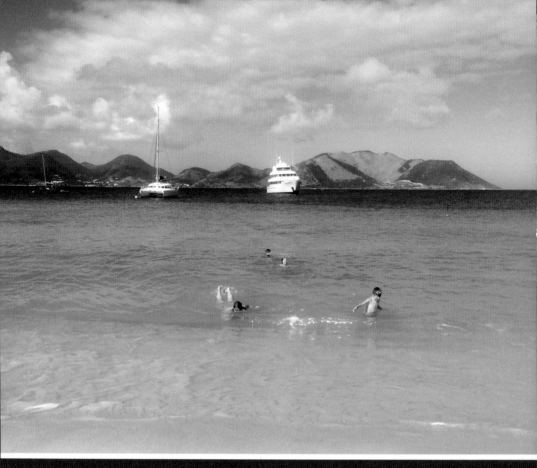

▲ Our first outing with *Fezywig* took us to Tintamarre,
a nature reserve just off Saint Martin.

▲ Eating simple and healthy in the cockpit.

▲ We ferried fresh water from shore to *Fezywig* using the large bladder and jerry cans loaned by *Day Dreamer*.

Sarah Jane in the famous ▶ shaft of light—the Baths, British Virgin Islands.

▼ Erik and SJ taking in the view from atop the Witch's . . . hat.

▲ Erik steering with his feet as we make our way
into Marigot Bay, Saint Martin.

▼ Driving our family across Simpson Bay Lagoon in our small dinghy.

▲ On our way to winning the Audience Choice Award at Lagoonies.

Photo credit: Ty LaMont Mecham

▲ We washed our laundry in a bucket and hung it out to dry in the fresh trade winds.

▲ Emily and Lily cleaning the bilge under the floorboards.

▲ Erik and John shuttling the Littles from shore back to *Discovery* on Dog Island, Anguilla.

▲ Pat installing our rebuilt engine, Oyster Pond, Saint Martin.

▼ SJ following her bliss on the rope swing.

▲ After church with Grandma and Grandpa Orton in Sint Maarten.

▶

Getting into our dinghy to head back to *Fezywig* felt like the land equivalent of getting in the car.

▲ Simpson Bay Lagoon.

◀ Karina snorkeling the south edge of Saba.

▼ *Fezywig, Day Dreamer,* and *Discovery* at anchor. Columbier, St. Barthélemy.

◀ The Bigs making shadows on the sand, St. Barthélemy.

▼

Everyone from *Discovery*, *Day Dreamer*, and *Fezywig* (except Emily and Lily) atop the Quill, Sint Eustatius.

▲ *Day Dreamer* and *Discovery* waving goodbye as
we leave Saint Martin bound for the BVIs.

▼ Living room, dining room, play room—northern edge of Tortola, British Virgin Islands.

▲ Getting the family to shore—the Baths, British Virgin Islands.

▲ Keeping our promise to take the kids to
the Baths, British Virgin Islands.

▲ Strolling for shade at the Bitter End Yacht Club, British Virgin Islands.

◀ Eli contemplating which direction to go in life, Sint Eustatius.

▼ No shoes required at this library— Culebra, Puerto Rico.

▲ Home Sweet Floating Home—Hog Cay, Exuma Chain, Bahamas.

▲ Scrubbing *Fezywig*—Hog Cay, Exuma Chain, Bahamas.

▲ Just before things went hog wild—
Staniel Cay, Bahamas.

Lily learning to love the ocean
one rung at a time. ▶

▼ That intangible something—
Great Inagua, Bahamas.

▲ Mugging with mugs in between squalls—ICW, Florida, USA.

▲ Parents optional—Hampton Bay, Virginia, USA.

▲ Crossing from North Carolina to Virginia on the North Landing River.

▲ Done—Dyckman Street Marina, New York, NY, USA.

We had been hustling since Saba, survived an unexpected squall, and kept our promise in the Baths. Those memories were made. Now on the other side of the island, *Fezywig* bobbed at anchor in Virgin Gorda Sound. The next day was Sunday, a day of rest. It was the first day of the week, but the last day we had planned. I felt the refreshing calm of an empty calendar like a blank canvas. Erik once said the seven of us on a boat would be enough universe for him. It was enough for me, too. With full holds, a water maker, and sails, we could go anywhere. Sunday afternoon we gathered the kids in the cockpit.

"Okay. We've made it this far," Erik said.

"I never thought we'd make it this far," Karina and I quoted Erik together.

"The Baths were really cool and beautiful," Karina said.

"Yeah, thanks for taking us," Alison said.

"I liked it," SJ added. Eli and Lily waited for the talking to be over. They didn't yet appreciate how informative these family chats could be.

"We've been planning to bring you here for a long time," Erik said.

"Funny how this was our main destination goal when we started, and it's cool," Karina said. "But not as cool as the stuff we had not planned on doing, like Colombier, Statia, and Saba," Karina said.

"And the people we met," I said. Everyone nodded their heads. We were all thinking of *Discovery* and *Day Dreamer* and so many others, but left their names unsaid.

"Tomorrow we can head out to Anegada or start west to Puerto Rico. What do you want to do?" Erik asked.

"What's in Anegada?" Alison asked.

"It's a super flat island with beautiful white sandy beaches, and we hear the lobster is amazing," Erik answered. "But we're not going out for lobster." The *Fezywig* crew are not big into seafood. We hadn't eaten any on the entire trip. Plus we were sure it was pricey.

"So it's nothing we haven't seen before," Karina said.

"Sure, but you never know," Erik said.

"How far is it?" SJ asked.

"About twelve miles."

We batted things around for a few minutes and the kids weighed the pros and cons. I was outwardly neutral, but after the storm I was looking toward the comfort of home. Well, our land home. We were always home, as Erik had promised, because we were always together.

"I know we're not going back to *Discovery* and *Day Dreamer*, so I want to go home," Jane voted.

"Me too," Alison said.

"I'm fine either way," Karina said.

"I want to go home," Eli was firm. He continued, "Lily? Do you want to go home and sit on a couch and watch movies and have your own bed?" That trumped sailing the Caribbean.

"Yes," Lily said, "I want to go to New York City."

"We could still go to Anegada," I told Erik. "This is not a democracy." Erik and I always aimed for unanimity. That made all our lives easier. But in the end, we were the parents and had the final say. Erik had missed Anegada twice already. The first time we didn't go to Anegada was with our sailing instructor, Matt. We'd told him we'd rather go to the Baths. The second time was when trying out a catamaran with friends. We'd sailed out far enough to see Anegada but had turned back to Virgin Gorda. This was the third time Erik might leave Anegada over the horizon.

"Some things can wait," he said.

No more shakedown cruises. No more circling islands to explore a new anchorage. No more detours. I didn't know how we would keep our girls' camp promise to Karina, Alison, and SJ. There was no possibility we'd be in New York by August. *Fezywig* only moves about five miles per hour on a good day. We would drop anchor and take our time, but from that day forward, our destination was home. Erik committed our plan to a clean sheet of paper and taped it next to the navigation desk.

A few hours later we tucked into Trellis Bay on the capital island of Tortola. Erik and I wanted to say hello to our sailing instructor, Matt, from our first visit to the BVI. Just like Matt had taught us, Erik sailed straight up to a mooring ball without motoring, something he was proud of. I knew we were in trouble at the bow. Ali, Jane, and I were struggling with the lines. We weren't ready, so Erik released the line on the front sail to keep the wind from pulling the nose of the boat away from the mooring ball. He was trying to make it easier for us. Unfortunately, when he released the line, the wind took the front sail and thrashed it around the deck. The line whipped and tangled around Alison's shoulders, neck, and head. She screamed.

Jane and I grabbed the lines and freed her. Alison covered her neck with her hand and steadied herself on the lifelines while we tied off. Erik came to the bow.

"What happened?" he demanded.

"Sorry," I said, "we were having trouble with the ropes. We weren't fast enough." I could see he was frustrated. "Ali, show Dad your neck." She moved her hand, revealing a bright red rope burn. She whimpered and Erik's shoulders sagged.

"Come here," he said hugging her. She buried her head in his chest and cried. Erik had come to blame us for fumbling the ropes, but Alison's injury sobered him. It wasn't hard to imagine how quickly that could have gone from bad to worse. He apologized and hugged our crying daughter. His tenderness stabilized morale generally, and we prepared to go ashore. Trial and error, works every time.

Pulling into Trellis Bay was like a homecoming. The airport where we had first landed in the BVI was accessible by flip-flop. We showed the kids the bay.

"Eli, this is the 'biggest hammock in the world.' Remember the picture of me and Dad sitting in this?" I asked.

"That's gigantic," Eli said. "We could all fit in there." So we did, and we took a new picture.

"That's the art studio where Matt's wife, Deb, makes pottery," Erik pointed from the hammock.

"I want to go there," Karina said, getting up.

"Let's go see if Deb is in," I said. She was. She showed the kids the studio and took a photo with us.

"Where's Matt?" Erik asked. "We were hoping to catch him while we're here."

"I think he was in Virgin Gorda Sound last night," Deb said.

"No way. We were there last night too," Erik said.

"Do you want to go back to see Matt?" I asked as the kids browsed the shop.

"We're not going back. It's okay," Erik said. "Come on, Eli. I want to show you the airport. It has roosters and chickens everywhere."

"Real ones?" Eli asked.

"Real ones," I said, hefting Lily onto my back. She held on around my neck. The older girls would catch up with us.

"You should see what SJ bought," Karina said.

"You bought some art?" Erik asked. "With what money?"

"I brought my own money," she said. She fished into her brown paper bag and pulled out a glazed ceramic snail with its mouth open and its eyes going in two different directions.

"Like us," I said. "We take our home wherever we go, too."

We pulled anchor and headed west. We slipped through the cut between Tortola and Guana Island and turned south, running along the back edge of Tortola. The wind was at our stern, so we spread the sails out to a full wing-on-wing and enjoyed the slow, gentle sail toward Jost Van Dyke, our destination for the day.

"This is like a playground after Saint Martin," Erik said. "We can always see where we're going. But it's weird because everyone here is on vacation. There aren't any cruisers."

"I still like it," I said. "Especially with the kids."

We listened to music and gathered in the cockpit, as we often did during short sails; nothing major happening. No big deal. Just gathered around, talking a little bit, taking in the view, feeling the wind, singing songs, the little kids climbing and dangling off the bimini. This no-big-deal time *is* a big deal. We were aboard *Fezywig* for this agenda-free time as much as were out here for adventure. Maybe this time simply being together was even more important.

That afternoon we pulled into Long Bay, right between Jost Van Dyke and Little Jost Van Dyke, and set the hook in an empty anchorage. There was a restaurant onshore called Taboo with an elevated patio. By evening the place would fill with the happy noise of relaxing tourists. Now it was empty, and we chatted with the manager, Marylin. SJ and Ali piled into a hammock hanging between two trees by the shore for a few minutes and then wandered off.

Talking with Marylin, I hadn't noticed someone lie down in the hammock. I knew it wasn't one of my kids, because one dark leg hung out as it swayed. Lily held her arms up to surprise the stranger with a big push. I jumped to stop her, but a bright, smiling face lifted slightly from the hammock.

"Hello. What's your name?" said a young man with long black cornrows tucked under his black cap.

"I'm Ocean Orton," she said, still calling herself Ocean. "What's your name?" Amir. He worked at Taboo with his mother, Marilyn. He was in the hammock awaiting the dinner crowd. Before long Lily was done pushing, and the tables turned. Amir pushed Lily "to the stars" and told her a story.

"Once upon a time," he said, "Queen Ocean swung up to the stars, where she saw a purple moon. All of her brothers and sisters were there. They had a picnic. Then Queen Ocean returned to her hammock."

"Who is your favorite superhero?" Amir asked.

"I'm Batman," Lily quoted the movie. "Who is your superhero?"

"I'm Thor. I have to be really strong to push Queen Ocean so high." Lily rolled out of the hammock when it was time to go, and Amir helped her to her feet. "Don't forget me," he said.

"I won't," she said. "I'll miss you. I'll call you tomorrow on the radio." Lily had once again worked her magic.

ERIK

I wrote in my journal:

"I think we're going to make it home to the U.S. I think we'll see friends and family as we travel up the East Coast. I think we'll pull into VA, somewhere near Occoquan, or the Potomac, or the Chesapeake. We'll sail up the Jersey Shore and into New York Harbor. We'll motor or sail up the Hudson. We'll anchor or tie up at the Dyckman Marina. We'll be home.

"We won't starve. We won't be homeless. We won't die. Eventually, we'll have money to pay for the things we need and want. Karina will probably go to college. And things will roll on. We'll see how it goes. But for now, I'm sitting here, at anchor, the blue and green water rolling past, the sun coming up in the east, the trade-wind breeze cooling the morning, the flag flapping in the breeze, the dinghy lapping off the stern. My hair is long, but clean. It's blond. Blonder than it's been in a long time. When it's not trying to beat me up, I really like the ocean. I still think I'll want a stone and wood home with a fireplace, but I'm happy with this for now. I'm a fortunate man. I'll try to be more grateful."

It felt good to be grateful.

Before heading out the next morning we hiked to the Bubbly Pool. It sounded like the right place to take a bunch of kids, and it was close. The short hike was through the tidal neck that separates Jost Van Dyke from Little Jost Van Dyke. Beyond the neck, the Bubbly Pool was a little cove of rocks encircling a small, sandy beach. The incoming waves pushed through a narrow opening in the rock that churned the water into white bubbly sea-foam. When the tide was high, it would send geyser-type spouts of water high into the air and fill the round cove like a fizzy swimming pool. But it was low tide, so there was a small puddle of water and some water swooshed in, but nothing too dramatic. All the Fezywigs cozied up in the little pool and had fun splashing and taking goofy underwater pictures. In the midst of our silliness, another family walked in from the surrounding brush and surveyed the site.

It was a handsome couple with two young children. Charterers. Plus the family had a guide with them, a large, gregarious man with a handlebar mustache and long, bushy beard. I'm sure he could tell a mean pirate story.

Having arrived, the family looked underwhelmed with their destination. The guide tried to explain, "At high tide the water can shoot as high as twenty, thirty feet into the air! And . . ." He was trying to sell it. It probably would have been better for them to come at high tide rather than imagine it.

"How long are you sailing?" I asked.

"Four days, three nights," the father replied.

"Nice," I said, nodding and smiling. But inside I kind of felt bad. Four days and three nights is better than no days and no nights, but I felt like they were missing out. Every moment of their trip was going to be in the company of some expert who was a complete stranger and whose goal was to get as big a tip as possible, and maybe a good review on his website. Maybe that's a jaded view, but I was glad we had the luxury of stumbling and fumbling as a family. It was a more difficult and scarier path, but more rewarding.

BRITISH VIRGIN ISLANDS (U.K.)

UNITED STATES VIRGIN ISLANDS

Culebra

Vieques

SAN JUAN

PUERTO RICO (U.S.)

PUERTO RICO TRENCH

MONA PASSAGE

Samana Bay

Luperón

DOMINICAN REPUBLIC

SANTO DOMINGO

HAITI

PORT-AU-PRINCE

HISPANIOLA

CHAPTER 12

AMAZING AND UNEXPECTED

NORTHWEST OF TORTOLA, BRITISH VIRGIN ISLANDS

5 Months aboard *Fezywig*

EMILY

"Hey!" Erik said, "I'm picking up AT&T." We could see the U.S. Virgin Islands across the channel. Everyone on the boat was required to check in on Saint John, which was annoying after the casual policies in the other islands.

"Should we bring spoons?" Karina asked. What the heck? We celebrated our first day back on U.S. soil with ice cream for everyone, playground time, and a social media splurge. But we couldn't play all day. We still needed to get out of the Caribbean before hurricane season. We needed provisions and charts for the Bahamas. We could get both in Benner Bay, Saint Thomas.

Erik headed toward an empty T-slip at one of the docks. There was a well-maintained catamaran with yellow trim ahead of us already tied up. As we got closer, the couple aboard saw us coming in. They hopped onto the dock and waited to take our lines.

"Thank you, that's so nice," I said, tossing the woman my line. "We're making a quick stop for food and charts."

"It's a long walk around on foot, but a shortcut across the water," the woman said. "I'm running to the grocery store before we take off in about thirty minutes. Can I offer you a ride?"

Her name was Rebecca. She took us to Budget Marine. The guys were helpful and efficient. Erik found our charts and got some advice, and we moved on to the grocery store. I thought Rebecca would be long gone, but I ran in to her on one of the air-conditioned aisles. We were both freezing. And it turned out we both knew *Silverheels*: Ken and Lynn, our first mentors in Sint Maarten, who had given us a giant mixing bowl and lots of great advice. Small, small world. She gave us a lift back to *Fezywig*. Rebecca and Mike finished crewing a charter and had to head out again right away. Before they left, Rebecca gave me their boat card: Zero to Cruising.

"Hey, I know you guys!" Erik said. "I read your blog. Your article on buying a boat out of charter convinced me to do the same thing."

"Really?" Mike said. "I'm so glad that was helpful to you. It was nice to meet you. Good luck out there."

"What a small world," Rebecca said. Erik gave them one of his business cards and helped them cast off their lines. We were right behind them heading out the channel.

"I wondered why they were so helpful," Karina said. "They were cruisers."

ERIK

We turned west. Our next anchorage was Culebra, an outer island of Puerto Rico and the last island in the Virgin Island chain. It had been good to be in familiar territory, but I knew it couldn't last. The airport on Saint Thomas, where we'd landed with our friends on our second trip to the BVI, was the last familiar thing we saw. We knew we were heading back into the unknown.

It was a gorgeous downwind sail to Culebra. We sailed wing-on-wing, with the waves pushing us forward for a solid three hours. When we turned up into the main bay at Culebra, the sailing only got better. The entrance narrowed, keeping all the waves outside. The water went lake-flat, but the wind stayed brisk. We sailed a mile in fifteen-knot trade winds on a perfectly flat lagoon. I was in sailing heaven. The beautiful, tucked-away island of Culebra welcomed us in.

Everything was quiet. Everything was calm. We passed a man who was rowing his dinghy far from shore. His outboard motor was tipped up out of the water. I called out and asked if he needed help. He didn't. He was rowing for the pleasure of it. This was a good sign.

It was so peaceful I didn't want to break the silence by starting the engines as we pulled into the anchorage. We simply turned up into the wind, dropped the anchor, and drifted backward on it.

It had been about a week since we'd left Saint Martin. We still missed our friends there. They were our tribe, our people, our new comfort zone. The BVI had been a good place to transition. But more uncertainty loomed ahead, and I could feel it wearing on me. This was where I had to step up. It was now really up to me—no wingmen, no mentors at my side. I had to be the captain.

Emily and I went to shore to scout things out and take care of official business. We needed a special decal to make our boat officially registered in the U.S. We waited for border patrol at a small black cafe table outside the airport in Culebra. We were keeping an eye out for an official-looking border patrol guy. Then Emily saw him. Black baseball cap. Black sunglasses. Black short-sleeved button-up shirt. Black pants tucked into thick black boots and a black holster housing a black gun at his hip. "I think this is our guy," Emily said. I snapped the laptop shut.

As I filled in our paperwork, Emily and the officer talked about Spanish poetry. Gabriel García Márquez was his favorite, but of course he read Neruda. "Who can deny Neruda?" Emily asked rhetorically.

"I'm happy to fax your application," Officer Border Patrol said. Suddenly, Emily's seat scraped against the cold tiled floor and I looked up from my binder to see the officer wielding a serrated buck knife. "It's for removing staples," he said. He submitted our application and rattled off a list of his favorite beaches. In typical island style, this errand had filled almost the whole morning.

On our way back to the dinghy, I noticed a sign for a library. We'd seen enough beaches this week. After lunch, I brought Emily and the kids to the library. It was two trailer homes set parallel to each other with a trellised patio in between. On one side was the library itself. The other side was divided into two parts: a fifteen-seat movie theater and a sewing/craft room. Half the library trailer was a small computer lab. I was going to need that. The other half was covered in carpet and lined with fun books and games, all preceded by a sign: "Shoes Off. Naked Feet, Yes!"

The kids tossed off their shoes, settled on the floor, and dug into the shelves of books. As much as I wanted to relax with my kids and read a book, I couldn't. I had things to do. I was the captain.

We were closing in on a deadline. In a few days our insurance would be null and void. If we weren't outside the "hurricane box" by July 15, our boat would not be covered if it was damaged by a named windstorm. We couldn't afford to have that happen. This all meant we either had to be north of Jacksonville, Florida, a thousand miles away, within the next forty-eight hours—which wasn't going to happen—or else have a provision in place. To get the provision we had to provide a planned route and itinerary, including hurricane-proof anchorages and our hurricane boat preparation plan. If our insurer approved the plan, they would—for a not-too-small fee—extend our coverage within the hurricane box for an additional thirty days. I sat at the picnic table on the patio with the charts spread out in front of me, my hands knit through my hair and my eyebrows scrunched together.

Emily and I both readily admit sailing comes more naturally to me, as do navigation and technical know-how. She checked in on me from time to time, but I knew I had to tackle this project solo, and part of me resented that. I missed my cocaptain dads with stuff like this on the line.

I did my best to piece together the distances and locations based off the charts we'd purchased the day prior, but I had no firsthand knowledge and no one to ask. It was all theoretical.

Emily came and sat next to me for short spells. She looked up "how to anchor amongst mangrove roots" and other such nonsense. "How many docking lines do we have?" she would ask. I couldn't believe it. What I wanted to say was, "Can't you see that doesn't matter right now?! The insurance needs an itinerary, not an equipment list." But what I said without looking up was, "Six," and I got back to work. If there was a hurricane, we'd anchor the boat and get off. I didn't care if it sank to the bottom, as long as it was insured. Emily thought she was saving our lives. I thought she was being irrelevant.

It was a cool day with a nice breeze, but I had sweat on the back of my neck and I kept grinding my teeth. Eventually the library closed and we went back to the boat.

That night a storm blew in. The clouds covered the moon and the wind howled all night. Emily and I lay in our cabin, glad we were at anchor and not out on open water. I sat up to peer through the side hatch. There was a fair bit of chop in the water, and I could see the boats around us bucking into the wind as they pulled tight against their anchor chains. I pulled up the blankets around me and pushed deeper into my pillow. We turned off the lights and went to sleep.

The next morning I walked up on deck, stretched, and took in the beautiful morning. I looked around, thinking to myself how unique this place was and how much I liked it. It wasn't a wide bay. All the edges felt close and snug but not too close. Then I realized things looked different than they had the day prior.

I walked around the boat trying to figure it out. Emily was now awake and came up on deck. The kids were dozing in their beds. The boat that was behind us was in the same place. We hadn't dragged in the night. But everything else felt like it had moved.

A voice called over from the boat off our starboard side, about fifty yards away, "Good morning!"

"Good morning!" I called back. It was a large-bellied gent in his sixties with long shocks of blond hair blowing up in the wind.

"You dragged anchor last night," he called across the water.

"We did?" I called back.

"Yeah, we were up in the night shining lights on the boat and shouting. We didn't think anyone was on board."

"Wow." I looked at Emily. We both blinked.

"We had our fenders out because we thought you might hit us," the big-bellied man called out.

"I'm really sorry about that," I called back. "Is everything okay on your boat?"

"Yeah, we're fine. That was a lot of wind. You and the boat behind you were both dragging. I'm glad you didn't drift all the way back to the seawall." Fortunately the anchors for both our dragging boats had caught and reset while we were sleeping.

"Wow. Me too," I said. "Thanks for looking out for us."

"You're welcome. Glad you guys are okay," he said. By now his wife had come on deck and we all waved to each other. All's well that ends well.

Emily and I sat down in the cockpit. "Wow," I said. For a third time. "Maybe I should have set the anchor better. It seemed like such a calm spot."

"It was," Emily said. "That was a lot of wind last night."

I looked out over the water and realized I was grinding my teeth.

After breakfast we went back to the library. Emily and the kids went to the books. I sat at a picnic table on the covered patio, logged on to the Wi-Fi, spread out my charts, guidebooks, and laptop, and resumed work on my first-world bureaucratic project.

It was Friday, and everything had to be in place by Tuesday. I knew they wouldn't do anything with it over the weekend. I had to send it off that day to have a hope of being covered. The deeper into the project I got, the more I looked at the library where my family was relaxing and squinted my eyes. My mouth tightened, and I scowled at my mostly empty spreadsheet. I didn't know how to ask for help, and even if I did, I wasn't sure what kind of help they could offer. I went for a walk. Emily joined me, but we didn't talk much. When we returned, the librarians had brought out the puppies.

Alongside the library were several orphaned puppies in dog crates. The librarians cared for them, and it was bath day. Eli and Lily laughed as they and a few Puerto Rican kids washed and rinsed the wriggling dogs. There's not much of a language barrier when it comes to washing puppies. I smiled a little bit.

We stopped by our neighbors' boat on our way home for dinner. The big-bellied guy with wild blond hair and his wife came out on deck.

"Hey, I wanted to apologize again for causing any alarm last night," I said as they leaned over the rails on their boat.

"No worries. We're glad you and your boat are okay," Don said. We'd learned that they were Don and Janis. From there, as sailors often do, we got to talking about weather. They had recently sailed down from the Bahamas and had charts, routing info, and weather forecasts. Hallelujah.

"You've got an ideal weather window starting on Sunday," Don said. "Chris Parker says it's the kind of weather window you only get every few months." Chris Parker is a weather guru. Sailors pay to subscribe to his weather reports via email. I hadn't subscribed, but I wanted the info.

"Would you mind if we swung by later to look at your charts and ask you a few questions?" I asked.

"Not at all," Janis said. It was set. I breathed easier knowing we could talk later that night. On the way to our boat, Eli complained about getting wet from the seawater. Didn't this kid appreciate this amazing experience we were giving him?! I resisted the urge to throw him overboard. Alison put a pot of water on the stovetop and played ukulele in her cabin while she waited for it to boil. Since I hadn't had a chance to read at the library, I grabbed a book and went to the bow to unwind.

I had settled in when Karina asked, "Dad, where's our dinghy?"

You gotta be kidding me! I thought to myself. I'd just gotten comfortable, but I got up and went back to the stern. Our dinghy was gone. Emily was the one who had tied it off. She must not have tied the knot correctly. It was a basic knot. How hard is it to tie a bowline? I grabbed the binoculars and scanned the bay off our stern. I spotted it half a mile away, pressed into the mangrove bushes. I clenched my teeth.

I flagged down a guy going past in a motorboat. He was going to pick up some people, but he'd swing by on his way back. I walked into the kitchen. The water was boiling. I looked in the pot. Almost all the water had boiled off. "Alison!" I shouted.

"What?" she called back from her cabin.

"You wasted water. You wasted fuel. And you're wasting our time." I slammed the lid on the pot and went to my cabin. Alison sheepishly restarted dinner.

Half an hour later she called out, "Dinner is served," and everyone gathered in the cockpit. I came out, ready to try and not bite anyone's head off.

As we finished eating I thought to myself, *This guy in the motorboat isn't coming back. We can't wait any longer. It's going to be dark soon.* I asked the kids, "Who wants to float downwind and get the dinghy?" Emily raised both light-blonde eyebrows.

"The wind has been steady all day, and it's right there," I said, "less than a thousand yards to the seawall." All the older kids shot each other sideways glances. "It's at the closed end of the bay. The inner tube will drift to the same spot as the dinghy. I want two of you to go together."

Alison and SJ volunteered. I equipped them with the waterproof VHF, and they plopped into the double inner tube and drifted off. Half an hour later they motored up to the stern in the dinghy.

I immediately jumped in the dinghy and went to shore for another walk. What was wrong with me? Why was I so angry at my kids? At my wife? I was on a beautiful, peaceful island in the Caribbean with my family. The breeze was blowing and there was a clear sky overhead. I kept walking.

At sunset I headed back. Before I left I'd turned on the generator to charge the batteries. When I returned, the generator was still running. I figured someone would have turned it off by now. The batteries should have been fully charged. I went to the nav station and checked the battery charge monitor. The batteries weren't charging. Great! Nobody had noticed.

"Come on, guys!" I bellowed at the whole boat. Everyone stopped what they were doing and looked at me. They had no idea what I was talking about. I thumped myself down on a cockpit bench. They quietly went back to whatever irrelevant thing they had been doing. I leaned my head into my hands and put my mind to work.

I went to my toolbox and pulled out a screwdriver. I turned off the generator and opened up the screws that held the plug in place at the end of the connector cord. I had installed the connector myself, so I knew what it was supposed to look like. Inside, the ground wire had come loose. I put it back in place, reinserted it to the shore power outlet, started up the generator, and checked the charge monitor. The batteries were charging. I didn't want to talk to anyone, but it was time to visit Don and Janis.

Emily and I lowered into the dinghy and puttered over the short distance. We didn't speak. Don and Janis were bubbly and beyond encouraging. He was a retired firefighter, and she was retired from health services. They were from Texas. Their accents made us feel welcome. He owned a plane back in Texas. Had his own runway and maintenance hangar. He made owning and taking care of an airplane sound like a breeze. I liked people who talked like that: competent, capable, relevant. They'd recently bought and renovated some beachfront property on the south coast of Puerto Rico. Now that it was rented out, they were taking a two-week break to sail with some friends. Everything about them encouraged me.

"With this weather window, you can make a straight shot to the Bahamas," Don beamed, his cheeks a bit rosy from the sun and his beer.

"Really?" I asked.

"Sure," he said. We came from Matthew Town straight down to Fajardo. It was great. Matthew Town has everything you need. Fuel, water, food. They have the best lobster. Huge!"

"Wow. Sounds awesome," I said. Emily and I hadn't made much eye contact since she'd lost the dinghy, but we looked at each other and nodded.

After a warm, boisterous visit, we climbed into our dinghy and motored back to *Fezywig*. Don and Janis had snapped me out of my funk about our uncertain future. The weather window would take us straight to the Bahamas.

I was claustrophobic. I still needed mentors and friends, but John and Peter were hundreds of nautical miles away on their way to Grenada. As much as Emily and I supported each other in our marriage, and we all supported each other as a family, we couldn't be everything to each other all the time. I needed outside input, as well as time alone with my thoughts. Journaling had always been therapeutic. I hadn't done much journaling, and aside from taking care of business, I hadn't spent time with anyone outside our family. I'd never been a husband, dad, and captain under these new circumstances. Sitting with Don and Janis broke the ice for me.

Emily and I still had work to do, as a couple and a sailing team, but we drove the dinghy back to *Fezywig* in peaceful silence.

EMILY

Erik carried the burden of being our most capable sailor and navigator. When he felt the world on his shoulders, I wanted to do something helpful. I apologized for tying the wrong knot and losing the dinghy. Within a day or two I knew he'd say, "Sorry I've been in a funk lately . . . ," and be ready to talk about it.

Processing intense feelings can require privacy. We didn't have much of that on *Fezywig*. It was the same in our apartment, so we have a few techniques to help maximize personal space in tight quarters. We all keep journals. Taking a walk helps, though it's not always an option at sea. We create audio cocoons by popping in earbuds and listening to anything from rock music to pre-recorded rainstorms. When one of us had that *do not disturb* vibe, we tried to respect it. Creating personal thinking space, however permeable, is essential for personal growth.

I preferred the struggles of too little space to having too much space. I had tried both. After Lily was born, while working on a project, we lived in a friend's 5,000-square-foot vacation home for six weeks. Coming from our 900-square-foot apartment, I fantasized about this palace with six bedrooms, a giant living room and, best of all, a playroom. With five young kids, I believed a playroom held the secret to happiness. I was wrong. A bigger home was a bigger responsibility. The larger space divided us while simultaneously multiplying how long it took to gather my family, tidy up, or find a lost shoe in a sprawling house. I was thankful for the place to stay for six weeks, but I was grateful every day for the simplicity and closeness of my tiny apartment. But that didn't make living in a small space easy.

If you laugh in a small living space, everyone else wants to know what's so funny. If you open a package of cookies, you draw a crowd. We can't hide our differences, either. Whether good or ill, we lived too close to let them fester. We addressed them and resolved them or let them go. It sounds more diplomatic than it feels in real life. I tell our kids, "People are messy." If you want people in your life, expect things to get messy.

Visiting Don and Janis helped. We got fresh stories and a fresh weather report. We decided to take Don's advice and leave after sunrise. We had a new mission to focus on. That helped too. It was a quick morning sail to Fajardo, Puerto Rico. We dropped anchor and went to work.

Our goal there was simple: get food, water, and fuel, and leave by Sunday afternoon. It was Saturday afternoon. We had twenty-four hours to make it all happen. But we were in a new place, so that involved figuring out where everything was and how to get there and back. This was especially tricky with provisions. We'd need a car to get them from wherever we bought them to the water's edge, and then we'd have to ferry them out to the boat. If we were lucky, we thought we could attend church Sunday morning. Never a bad thing before putting your life in danger.

"I want to check the ferry schedule at this marina here," Erik said. "Maybe we won't have to dinghy all the way to the main island, about a mile away."

"Let's see if that hotel-looking thing has a laundromat," I said.

I was tying off on the seawall when I saw this huge guy, well over six feet tall, with a big bushy beard and baseball hat. He looked like he was off-loading a guitar and an ironing board. My hopes for a laundromat skyrocketed.

"Is that an ironing board?" I asked.

"No, it's my surfboard." He had a big smile, too.

"Right, that makes a lot more sense," I said. Erik had the good sense to be embarrassed on my behalf.

"And you play music?" Erik asked, noticing his guitar.

"Yeah, I play at this little bungalow up around the bend."

"Cool. We play tunes too. We have a bit of a family band," Erik said.

"No way! It'd be great to hear you guys play."

A few minutes in, Erik asked, "Have you ever sailed the Bahamas?"

"Tons."

"Any route recommendations?"

"Sure. Which boat are you on?" he asked. I pointed to our catamaran a few hundred yards away. "I'm on that green sailboat behind you. Why don't I swing by after your errands and I can show you some route ideas?"

"That'd be awesome," Erik said.

Our scouting trip didn't turn up a ferry or laundry, but Erik was thrilled to get some expertise planning our route through the Bahamas. We returned to *Fezywig* for Jane, our volunteer for the day. "We met a guy named Ike, and he may come by later tonight," Erik said. "He plays the guitar."

"Cool," Karina said. "How long will you be gone?"

"A couple of hours," I estimated. We had a lot to do in a couple of hours.

"Let's see if we can find the local chapel first," Erik said. "Maybe someone will be there who can recommend a place to rent a car." The church was a mile away—if you knew right where it was and your smartphone GPS didn't glitch like ours did. I called on my rusty college Spanish to ask for directions, and we finally made our way through the humidity to our destination. As best I could tell no one was at the chapel, but we called out "Aló!" anyway. Down a darkened hallway, a doorway opened a pocket of light and a slim Puerto Rican gentleman in a white shirt and tie stuck his head out. He invited us to sit in the small office where he was doing family history research. We briefly explained who we were and asked if he could recommend a good place to rent a car.

"Toma el mío," he said without hesitation. "Take mine." He handed us the keys to his pickup truck in the parking lot.

"Gracias. What's your name again?" Erik asked.

We piled into Rafael's truck. We hadn't moved this fast in weeks. Traffic lights, stop signs, yielding and merging, all happening at ten times the speed of *Fezywig*.

"Can I ride in the back on our way home?" Jane asked.

"It's pretty fun," I said. "I did it as a kid—loved the eighties."

"We'll see . . ." Erik said. He pulled into the Walmart parking lot. My heart dropped. It was huge. It would take a while to find everything. I forgot how tattered and sun-bleached I was until I was around people with strip malls and washing machines. I may have been shabby, but I looked official. Officially shabby? Whatever. For the next two hours, I carried my clipboard and crossed off found items while Erik and Jane followed me up and down the unfamiliar aisles, each pushing a cart. Our list completed, we headed to the register to pay. $340 for two carts of groceries.

"That's way cheaper than Saint Martin," I said. "Maybe we should stay here for the next six months."

It was dark when Rafael handed the last bag of groceries to Jane to put in the dinghy. We'd been gone several hours.

"What time is church tomorrow?" Erik asked, putting on his headlamp.

"A las doce," Rafael said. Noon.

Dang it. That was too late for us. We had to be underway by then. Weather waits for no man—or family. We thanked him profusely for the use of his truck and drove our heavy-laden dinghy into the darkness. I radioed ahead. Karina and Alison were relieved to hear from us.

"Oh, and that guy Ike came by twice," Karina said.

"Thanks for the heads up," I said, and I reclipped the radio to my backpack. Erik stopped by Ike's boat so he'd know we were home.

The kids immediately started unloading the dinghy and putting away groceries. We had a system. And I had a surprise for them.

"Hey kids, check this out," I said, setting a rotisserie chicken on the salon table. Somewhere angels were singing. I couldn't remember the last time we'd eaten chicken. It wasn't from a can. Nothing from my galley kitchen could compare with the scientifically prepared poultry. It was like a surprise Thanksgiving without any of the holiday pressure. I removed the plastic lid and we pulled off chunks and stuffed our mouths.

"You guys are a bunch of barbarians," Erik said, reaching over the melee to get some for himself.

"Mom, this is so good," Eli muffled through his mouthful.

Ike pulled up with a guitar strapped to his back and a stack of charts under his arm. "Would you like some chicken?" I offered.

"Nah, I had an avocado for dinner already, so I'm good," Ike said.

"That must've been a mighty avocado," I said. This was not a small guy.

"More for us," Alison said.

"Let's clear this table so Dad and Ike can do their magic in here," I said.

Ike pulled out his charts, and the kids continued stowing groceries under the bench seats and floorboards.

"I'm starting to get my head around the Bahamas," Erik said. He'd already sent a plan to the insurance company and consulted with Don.

Ike showed us some of his favorite spots in the Bahamas. Erik took notes and felt better oriented talking to someone who had been there so many times.

"It's all going to be okay. There are good things ahead. Don't worry too much. You'll be fine," Ike said. That was reassurance I wasn't qualified to give. Erik stopped grinding his teeth.

"You still up for a jam session?" Erik said. "It's getting late."

"We don't have to worry about the neighbors," I said. No boats were within earshot, and the moon was full. We got all the instruments and all the kids on deck. We all lay on the trampoline under the moon learning new songs and improvising our own, the Fajardo Blues. We all felt the playful pressure. It's so much easier to sing somebody else's song than it is to make up one of your own, especially when others are listening.

Ike taught our songwriters, Karina and Alison, a bit about how to make a living as a live musician. "Have three hours' worth of material and take a fifteen- or twenty-minute break. Play tunes people know: Bob Marley, Jimmy Buffet . . . things they expect to hear when they're at the beach on vacation. But keep writing your own stuff. No one ever got famous playing someone else's stuff. You have to write, speak, and sing with your own voice. That's what I'm working on. Finding my voice." I think that's what we're all working on in some way or another.

ERIK

My biggest crossing to this point as captain had been eighty miles. We were leaving in the morning and our next stop was 500 miles away. We would be along the Puerto Rican and Dominican coasts for most of the way, but the last leg—from Luperón to Matthew Town—would be 150 exposed, vulnerable miles. By that time, we would be outside our weather window, we would have no fresh forecast, and we would be nearing the end of our fuel supply. Our only options to ditch would be Haiti and Cuba. We would technically be "outside the box" for windstorm coverage, and I still hadn't gotten confirmation that we would be insured come Tuesday. The next morning was Sunday, and we had to go. I'd have no way to check email once we pulled anchor. So many unknowns.

But that morning we'd been in Culebra, where Don and Julia had looked out for us and encouraged us. By midnight we'd met Ike and Rafael. We'd borrowed Rafael's truck and been to a Super Walmart. We had a boat full of groceries, Ike said our route looked good, and we'd learned a new tune. I snuggled closer to Emily and fell asleep.

I wrote in my journal: "Despite my fears, the amazing and the unexpected continue to happen."

The next morning we pulled anchor and motored the mile over to the marina to top up on fuel before setting out for Matthew Town, Great Inagua, Bahamas.

There was a small concrete room constructed on the dock. Inside was the cash register and a few items for sale like fuel cleaner, boat polish, sodas, candy, and ice cream. Around back were some restrooms. Emily and the kids took one last chance to use a land-based toilet, but Lily walked right behind the counter for the cash register and pulled the desktop calculator up in front of her. She'd already grabbed a few Snickers and bags of peanut M&M's and was ringing them up when I walked in the door.

"That's not going to work, sweetie," I said.

She looked up, smiled extra big, and then went back to work. I was irrelevant.

"Hey there. Time to get on the boat," I continued. She kept punching numbers. One of the guys in a blue polo walked in.

"Thanks for helping us out!" he beamed. "Can I get in here real quick?" He squeezed in and rang up the fuel.

"Come on, Lily," I said.

"You gotta go with your daddy, but thanks for all your help. Here's your payment." With that, he handed her a bag of peanut M&M's, a Coke, and a package of Oreos. Only Lily could work for two minutes and get paid in Oreos. She's a genius.

Only Lily could work for two minutes and get paid in Oreos.

I started up the motors. Other boats were lining up to get fuel. We pushed off from the dock and I went to spin the boat so we could head out the way we had come in. When I tried to spin the boat, it wouldn't turn. One engine would go in forward and reverse, but the other engine wouldn't do either. It ran fine, but the propeller wouldn't engage. Was I confused? Had I forgotten how to spin our boat? I prided myself on being a good driver. After three tries, I couldn't get *Fezywig* to turn around. It was bad enough I was confused; now I was embarrassed because the dockhands were watching, along with all the other boats waiting to get fuel. In the end, I drove the boat out of the marina backward. There's nothing quite as cool as driving backward at five miles per hour. Very Jason Bourne.

Once into Fajardo Bay, we quickly set the anchor and I opened the engine compartment. My palms were sweating. This was an auspicious beginning. Our weather window was open, and I didn't want to miss it. I sighed, climbed down into the engine compartment, and looked around.

The throttle cable had come loose. It was literally as simple as tightening a screw, which I did. Karina started the engines and moved the throttle forward and back. Everything worked fine. I wiped my palms on my shorts and climbed out. I closed the engine compartment and we pulled anchor. I pulled down my sunglasses and settled in. "It's no big deal. Everything will be fine," I told myself.

UNITED STATES

THE BAHAMAS

Georgetown, Great Exumas

CUBA

CAYMAN ISLANDS

JAMAICA

TURKS AND CAICOS ISLANDS

White Bluff Harbour, Great Inagua (Bahamas)

WEST INDIES

HAITI

DOMINICAN REPUBLIC

PUERTO RICO

MONA PASSAGE

BRITISH VIRGIN ISLANDS

U.S. VIRGIN ISLANDS

ANGUILLA

SABA

ST. EUSTATIUS

SAINT KITTS AND NEVIS

SAINT MARTIN/ SINT MAARTEN

SAINT BARTHÉLEMY

ANTIGUA AND BARBUDA

MONTSERRAT

GUADELOUPE

CHAPTER 13

80% BORING, 15% BEAUTIFUL, 5% LIFE-THREATENING

THE ATLANTIC OCEAN, NORTH OF PUERTO RICO

5 Months, 5 Days aboard *Fezywig*

ERIK

The reason we had left Culebra was because there would be no wind for days. That's what we wanted, at least for the Mona Passage. We wanted flat, boring, and safe. That's what we got. Reading made me queasy, the scenery changed slowly, and I could take only so many naps. So we motored along listening to Jim Gaffigan's *Dad Is Fat*. I like Jim Gaffigan. I think he's funny and I can relate to him. We both belong to an exclusive club: the married, father-of-five, living in a two-bedroom-apartment-in-Manhattan club. I think there are maybe six of us in that club. So it's like we're brothers.

We found out it takes quite a while to sail the length of Puerto Rico. We'd left early in the morning, and by 2:00 a.m. the next morning we were getting close to the other end of the island. We'd zigzagged our way along the coast to avoid having the wind directly on our stern. No more accidental jibes at night, thank you very much. The last town along the coast was Arecibo. We were cutting in toward it before turning out and committing to cross the Mona Passage.

I prepared to jibe when, in the abyss that is the open sea at night, I saw something off our starboard stern. It was big, black, and close.

"Holy crap!" I shouted.

"What is it?" Emily came out to the cockpit.

It was a boat. A black, silent boat. It took me two seconds to realize it was a coast guard boat, but with its lights off. Their goal was to sneak up on us. What they didn't know was we were about to turn—right into them. Boats don't come with turn signals.

After I pointed them out to Emily, they turned on their searchlight and "looked us up and down." I waved. What else do you do? There was nothing stealthy about us. We had all our running lights on. All the lights in the main salon were on. Emily and I were even wearing our big bulky orange nerd life jackets. We didn't mess around with safety when it came to overnight passages. We were the opposite of Miami Vice.

After another look they seemed to conclude we were harmless, or least not carrying cocaine, and peeled off. But jeez! Really? Did they have to sneak up on us like that? If they hadn't been on that boat with a mounted machine gun, I would have punched them in the arm.

We sailed on through the night and crossed the Mona Passage. It was a complete non-event. Flat and windless, as we'd hoped. We motored along at five or six knots and reached the other side by the end of the next day. That's when it got interesting.

We were skirting the northeast coast of Hispaniola.[15] It was right around noon when our starboard engine sputtered to a stop.

"Seriously?" Alison said. She and SJ raised their heads from the

---

15. Hispaniola: the fancy term for the island of the Dominican Republic and Haiti. Used in a sentence: "Hey, Columbus, should we call this island Hispaniola?"

cockpit table. Karina, who was filming giant clouds with my smartphone, stopped to find out what had happened. Eli and Lily kept watching Wallace and Gromit—surely this did not concern them. Emily popped her head through our cabin hatch where she'd been napping.

It was one of those dying engine sounds that was actually peaceful. In fact, it sounded familiar. It didn't seize up and grind to a halt. Even so, I could feel sweat pushing through my skin. We had a lot of miles to go. I tried restarting the engine. That didn't work. I opened up the engine compartment and checked the oil and sail drive fluid levels. They looked good. I went below, opened up the floor in our cabin, and tapped on the fuel tank. Big, empty, echoey sounds. Somehow I'd miscalculated the fuel consumption. Because of the lack of wind, we'd motored and motor-sailed most of the way.

"I'm not sure where I screwed up," I told Emily. "It's pretty basic math."

The truth was we hadn't done too much motoring up to this point. These were the longest distances we'd covered in a single stretch. And our fuel gauges didn't work. Peter on *Day Dreamer* had convinced me trying to fix fuel gauges and keep them working was a fool's errand. Whether he was right or not, we didn't have functioning fuel gauges, and now we had to deal with at least one empty tank, possibly two.

"What do you think?" Emily asked. "Should we stop and get more fuel?" It was a good question. I didn't know the answer.

"Let's think this through out loud," I said. "We still have some fuel in the port engine, I think. I'll open it up and try to see how much. Plus we still have two jerry cans. They're five gallons each. Let's pour some in to make sure it's actually a fuel issue. Assuming it is, we can sail." That was my logic.

Emily continued, "The scary part's over. We crossed the Mona Passage."

"Are you comfortable if we try and sail the rest of the way?" I asked.

"I think we'll be okay. What do you think?"

"We know there's fuel in Matthew Town. There's not really any-where to stop in the DR without backtracking. Let's check the engine first."

I unlashed one of the yellow fuel jugs and pulled out a hose. Karina held a funnel at the top of the hose and I did my best to pour in fuel while we sailed along. We decided to put in only two gallons. If this was an engine issue, I didn't want to put a whole jug of fuel into an engine that didn't work.

I climbed into the engine compartment and pushed the little metal lever with my thumb to manually pump fuel into the line. All those repair attempts were paying off. Karina turned the key and the engine started up. I closed my eyes and smiled.

"Okay, you can turn the engine off," I called from the compart-ment. Karina killed the engine. It was time to sail.

"Matthew Town?" Emily asked.

"Matthew Town," I said.

The sun had gone down and we were moving fairly well under sail. It was nice to have the quiet for a change. That's one of the peaceful things about a sailboat. You can move yourself, everyone and every-thing aboard, by harnessing the power of nature. We were well stocked from Fajardo and no one was seasick so we had a good lunch: home-made bread with canned New Zealand butter and strawberry jam. Dinner was black bean soup with corn chips and salsa. We cleaned up and were enjoying a quiet evening, moving toward bedtime for the little kids, when I thought I saw something over my shoulder. No ninja coast guard boat this time. It was the opposite. This was a light. I looked behind me but it wasn't there. A few minutes later I saw it again. I missed it a second time. I turned around and stood still, look-ing off the stern.

We were north of Samaná Bay, Dominican Republic, when I saw

the clouds light up like a flickering light bulb. My hands went cold. "There wasn't even supposed to be rain," I said to myself. Now this.

"Emily, we've got lightning," I called down into the boat. She was in the middle of putting Eli and Lily to bed. She immediately came up on deck. We both looked off the stern until it flashed again. We both looked up at our tall metal mast. We went to our charts.

I started to spill out my thoughts. "Samaná Bay is directly south of us. It's the only place to ditch for another hundred miles." I looked over my shoulder again to watch the sky. "The entrance is super out of the way, and even once inside it's a long slog to any kind of anchorage."

"But if that storm comes up on us, it'd be better to be in there than out here," Emily said.

"True. But it will use up most of our fuel."

"Can we get more in there?" she asked.

"We'd have to." We both looked at the sky. Another flicker. "Why don't we do this," I started. "Let's sail toward the bay. If the lightning looks like it's moving closer, we'll turn on the engines and high tail it in. If we sail for a bit and it keeps its distance, we can always change course."

"It still makes me nervous," Emily said.

"Me too."

We pointed the boat toward the massive bay. We watched the sky for a long, slow, sweaty-handed hour. The sky reminded me of a vintage light bulb with a shorted power cord; lots of bright flickers, but electricity never came down out of the sky. There were no bolts of lightning, just flashes up high, wrapped in the gauzy haze of clouds. Sheet lightning. If I hadn't wanted to pee my pants, I probably would have thought it was pretty.

The little kids were now asleep. Emily came and watched the night sky with me. There were still stars overhead, but we knew how quickly that could change.

"Looks like it's keeping its distance," she said.

"Yeah," I said. We kept watching. "I think it's pretty far away."

The older girls were below, reading in their beds. We would fill them in when we changed watch.

We turned the boat northwest toward Matthew Town.

We were grateful for our kids' trust in us. We were all in new territory in terms of risk, but we hadn't come here by chance. This was by design. We'd made deliberate efforts to prepare and be safe. We'd installed a new radio with distress-broadcast abilities. We had all the necessary safety equipment aboard. We'd trained and practiced together for years. We had a good plan for this crossing, including contingencies should something go wrong. But we've long taught our kids, all life is a risk. Driving a car is a risk. Getting on a plane is a risk. Getting out of bed is a risk. Quitting a job is a risk. Taking a job is a risk. Going on an adventure is a risk. But what about not going? There are big risks that come with playing it safe. We teach our kids, the safest thing is to learn how to handle risk.

A friend once said to me, "I want to take risks. But I don't know how it will turn out." It's an inside joke in our family reminding us that we can't predict the future. All we can do is our best. Here, just north of the Dominican Republic, we'd done our best. We trusted ourselves and we trusted each other. We sailed on through the night.

There was practically no sign of civilization on the northern Dominican coast. We sailed past uninhabited mile after uninhabited mile, not seeing any lights on shore: no houses, stores, or streetlamps, just a black ridgeline against the night sky. We were on our own. Sheet lightning continued behind us in the distance.

Luperón was our last chance to ditch. It was a small cove before reaching the Dominican-Haitian border. As a deep, well-protected harbor, it made for a good hurricane hole. It was one of the stops on the itinerary I'd sent the insurance company. Legend has it Christopher

Columbus once sailed his ships into this harbor to avoid a storm.[16] If we were going to stop anywhere, it was here. The only thing we wanted at this point was fuel and an updated weather forecast, but the guidebooks showed no fueling docks, and the storm seemed to be holding off.

After Luperón the coast fell away to the southwest while we continued northwest, making a straight line for Matthew Town. If anything went wrong, the only places to go were Haiti or Cuba. I found myself looking at Guantánamo Bay not as a name on the news but a port of call in event of a storm, injury, or some other accident. That was a direction I did not want to go.

We sailed past the lights of Luperón and watched as the coast beyond became black again and faded into the distance.

We were three days out from Fajardo. My throat went dry at the thought of leaving the coastline. I felt like my captain's training wheels were coming off. The only thing to do was continue sailing northwest and keep listening to Jim Gaffigan.

Our friend John said, "Sailing is eighty percent boredom, fifteen percent beautiful, and five percent life-threatening." I was starting to understand what he was talking about.

We'd left Fajardo on Sunday. It was now Thursday. When motoring, we were making about six knots. Sailing, we were now lucky to break four knots. There's nothing quite as tedious as waffling around at two or three miles per hour in the middle of the ocean.

Thursday I woke up and took a shower. We'd been rotating through night watches for the past three nights. Two hours on, two hours off. The girls were still nervous about the lightning, so they woke me up during my two-hour bits of sleep to tell me about it. I poked my head out of my hatch and watched the sky. Once I could tell it was

---

16. Luperón, used in a sentence: "Christopher Columbus, there's a hurricane coming. Should we sail into Luperón?"

still hundreds of miles away, I comforted them, closed the hatch, and grumbled into my pillow as I tried to get a few more minutes of sleep before I was back on watch. I like to think I'm generally a congenial person, but when my sleep gets broken up, my cheerfulness fades fast.

I dare say even the most organized of families would struggle with this kind of sleep schedule. We had been underway four days nonstop. Beyond breakfast, lunch, and dinner we had no structure to our days. Our boat looked slightly like the sloth enclosures at the zoo; a bunch of long-armed, funny-faced mammals sprawled across any flat surface, trying to find shade and stay adequately hydrated with the minimum amount of physical exertion. When any physical exertion did occur it was mild at best and was accomplished at a pace even slower than the speed of our boat. One exception was when Jane asked if she could get in the water and swim. She pushed on the stern and kicked her feet. The boat went from one knot to two knots. It didn't take long for her to remember we were sailing over the deepest spot of the Atlantic Ocean, the Puerto Rico Trench: 27,500 feet deep. We hadn't seen any sharks, and they were not likely, but imagining what five miles of depth could hold will get in your head. She got "tired" and got back in.

Our stomachs stabilized, and we'd long since finished Jim Gaffigan's *Dad Is Fat* in its entirety. But we still had gobs of time on our hands. Karina wrote a new song and wanted to make a music video, so she was shooting footage with my iPhone.

> *How to tell what I've felt*
> *Find my fit, find myself*
> *Ignorance and impatience are a bad mix*
> *Get out of the muck, ask for too much,*
> *Go with your gut, and make your own luck*
>
> *As mountains of clouds keep rolling by*
> *Castles I've built up for myself up in my sky*
> *Most of my ideas won't fit inside my wallet*

But if I hear a good band name you know I'm gonna call it
And keep building my castles in my sky

The rest of us were too drained for philosophy or poetry. We made a list: "How Long Does It Take to Sail from Puerto Rico to the Bahamas?" Here are a few:

- Longer than it takes Mom to get a tan (she's a redhead)
- Longer than it takes Dad to put a shirt on (I hate wearing shirts)
- Let's say Congress balanced the budget
- Long enough for Eli to reenact the *Lego Movie* five times (he'd memorized most of it while underway and could reenact entire thirty-minute sequences)
- Longer than a community production of Wagner's *Ring Cycle*[17]
- Let's say global warming has run its course
- Let's say all our kids have now gone through puberty
- Let's say Eli is now shaving
- Think of downloading *Gone with the Wind* over a dial-up connection
- Remember plate tectonics?

This was all the eighty-percent boring part John had talked about. I would say the sheet lightning went in the captain's log as the five-percent life-threatening part. Slowly the island of Great Inagua crept into view over the horizon. This was part of the fifteen-percent beautiful.

I can't say it was a particularly beautiful island from a distance. All the islands were blurring together for me. Although, you know how once you've been camping for a week, any warm food with sugar or

---

17. Wagner's *Ring Cycle*: if you don't know what this is, you need more opera friends in your life. It's the operatic equivalent of Tolkien's *Lord of the Rings*. It's a collection of four operas and takes about fifteen hours to perform the whole thing. Some people really like opera.

salt tastes amazing? Or a carpeted floor feels like a Posturepedic mattress compared to your sleeping bag? I'm sure that's part of why Great Inagua was so beautiful. After being at sea for five days straight, even a slab of concrete probably would have looked good. But now in front of our bow was land, a new country, and it was lined with palm trees and—as best we could tell—a lovely, white, sandy beach.

It took us most of the afternoon to get close enough to see any details, even with the binoculars. But land was on the horizon, so the sloths turned into something more akin to fifth-grade kids in a math lesson: sitting up straight and looking forward, but brains were still a bit mushy. This is when I started to do some math of my own. Given the distance to Matthew Town and the hours of daylight left, we would get into port after dark. I never like to pull into a new harbor or anchorage in the dark, and this was no exception. However, on the south side of the island were a couple options that looked okay.

I couldn't find anything about them in any guidebooks, but then again, this was the nether regions of the Bahamas. The only thing on this large, flat island was a flamingo sanctuary and one of the world's largest salt manufacturing operations. Let's say it didn't have a rich history of tourism.

"Okay, guys, here are our options," I said. "We can sail west around to Matthew Town, but we'll probably arrive after dark." A general groan ensued. "We can head east to Lantern Head. It's the next most protected anchorage, but it's the opposite direction of Matthew Town." Some head nods. Everyone wanted a flat anchorage. "Or we can go to White Bluff, which is that beach straight ahead. It looks like there's a hotel or something on shore, but I can't tell yet."

Emily chimed in, "Karina, it's your birthday tomorrow, so your vote counts double."

"I want to record my song while everyone is off the boat," Karina said, "and then get some Wi-Fi to post my video[18] and connect with friends."

We decided on White Bluff.

We had another couple of hours of light, so we were in good shape. The beauty of the island began to unfold the closer we got. The palm trees continued in both directions as far as we could see. The beach had the whitest sand we had seen. The water beneath us was crystal clear. After over a hundred hours of nonstop sailing and worrying, we were almost there. We'd made it.

That's when I saw the teeth sticking out of the water. I had to check several times in the binoculars, but it definitely looked like teeth—a long, continuous row of them.

"Emily, will you take a look at this?"

"What is it?"

"Do you see that?" She focused in. Then I saw her turn her head completely to the right, then back to center, and then completely to the left.

"Yeah. I see it," she said.

"Does that look like a reef to you?"

"I think so."

My mouth went dry. I called for spotters on the bow. Alison and Karina went up and began scouring the ocean surface with their eyes. Either option to the west or east would get us in after dark. Now there was an unmarked reef between us and White Bluff.

"This doesn't make any sense," I said. "The place is called White Bluff Harbour. They wouldn't call it *harbour* if there wasn't a way in." But there it was: an unmarked reef continuing in both directions for miles. Behind the reef was a safe, flat, turquoise lagoon lapping up onto a white powder beach. We could see the white bluff now; a small cliff

---

18. Search YouTube for "Karina Orton Castles in My Sky (Original song)" You can also find her on Soundcloud and iTunes. #shameslessplug

of white sandstone climbing directly up from the beach to a height of seventy or eighty feet.

As we continued our slow, steady headway toward the island, I pulled up my charts on the iPad. I zoomed in as close as I could. I zoomed and looked, zoomed and looked. Then I saw it. A single, tiny dashed line followed the contour of the ocean and shore. At first I thought it was another contour line, showing the depth of the ocean floor, but upon closer inspection this was indeed a reef. It definitely showed a line of small but fiercely sharp rock that encircled the whole lagoon. It made sense. Why else would there be a pristine, protected body of water facing the ocean if there weren't some barrier to keep the ocean waves out?

I zoomed to 3000 percent and swiped left across my charts, slowly, slowly, slowly. Then I saw it: a small break in the dotted line. "I think I found the entrance!" I said, and I showed Emily. "Right here. There are still a few submerged rocks, but it looks wide enough and deep enough for us to squeak through."

"I think you're right," she said.

"If we get there and it looks bad, we can keep sailing around to Matthew Town," I added. What I didn't add was we would likely sail in a circle until morning so we could come in with daylight. Another night at sea was not appealing to any of us. Okay, we had a goal.

"Everyone come here and look at the chart," I said. "We'll have about two feet of clearance between us and these rocks."

"That's tight," Alison said. Everyone nodded.

"For all we know, it will be low tide, which might mean we have even less clearance. Plus the channel will only leave about five or six feet on either side," I added.

"Dad's *boat* is fat," Jane said. Her siblings thought that was pretty funny.

Everyone went to his or her post. I began calling out our depth so they could have a frame of reference. "Forty seven feet," I said.

"We can see everything!" Alison said from the bow.

"Yeah, I can see rocks and the leaves on plants," Karina beamed. Again, fifteen percent beauty. "We're really at forty-seven feet?"

"Yup."

"Wow."

Half an hour before, our depth gauge had been blank. We'd been in thousands of feet of water and our sounder wasn't set up to handle reading that deep. But the ocean floor had come rushing up at us. We'd been at 300, then 200, 100, and now 47 feet of depth. It kept coming in fast: 40, 30, 20.

"I think I see the break in the reef!" Alison called out.

I scanned it with binoculars and confirmed there indeed was a break. But one mistake and we could tear a hole in the bottom of our fiberglass boat. Coral is a very unforgiving rock. It spends centuries and millennia keeping the ocean on one side and the land and lagoon on the other. It wasn't going to make any exceptions for our little thirty-eight-foot sailboat.

"Depth is seven feet," I called out as I lightly touched the helm wheel. We needed four feet to clear our keel. The tide was anyone's guess. That all affected the depth.

Hours earlier we had been listless and exhausted. Now everyone was up. Alison and Karina on the bow; Jane, Eli, Lily, and Emily lining the beams looking at the ocean floor and horizon. After five days, safety was a few hundred yards away. If we didn't make it in, it was either another night on the open ocean or a sunk boat on the rocks.

"Six feet of depth," I called.

"I can see the boulders, one to port. The other to starboard," Alison said.

"Anything that's going to pass beneath us?" I asked.

"Not that I can see," she added.

"Me neither," Karina called out.

We'd taken down the sail to avoid being pushed to one side or the other and had the motors running but throttled all the way back. We moved forward at one to two miles per hour. We weren't even at a walking pace. We'd saved our last gallons of fuel for a situation just like this. Then I saw the reef to my right and my left.

"Five feet of depth," I called.

"The boulders are behind us," Karina called out.

"The reef is behind us," Emily called out.

"Six feet of depth," I called. "Seven feet. Eight feet." We'd passed the shallows and the boulders. We were inside the reef.

We pulled up close to the beach, powered in reverse to set the anchor, and drifted until the chain went slack. After 104 hours of continuous motion, five days and four nights, I killed the motors. A silence and a peace descended on the boat. There were no sounds except the ocean pushing against the reef behind us and lapping up on the beach in front of us. The white, chalky cliffs climbed up from the beach. To our right a pristine powder beach ran until the island bent and we couldn't see any further. To our left a blue lagoon sat against the setting sun. Two small, white, one-story shacks were the only evidence of humanity in sight. We saw no people, no lights. It was quiet, calm, and peaceful.

As the sun set, the water turned from sparklingly clear to dark and opaque. Sitting on the side of the boat, Emily saw bioluminescent light flickering around our boat. Flashes of neon green, red, and purple. Fifteen percent poetic beauty. She then prepared a big, fat dinner: Indian tikka masala with chickpeas and corn, and homemade cinnamon rolls for dessert. All Karina's favorites. We ate until we were stuffed. The sun went down and we all went to sleep, at the same time, for as long as we wanted.

I think this was the first time the Orton adage, "It will emerge," entered my head. I don't know when it occurred to Emily—probably sooner, because she's bright—but this concept eventually became bedrock for both of us. For so many weeks, I'd been trying to push and force the situation. I wanted the engine fixed on my timeline. I wanted to hustle off to the BVI. I wanted to know when and where we would arrive in the Bahamas. The truth is, there was no way of knowing. I would have to let it emerge. I could predict, plan, and hope, but in the end, the wind, sea, and a thousand other breezes would shape the unfolding of events. I had to wait, just like everyone else. No amount of planning or willpower could make it otherwise. I learned to become fairly zen about it. "It will emerge" was the yin to the yang of "trial and error works every time." Tenacity has its place. But so does waiting; engaged, curious, and resourceful, but patient. White Bluff Harbour was nowhere in our plans, yet here we were.

N
E
W
S
Florida
(U.S.)
GULF STREAM
Bimini
Islands
Cat Cays
Chub Cay
NASSAU
THE BAHAMAS
Thunderball
Grotto
Staniel Cay
EXUMA CHAIN
Great
Exuma
George
Town
Hog
Cay
Long Island
CUBA
TURKS &
CAICOS ISL.
(U.K.)
Inagua
Matthew Town
White Bluff
0
50 km
0
50 mi

CHAPTER 14

IT WILL EMERGE

GREAT INAGUA, BAHAMAS

5 Months, 10 Days aboard *Fezywig*

EMILY

There was nothing in White Bluff Harbour. No pier. No shops. No people. No Wi-Fi. Nothing but safety and rest after a long journey. The whole Atlantic Ocean ebbed and flowed outside the blessed reef. Miles of white, sandy beach spread before us. Erik and I lay still until the kids woke up.

In a moment of passage-making bleariness, Erik had told them, "You can do whatever you want when we get to the Bahamas."

"Anything?" Jane double-checked. As soon as we set anchor, she climbed the shrouds.[19] Now she and Alison wanted to swim in to shore to explore.

---

19. Shroud: cables—maybe as thick as a #2 pencil—running from the deck to the top of the mast. Sometimes the best thing a mom can do for her child is look away. That's what I did. Jane is our child most likely to run away and join the circus.

As soon as we set anchor she climbed the shrouds.

"Dad and I are going to scout it first. You guys watch Eli and Lily until we get back." Karina was getting the whole day off for her birthday.

We drove along the lagoon, pulled the dinghy ashore, and started exploring. "Look how pink it is inside this conch shell," I said, showing Erik one of dozens of large conch shells scattered in the wet sand.

"I'm guessing this place is a fried conch bar," Erik said, gesturing to two one-story structures farther down the beach. "It looks like there are piles of conch over there."

I knocked on the door and peeked in the windows. Nobody was there. It didn't look like anyone had been there for a while. There were a couple other bungalows back farther from the beach; four wooden walls with a tin roof and a door and a window. Anywhere else I would guess they were storage units, but here it could be an artists' colony— a place to write or paint in isolation and solitude. It was quiet and peaceful.

"This place seems pretty private," Erik raised his eyebrows at me.

"Excellent point," I said.

Erik found a shaded spot out of sight of *Fezywig* and we made love. It had been a long week, but the Bahamas were off to a good start.

"Check out these conch shells," I called as we pulled up to *Fezywig*.

"Those are huge," Alison said. "Can we go now?" She and Jane hopped into the water and swam to shore. I left my stash of sandy conch shells in the cockpit and helped Lily into the dinghy. Erik called Eli, and we were ready to go.

"You sure you don't want anything else?" I asked Karina.

"I want Wi-Fi," she said. I shrugged and hugged her. There was nothing I could do about that.

"I'm sorry you can't get your birthday messages from Facebook. We'll try again in Matthew Town. Good luck making your music video. We'll keep the kids out of the way for a few hours. I love you," I said.

I'd never seen finer sand. It was like powdered sugar, and the girls were covered in it.

"Hey, Mom," Alison said. "Isn't this place like being on set for *The Pirates of Penzance*? I thought the palm trees were really tall like the other ones we've seen, but everything is really short—like this cliff." From sea, Erik had estimated the sandy bluff to be about seventy feet tall. It was half that height.

"It's a little disorienting, like *Gulliver's Travels*," I said.

"We found all this washed-up trash. Me and SJ are digging up a buried net. Then we're gonna make a fort," Alison said.

"Look at these glass bottles I found," SJ said, pointing to a small collection at the base of the cliff. By this time, Lily had stripped off her swimsuit. I didn't worry about sunscreen because she was covered in the powdery sand. Alison and Jane ran off to write messages in the sand for some sky viewer to read while Eli worked on a sandcastle. These guys were having a party. I hoped Karina was having fun too.

Erik and I sat side by side on the beach, the ocean horizon wrapping up our whole field of sight. The waves came in quietly and then went out again just as quietly. We swayed ever so slightly, even though we sat perfectly still in the sand. Five days at sea can do that to you.

"I never thought we'd make it this far," Erik said.

"Really?"

"I hoped we would, but I didn't know for sure," he said.

"You were great out there."

"Thank you." He looked out over the ocean. "I needed to hear that."

The Virgin Islands, Puerto Rico, the Dominican Republic, Haiti, Turks, and Caicos were all behind us. We sat there as the trade winds came up to meet us and then continued on their journey west. We would follow them soon enough.

Sarah Jane came running up, her white hair flinging and flopping from side to side, her white teeth gleaming a huge grin, and her eyes sparkling like a Bahamian lagoon.

"Dad, can we have a fire tonight!?"

"We need more fire in our life," Erik said. He always said that, but this was the first place remote enough to have one. "Gather up some wood and we'll build it right there." He pointed to a spot a few feet away by a big log near the cliff.

Erik went to check on Karina's project and returned with her a few minutes later.

"The cable for the microphone isn't working," she said. "It won't record. I've tried so many times. I can't even do this one simple thing for my birthday." She was close to tears. "I have all the cloud footage." She hadn't asked for much—a little time alone to record her beautiful song about dreams for the future. She didn't feel like singing anymore. She sat in the shade of the cliff and poked at the sand with a stick.

"I offered to help troubleshoot," Erik told me. "She said, 'I just want to get off this stupid boat.'" Karina still needed some space, so we gave her the beach. Erik and I went back to *Fezywig* to work on a few things that had been too arduous to look at while underway.

With the sail down for the first time in six days, we fixed the fiberglass rods that held the lazy jack open. The lazy jack is a canvas taco that holds the mainsail when it's lowered, protecting it from the punishing Caribbean sun. We opened the lower hatches that remained closed during the crossing and gave them their first breath in nearly a week. We hung sheets and clothes in the sun. I love the fresh feeling of tidying up. When I got to Eli and Lily's cabin, the hatch was already open. I wailed.

"What is it?" Erik asked. I could hear him making his way to the starboard pontoon. I held up a picture book. The pages were puffed and wilted with saltwater. Black speckles of mold were already growing on the cover.

"They're all like this. Eli must've opened the side hatch days ago. After all the trouble picking out our favorites . . . " I caught myself. "Sorry. That was a dramatic response. It's only stuff. They're all replaceable." We knew all the books were ruined, but Erik helped me set them out to dry anyway.

Erik pulled out his guitar and went to the bow. He hadn't played since Fajardo with Ike. He played for the ocean, the sky, and me. Then he rested. The world of news, information, banks, and email awaited around the bend at Matthew Town.

That evening we gathered around the fire as the sun set into the ocean. God doesn't disappoint in the Caribbean sunset department. Karina mellowed.

"I know it sounds ridiculous to complain about having my birthday on some remote island in the Bahamas . . ." she started.

"I get it," I said. "You only wanted one simple thing and it didn't work out. It's frustrating. I'm sorry."

"It's okay." We all talked about our friends back in Saint Martin. We missed them. We talked about our friends back in NYC. We missed them, too. We talked about being together. Despite being completely bored out of our skulls for five days dying to talk to other people, we sat around the fire content to be just us.

I want to capture my family as we were that night. Eli wore his felt Indiana Jones hat, the same one we'd almost lost overboard in the Florida Keys. A red bandanna hung triangled around his neck. His baggy black clamdiggers flapped around his skinny legs as he picked up driftwood and smacked it against anything hard. Lily had run naked all afternoon, sand sticking to her whole body and her tan lines on full display. Alison's copper hair was growing out. The sun-bleached tips hung over her tanned face in stark contrast to the black rash guard she'd paired with her orange swimsuit. In her green T-shirt, Karina's eyes looked like the sea and she was patient against the backdrop of frustration. I wore an aqua tank top and cutoff black Dickies. Forty was probably too old for pigtails in New York, but here they made sense. We were all sun-bleached and faded.

Erik's gray-blue Patagonia board shorts were a running gag as they slung ever lower around his shrinking waist. A pale yellow T-shirt provided some protection from the sun, but now the sun was sinking into the ocean.

SJ streaked her face with the beach sand. It was fine enough to simply stick to her skin. She squatted by the fire with a large stick next to her. With a patch of white sand on her chin, and the rest of her covered in the same white powder, she looked aboriginal. The fire flickered in the blacks of her eyes.

There was something new about each of these kids. As we sat in a circle watching the fire burn to embers, I noticed something in their eyes and in their shoulders: night watches, sheet lightning, miles of ocean depth beneath their feet, the Mona Passage, doldrums, watching the ocean floor and spotting the reef as we laced through to the safety of the lagoon. They were still children. We hadn't had any tragedies, but they knew they could do something they didn't know they could do before. We all did. As the fire burned down, the conversation gave way to watching embers. Erik threw sand on the fire. We walked to the dinghy, untied it, and rode the short distance to *Fezywig*.

We stayed for three days.

CHAPTER 15

APPARENT WIND

MATTHEW TOWN, GREAT INAGUA, BAHAMAS

5 Months, 13 Days aboard *Fezywig*

ERIK

We cleared in with customs and I checked email for the first time since Culebra. I had a lot to be grateful for. My old job wanted me back. They just had to check with the client first. The Andersons had signed the lease agreement and sent a deposit. Our named storm insurance provision had been approved. We now had an additional month to get north of Jacksonville. I shifted from leaning forward to leaning back in my chair.

With pieces falling into place, we bought the girls' airfare from Florida to New York. They would fly out in a couple weeks. We would keep our word, and SJ would get to go to camp with her sisters. We had some expectations. In Matthew Town, there were several things that we didn't expect. A stranger gave us a ride into town. We found the library and Emily read to a group of children. Her dream job. A former mayor and his daughter taught us to eat guineps, a tart fruit, on the dock. They played us their favorite country songs until their truck battery died. The kids found a public trampoline next to a BBQ shack. We were deemed harmless by homeland security, and we killed hundreds of flies. We were there only two nights.

Our next stop was Long Island, Bahamas, a 120-mile jaunt. We had full water and fuel tanks, and all the bureaucracy was behind us. Plus our confidence had grown. Before, our biggest crossing had been 80 miles. That had grown to 500 miles. We were inside our new comfort zone.

The only spot that gave me pause was the Mira Por Vos Passage, a narrow squeeze we would pass through at night around the halfway point of the crossing. It was not quite as notorious as the Mona Passage, but the meaning behind the name unnerved me: the "Look Out for Yourself" or "Be Careful" Channel. We pulled anchor and headed north.

From the minute we cast off it was night and day from our previous crossing. We hit eight knots even in the lee of Great Inagua, and it was off to the races. Like so many things in life, it's easy when you have momentum. With the strong winds we cruised along, skimming across the waves as the water quickly turned from turquoise to emerald green to cobalt. We were now in open water, out of the lee of the island, and the trades coming across the Atlantic hit our sails. We picked up an extra knot and a half of speed. For our little boat this was quite a ride.

There's a beautiful balance you can feel when a boat, a course, and the wind align. I would call it harmony. In this case the wind came across the side of the boat, creating forward momentum. The only reason there's forward moment, instead of sideways momentum, is because under the water are two keels—thin, large, and heavy fins at the center of each side of the boat. The key, though, are the rudders: two small dagger fins at the stern. They pivot left and right to steer the boat.

With the wind coming from the side and the boat racing forward across the wind, a vibration starts to occur in the boat. As the sails are adjusted and rudder tweaked, the boat gets tuned. Sailors actually use the term 'tuning the sails.' The vibration quiets and the boat is in harmony. *Fezywig* was tuned, and we sliced northward gracefully and smoothly as the sun set on our portside.

I'd felt out of tune, out of sorts, for some time. I'd felt alone, frustrated, worried. I'd felt pulled in many directions and was struggling to make forward progress. But I felt like with the good news, the successful crossing, and more confidence, I was more in harmony.

The trick with the Mira Por Vos passage was you sailed through it going north, with an island on the right and coral rocks on your left. The wind and current come from the right, wanting to push any boat left (west) onto the rocks. This is what we didn't want to happen. To be extra sure, I stayed up and did a double watch.

The passage was plenty wide, roughly eight miles. But we cheated toward the island to the east, knowing the current would try to carry us west. Given our speed, we were through the channel before the current could carry us far.

Emily was with me on the first watch. Alison joined me for the second watch. "We're going too fast," I said. I'd clocked our top speed that night at around 10.4 knots, a speed record for short, stubby *Fezywig*. The winds were holding steady at about 20 knots. "We're going to get in before sunrise. We need to shorten the sails."

"Okay. Do you need me to do anything?" Alison said.

"Can you help with the winches?" We peeled ourselves off the benches where we'd been chilling and went to work. Trimming the jib slowed us a bit. We left out a small triangle of it to keep the boat balanced.

Now for the mainsail. I'd vowed not to do any deck work at night, but we'd been getting the hang of things over the past couple weeks. Alison and I were both tethered in and she was a good sailor, so we went for it.

As she lowered the sail, something wasn't right. The boom[20] was coming down with the sail. That wasn't good.

"Hold on, Alison," I said. I looked around but couldn't figure it out. "Lower it a little bit." She started to lower the sail and again the boom lowered as well.

"Okay, stop," I looked some more. I saw a scrap of snapped rope hanging out from the end of the boom. I looked up and could see the rest of the line from the top of the mast wafting back and forth in the wind. Sometime in the night it had silently broken.

"I guess we worked it too hard in the night."

"Guess so. So what do we do?"

"Just leave the mainsail up. I don't want to deal with this in the dark."

"Okay." Alison hoisted the main back up to full height, I pointed the boat north again, and the sail filled with wind.

The sky started to lighten and the stars slowly disappeared against the twilight. We caught sight of Long Island and watched as the depth gauge came up once again from unfathomable to less than ten feet. The water was clear and the bottom was sand in every direction.

I pointed the boat into the wind, and we slowly lowered the boom and rested it atop the bimini frame. Alison went to the bow and lowered the anchor. It set easily in the sand, and I cut the engines.

"Thanks for all your help, kiddo."

"I'm going to get some sleep," she said.

"Good idea." I stopped and looked around. We sat tucked behind the tip of Long Island. The ocean, as usual, extended forever behind us. The sun continued to rise in the east. It was a lovely spot. We were getting better at this. I went below and promptly fell asleep.

We'd been away from civilization for quite some time. By

---

20. The boom: big metal bar that spans the base of the mainsail.

civilization, I mean grocery stores. Our last good shop was the Super Walmart in Puerto Rico. We needed a proper shop, and we missed cruisers.

We knew we'd find both in Georgetown on the Great Exuma chain.

The Bahamas are a series of oceanic shelves that create expanses of shallow water surrounded by steep drop-offs back into ocean depths. Crossing from Great Inagua to Long Island brought us across more of the deep ocean, but now we found ourselves on the shelf of the Great Bahama Bank. We had to pay careful attention to our depth.

Day Dreamer had told us about a place called Hog Cay, and we wanted to check it out. It was the most southern tip of the Great Exuma chain to our north. It was a small, uninhabited island, but the perfect stopover on our way to Georgetown. To get there we would sail in the lee of Long Island following an underwater channel that got increasingly narrow and shallow until it wove between Hog Cay and the Exumas. The only slightly scary crossing that remained was jumping the Gulf Stream to Florida, but for now we had everything to look forward to about the Bahamas. The wind was steady and plentiful. Aside from our topping lift, the boat was in great shape. We were long since reacclimated to being at sea (no nausea), and we knew more than ever what we were capable of.

The turquoise water met the blue sky at the horizon. Overhead were wisps of white clouds, and in the middle of it all was a little white sailboat with thin blue stripes down the side and sails with red trim. If I could have floated overhead and looked down on ourselves at the moment, I would say it was the perfect moment of sublimity.

Approaching the cut leading into Hog Cay, we could see sand dollars resting on the ocean floor as we passed over them. We worked our way around and through the rocks. The tide must have been out, because the water got extremely shallow. I would not have been surprised if our keel fins carved two lines through the sand beneath us.

But I wasn't worried. Sand is forgiving, and we'd been through much worse.

Once through the cut, the water deepened and we knew we had arrived. We motored close to the cay and dropped the anchor into a perfectly clear field of sand. We bore down to set the anchor, and once again everything came to rest.

One of the frequent tasks that had evolved since moving more often was *diving on the anchor.* When you park a car, you can generally walk away knowing it's secure, unless of course it's on a hill in San Francisco. With a boat, once you park it, it's a good idea to check the anchor to make sure it's secure. Sometimes this is a dreaded task, because the sailing has been lousy and everyone's tired. It involves putting on fins and a snorkel mask and getting wet. The ridiculousness of this strikes me as I write, because sometimes nobody wanted to do it. After all, who would want to go snorkeling in warm Caribbean waters at the end of a day of sailing? But alas, such was the case from time to time. Fortunately, on this day, it was a welcome task and Jane won the lottery. As a young, kinetic twelve-year-old she was quick into the water and quick down the chain, which was easy to spot against the white sand in clear water. The anchor was buried in the sand. Perfect.

Some people tend to think a sandy seabed is a terrible place to set an anchor. In fact, it is ideal. They think you want rock in which to set your anchor. This is the worst scenario. An anchor holds fast by digging into the ground beneath the boat, not by latching on to it somehow. Sand is ideal; mud is next best. The anchor is designed like a plow, so the more it is pulled from the end of a long chain at a narrow angle, the deeper it digs and the more secure the boat. The longer the chain, the more secure the anchor. To pull anchor, you simply move your boat over the location of the anchor, pulling in the chain as you go. Once you are directly above the anchor, you pull up, much like pulling the tab of a soda can. It pops the anchor free from its embedded place in the sand or mud. Suffice it to say, it was sand down there and we had a perfect anchorage.

I was learning anchoring was much like life. Locking onto something with no flexibility was the surest way to destroy it. The worst kind of anchor would be to bolt a boat to the ocean floor with a short steel cable. Gripping too tight would rip the bow off the boat. An anchor worked on these principles, and these anchoring principles were sound and fast. Correctly applied, a boat would always be secure. I wanted to be sound and fast, as well as flexible.

The kids knew we would be arriving in the evening, so they had taken the initiative and prepared food while underway. Dinner was served upon arrival: curried red lentil soup. We'd sailed nine hours over forty beautiful miles. After dinner we all went to the front of the boat and settled in on the trampoline.

"I love it here," Jane said.

"Me too," Alison added.

"I miss *Day Dreamer* and *Discovery*," Karina said. "But it's kind of nice being just us."

"Yeah, but we'll see them again," Alison said.

"How do you know?" Emily asked.

"I just know. I think things just work out like that."

"But there's no Wi-Fi," Eli smiled—not a happy smile.

"I like it that way," Emily smiled back.

The sun set and stars twinkled against the darkening sky.

"I think *Day Dreamer* was right," I said. "This is a lovely spot." I missed my dad cocaptains, and Emily missed the other moms, but Karina was right. This was what we'd come for: to be together as a family, just us.

Below, the water lapped quietly against the inside of the hulls. Looking into the sky we spotted two falling stars. There was almost no moon that night, so we lay there watching the stars become clearer and clearer. It had been a good day. We all went to bed early.

We had two more weeks to spend in the Bahamas. That's kind of like walking into a library and saying, you have two weeks to read as much as you want. There's no way to read everything, but you can undoubtedly find a couple good books and really enjoy them.

I awoke the next morning and couldn't have been more pleased. The night had been calm and flat. The tide had gone out quite a bit. A fleshy sandbar had emerged from Hog Cay and now extended out about a hundred yards toward us. It looked like a thigh almost entirely submerged in a bathtub, with the topmost section peeking through the water. With the sun rising higher in the sky, the cove felt like a bathtub. "I vote we stay a while," I said as we all munched on our breakfast.

"Okay," was the common consensus from all the other munchers.

We still had plenty of food and fuel. I'd put in the water maker for situations like this. We could create fresh water, and the weather was perfect. Why go anywhere else?

I intended to wait until Georgetown to look at the topping lift, but this was as good a place as any. I used my lighter to fuse the frayed end of the rope descending from the mast. I then asked Emily to open the deck cleat so I could pull down enough rope to reach the end of the boom.

"Which one?" she asked.

"It's that one."

"This one?"

"Yeah."

She opened the cleat and I pulled slightly on the line. I needed only a few additional feet. That's when Emily's end of the line slid all the way through the cleat, up the mast, and over the pulley at the top and dumped the entire line, limp on the deck.

I looked at Emily and she looked at me. Technically it wasn't her fault that *she* had let the line slip away. There was no stopper knot on the end to prevent it. But she also hadn't thought of checking. This two-minute project became a two-hour project. I would have to go to the top of the mast, rethread the line through the pulley at the top, snake it down through the inside of the mast, and lace it out of the mast and through the deck cleat. I tried to not let daggers come out of my eyes.

I went to get my climbing harness. Several hours later, the project was completed. The line had been rethreaded through the top of the mast. I ran it through the cleat and locked it in place. I tied a stopper knot on the end. Emily had done her best to be cheerful throughout the afternoon, but I did not smile back. With the project completed, I put on my snorkel fins and jumped into the water. I was trying to get out of my grumpy-pants mood.

"I'm swimming to shore. Anyone else want to come?" I asked.

Alison joined me. Emily followed later in the dinghy with the Littles. Once Lily was to the sand, she could not have been happier. She lay on her stomach and kicked her feet.

"Daddy, I so happy," she said as she smiled at me.

"Yeah, this is pretty nice, isn't it, Lil?" I said.

"We stay long time?" she asked.

"We'll see."

In true *Fezywig* fashion, we worked hard and we played hard. The next morning we did boat cleaning. The water was shallow enough that we could stand on the sand and clean the hull. Alison and I worked on the submerged portions. Matthew Town's dock had left a big black smudge on the starboard side. Emily, Eli, and Lily piled into the dinghy and scrubbed that away. Karina and Jane scrubbed the deck, washed the windows, and wiped down the kitchen. Everyone got to take turns picking the music and, with no one else around, we cranked it up.

We spent three days and two nights at Hog Cay. Then it was time to go find another book.

We pulled anchor and headed north, skirting the east edge of Little Exuma Island. It was about eighteen miles to Georgetown. A down-wind sail.

Sailing downwind is ironic. Most people have an image of good sailing. It involves a boat with full sails, heeled over slightly, or a lot, slicing through the waves with the wind in your hair, and maybe the people aboard look and dress like the Kennedys. We don't look like the Kennedys. Nor do we dress like them. Sailing with the wind in your face can look dramatic, but it also turns out to be a long way to anywhere. Sailing into the wind is what you do when you're out for some kicks and thrills on a day sail, or you have no other choice.

If the wind is coming from behind you, that's a good way to get where you want to go, but it's also boring. It's slow and boring because it feels like nothing is happening. Sailors use a fancy term called "apparent wind": the wind you perceive because of your movement through the air. When you ride a bike it feels windy. When you stop, it's no longer windy. Apparent wind. When you sail *with* the wind, the wind is moving but you're moving with it, so it feels like there's no wind, which makes it feel like nothing is happening. This is when you have to look at the water and watch the speed of bits of floating reed and sea-foam gliding past. You have to look closely at the things right under your nose to notice the movement.

I knew I was learning things on this trip, but I wasn't sure what they all were. Some things were deathly boring, and it didn't feel like I was making any progress. I knew I got frustrated easily. I yelled at my kids. I held grudges. I was often antsy to go and do something. It was hard for me to slow down and sit still. I missed the exhilaration of being busy. But I wanted to take time to be slow with my family, my wife, and myself, both during this trip and in my life. Things could never move fast enough for me. I liked how it felt to sail into the wind. But for now, I was sailing downwind, to Georgetown. It was peaceful and soothing. I was trying to practice slowing down.

CHAPTER 16

THAT ESCALATED QUICKLY

GREAT EXUMA CHAIN, BAHAMAS

5 Months, 18 Days aboard *Fezywig*

ERIK

At high season, we knew the anchorages around Georgetown were packed with boats, vacationers, retirees, cruisers, you name it. It was a field of masts. Now, as we pulled in at almost the end of July, perhaps a half dozen boats floated at anchor. We chose a spot not too far out and not too far in. Setting the anchor was dead easy. All sand.

With the dinghy lowered, Emily and I headed to shore. We motored up to a low concrete seawall, tied off, and hopped up onto land. The main road through town stood a dozen feet away. I pulled on my red backpack, which had become my customary first-time-to-shore kit, adjusted my broad-brimmed straw hat, and put on my flip-flops. Emily and I walked down the road, enjoying the shade of the occasional trees. The "town" itself was small. We saw the grocery store and headed straight there.

When we walked in, we knew we had arrived. Although nowhere

close to the Super Walmart in Fajardo, this was indeed a respectable grocery store, even by Caribbean standards. There were five checkout registers and a dozen or so aisles. We walked along the refrigeration aisle, enjoying the cold leaking out. They stocked cold cereal, vegetables, meat that was not in a can, all kinds of laundry and cleaning items, soda, and the holy grail of sailing provisions: ice cream. Deep shelves of ice cream, sorbet, and other frozen delicacies. Emily and I selected two individual pints of sorbet, making sure to pick the most extravagant flavors, and headed for the checkout register. We would be back for the more practical stuff. We'd brought two metal spoons in my trusty red backpack should such a contingency materialize. Our faith was rewarded.

However, on our way to pay for our frozen treasure, we heard the word "laundromat" and our ears perked up. Along with food and Wi-Fi, a laundromat completes the triumvirate of cruisers' essentials. We stopped instinctively and spoke to the mother and two teenagers perusing the cold cereal selections.

"Excuse me, we heard you mention the laundromat," Emily ventured. "You wouldn't happen to be sailors, would you?"

"Yes, we are," said the woman with brown curly hair. Within a few moments we knew where they were anchored, exchanged kids' names, and invited them over for brownies that evening. The invitation was extended to the other boat next to them, which also had teenagers. We were headed north and they were headed south. They wanted to know all about what awaited them. We had met *Day Star* and *Palenteer*.

Emily and I paid for our sorbet, walked to a picnic table by the seawall, and got comfortable. There's a certain joy to having your own pint of frozen sorbet whilst sitting on a hot Bahamian island. The *pièce de résistance* is having your own metal spoon with which to enjoy it. Emily and I exchanged a few bites, but otherwise we hunkered down and made for the bottom of our own containers.

That night the kids of *Day Star* and *Palanteer* sat on our trampoline peppering each other with teenager questions while the parents peppered us with cruiser questions.

"Can you get fuel in Matthew Town?"

"What about docking in the DR?"

"How was the Mona Passage?"

"Do you have to clear customs in Puerto Rico?"

"What are the best places to see in the BVI?"

It was a switch to pull into port and be confident enough to host a gathering on our first night.

The next day was Sunday and we spent it quietly aboard. We did church on the boat as a family. The rest of the day we would stay close to the boat and enjoy some quiet and solitude. It was simple and I liked it. That evening we had a farewell visit with our new boat friends.

When we traveled with *Day Dreamer* and *Discovery* there had been twelve kids total—ten girls and two boys, Eli and Jack. Jack was half Eli's age. Now Eli was in the water playing with the big boys, teenagers. They had pecks and abs and they picked up Eli and threw him around in the water like a rag doll. After a series of dunkings he got his head above water and grinned.

"This is living life!" he shouted as one of the boys grabbed him and threw him like a skipping stone. Boys.

In the morning *Fezywig* would provision, pull anchor, and move north. It was good to be with other families again, but we knew we could stand on our own whenever we needed to. We were realizing how much we'd learned. They had questions, and we had answers. They had concerns. We could give assurances. We were becoming seasoned.

We were spending a lot of time together as a family, and that can be good and that can be bad. Before we left, a lot of people asked, "Aren't you going to drive each other crazy?" We were never really too worried about that going in. I think when a family or couple are in crisis mode (or at least what feels like crisis mode), it's easier to set aside differences and hurt feelings and focus on the problems at hand. Something needs to happen now. A problem needs to be solved immediately. There is no time or energy for petty arguments or squabbles. When the seas are calm, the wind is steady, and things are shipshape is the easiest time to slip into complacency or for unresolved problems to surface. We were in calm seas, with steady winds, and the boat was shipshape.

When Emily and I had first gotten on the boat, we had been intensely united. We had problems to solve and everything was new. It was good to constantly give each other moral support as we tackled unknown after unknown. This had worked well in Sint Maarten through the BVI. But now I wanted competent help dealing with the logistics of running a boat.

Every time we moved or pulled anchor—which was a lot once we left Saint Martin—a long checklist came to mind of what needed to get done. The same thing was true for when we were underway. For me these were obvious tasks, and I felt an urgency about them. But it was often a chore to get the crew moving to get it all done, or the alternative was I did them all myself. Both created resentment. I wanted a crew that was on point. But as much as we were a crew, we were a family first. I was starting to suffer from something I might call Togetherness Fatigue. It came to an unexpected head a few miles north in Staniel Cay.

Staniel Cay had two great tourist spots: Thunderball Grotto and Pig Beach. I figure anything with "thunderball" in the title is worth a look-see, but Pig Beach was purely based on tourist marketing. At least half of the Bahama-related pictures we found online had pigs swimming. They're super cute. What's more adorable than a little pink pig swimming in perfect, turquoise water up to your dinghy and nuzzling his head into your hand while you feed it baby carrots? Nothing, that's what. So we had to go.

It was almost two miles, via dinghy, around the point to see the pigs. As we got closer, the size of these pigs came into perspective. These were not cute, cuddly piglets like in *Babe* or Wilbur in *Charlotte's Web*. These were the big-mama, semi-truck versions of pigs, and they knew what they wanted. They didn't swim a stroke more than was necessary to get themselves astride our dinghy, and they essentially opened their mouths and looked at us out of the corner of their eyes with a look that said, "Just dump it right here." They knew the routine. We were being hustled. It kind of reminded me of trying to walk past the aggressive photo-op characters in Times Square dressed up like Elmo or the latest Disney character. They want to take a picture with you but get ticked if you don't give them a tip.

The kids fed a few pigs some carrots, being careful to draw their fingers back quickly to avoid being bit, and then we beached the dinghy so we could get out and walk around. The little pigs were on-shore. The instant the gargantuan pigs realized we were not handing out any more food, they turned their butts toward us and swam—very slowly—toward another boat full of tourists with armloads of carrots and potatoes.

The little pigs were indeed cute. What's cuter than your little son, with a red bandanna around his neck, petting a spotted pig half his height? Nothing, that's what. So it was delightful to see our children amongst these little, wild beach urchins. Eli bent down and opened the container with his leftover oatmeal. A couple of pigs nuzzled in their snouts and snarfed cutely on their hearty snack. But in about a nano-second, my son was swarmed by a stampede of thronging mini-pigs clamoring for a bite of whatever was on the menu. Alarmed, Eli simply dropped his oatmeal and fled.

Emily and I sat on the beach watching the pigs and watching our kids as they ran around both trying to pet and stay away from the pigs.

We walked back and forth in the calm shallow water, letting it lap up around our shins and knees. That's when Alison asked, "What's that?" as she pointed to something floating on the surface of the water. It was a nine-inch long pig turd.

"Okay! Everyone in the dinghy," I called out. I started to put the dinghy off the beach before Emily and the kids gathered up. The pigs were closing in. They could sense our fear and our imminent departure. They began to gnaw on the lines running the length of the dinghy. We splashed the water with oars to scare them back, but they kept coming. I tipped the outboard motor down and started it up. I like to think I looked to make sure there weren't any pigs in the vicinity of the propeller.

The kids jumped over the side and into the dinghy like it was the last chopper out of Saigon. I threw the outboard into reverse and opened the throttle. As we moved into deeper water the pigs started to swim and squeal, thrashing toward us. But then, like couch potatoes who grow bored with a show, they gave up and turned back to shore, looking for another boat of suckers headed toward the beach.

We made it back to *Fezywig* alive.

It was going to be low tide soon, so we quickly ate spaghetti with canned marinara sauce and got ready to head over to Thunderball Grotto. On the outside, it was a tall rocky crag that rose fifty feet above the water's surface. Inside it was like swimming into the basilica of caves. It was best to swim in at low tide, when there was a pause between the tide flowing out and the new tide flowing in. Emily put life jackets on Eli and Lily, everyone piled into the dinghy, and we motored over to the cave entrance. We put on snorkel masks and flippers and swam in. Once inside, the ceiling rose in a majestic dome, with a small opening at its apex that let in clean shafts of light that hit the water and illuminated the sandy bottom beneath.

We were not the only ones there. A couple brave souls had gone back out of the cave and clambered to the top. They were now peering

down from above. With conflicting shouts of encouragement and cau-
tion from their friends below, they jumped through the hole above and
plummeted into water. Immediately Alison and SJ looked at each other
and raised their eyebrows.

"We're gonna jump," SJ said, and they started to swim for the exit.
She looked at me and asked, "You wanna come?" I don't know if it was
fatherly concern or macho pride, but I looked at Emily, shrugged, and
swam after them.

The climb to the top was sharp and jagged. I was glad I'd brought
my water sandals. Alison and SJ were barefoot, so I beat them to the
top. Point 1: Dad. I encouraged them from above and pointed out
the best path. Then we all gathered at the top. The funny thing about
looking into a bottomless pit of darkness is it always looks higher from
the top. Inside the grotto we had been able to see the silhouette of
the jumpers, and we could see the water, clear and inviting, below.
But from above, the sun is bright and blinding. Your eyes dilate and
you can no longer see anything inside the grotto. You can hear voices;
some are warning you off and others are encouraging you. And in
your head you're saying to yourself, *Am I gonna jump? Am I really this
stupid? This looks like a bad idea. But I just saw somebody else do it. Is
there really water down there?* In all honesty, you can't see anything.
Meanwhile you're standing on a razor-sharp circle of rock with a three-
foot-diameter hole, heading into what feels like a fifty-foot drop into
water you hope is still there. I know metaphors abound with this kind
of stuff: fear, trust, the unknown, God, danger, safety, risk, reward. I'll
trust you to make up your own.

If I waited another second I was going to chicken out. "Okay, girls,
see you down there." I jumped.

My feet hit first, then my hands. I'd used my right hand to plug my
nose. I didn't want water going up there. But the water had yanked my
hand away and sent saltwater up my nasal passage all the way back to
my eardrum. No exaggeration. I was fine, but it hurt.

Karina, the Littles, and Emily cheered when I surfaced. I swam to the side and looked up. Alison stood on the edge, pausing for a split second, and then jumped. We cheered. She swam to the side. SJ peered over the edge. SJ, our daredevil. We called to her and told her we were fine. She stayed where she was and continued peering. One minute turned into five minutes. She was up there all alone. "It's fine! We're down here. You can do it!" Alison and I called up.

This was not the kind of edge you can sit down and ease up to. When I say the rock was sharp, I mean it was razor sharp. It was all or nothing. Five minutes turned into ten. The tide was coming in and the entrance was almost covered.

At the moment, Jane was happier to be at the top of the grotto, barefoot, hot, and scared, than she was to be in the cool, clear water below. Her anxiety over what she could no longer see, and the fear of what it would take to get there, were more powerful than her will to jump. We did our best to help her shift the balance, but it was up to her. Only she could decide when she wanted to move and how she would do it. She could climb back down or she could jump. The push of her current situation, the pull of her new situation, her anxiety about her future, and her loyalty to her present were all shifting moment by moment. We change when we're more excited about getting the new thing than we are scared about losing the old thing. I go through this same semiconscious process every time I face my own fears. I think we all do. It's very personal. I internally weigh all these factors in the balance, and something happens or it doesn't.

"Janie, you can do this," I said. "We believe in you!"

We kept treading water, being pushed stronger and stronger by the rising tide. Then the balance shifted.

The hole above filled with a black silhouette, and down came Jane. She sliced the water's surface feet first and swooshed into the clear basin below. She came up through the white bubbling foam with a huge grin on her face. We all cheered. A quick group hug while treading water, and out we went.

My sinus hurt pretty bad when we got back to the boat. I pathetically lay in our bed and asked for ibuprofen. Emily brought some down and went back to fixing dinner. As I lay there suffering, I heard a panicking scream come from the bow. I jumped out of bed and ran upstairs.

Alison and Jane were encouraged by their jump into the grotto, so they'd continued the theme when they got back to *Fezywig*. They were taking turns running down the side of the boat and jumping off the bow. A cable ran down the side of the boat to make a railing. That cable was fastened at the end by a pin, and that pin was held in place with a ring, similar to a keyring, but smaller. Jane had caught her pinkie toe in the ring just before she'd jumped off the bow.

"There's a lot of blood!" Alison called out. She was in the water with Jane.

I jumped in the water and grabbed Jane.

"Everyone out!" Emily called. It was almost sunset. She knew this was the time sharks would be looking for dinner, and there was blood in the water. We weren't sure how far sharks could smell blood, but Emily had seen enough nature documentaries to worry. We helped Jane onto the steps at the stern, and the blood, mixed with dripping salt water, started to spread across the deck. Her toe was securely attached, but there was a deep cut.

We got her up into the cockpit and grabbed the first aid kit. We flushed the cut with freshwater, dried it, staunched the bleeding with gauze pads, and taped her toes together. It could have been much worse. I was grateful. I still had the ibuprofen out, so Jane took some and we both went to our cabins to lie down.

My ear was throbbing. Emily brought me a hot compress to put on my ear and dug into her internet research on the subject. I promptly fell asleep.

That night, when Emily came to bed, I found this note next to my head:

"For my favorite Mom and Dad, Love SJ

"For my favorite Dad: Dad thank you for keeping me safe last afternoon. Even in your pain. I feel much better now. And thank you for making me feel safe as I jumped through that hole, and when we were at the beach with mega pigs. I really want you to get better. I'm praying for you. You are the best Dad in the world, and I love you. SJ

"For my favorite Mom: Mom thank you for re-doing my Band-Aid last night. It made me feel loved. And thank you so much for loving and taking care of Dad. I bet it makes him feel loved too. Thank you for taking care of me and everyone, with Dad. I love you, you're the best Mom in the world. SJ"

What's cuter than that? Nothing.

When I woke up the next morning, my ear wasn't aching. I rolled over and saw Emily was gone, probably doing yoga on deck. I climbed the two steps into the galley and saw her at the salon table in her striped PJ pants and aqua T-shirt. The laptop was open and she was slumped over the table, her face buried into a folded beach towel, crying.

I put my hand on her back to let her know that I was there and that I was there for her. I didn't know what to say. I didn't know what was wrong. At my touch, she sat up and looked at me. Her face paled under a mask of freckles, her puffy eyes bloodshot. She sounded slightly congested as she asked, "Are you happy?"

I didn't move. I needed more information. "What do you mean?"

"Everyone was asleep when I woke up, so I thought I would have a turn with the laptop, do some writing. I didn't mean to see it, but when I turned it on, your journal was open. I wasn't trying to read it, but the words were already in my head before I had a chance to close out your document," she continued.

I believed her. What little privacy we each had, we respected. My last journal entry was from the night before. It had been a good day in Staniel Cay, with the pigs, the grotto jump, and the notes from SJ. My favorite part of the day had been helping SJ with her toe injury because it was unselfish. In my private writing I struggled with selfishness. Not only was I the only one who really understood how to navigate, sail, and maintain *Fezywig*, I'd been reading two books, one about a dutiful politician, Harry S. Truman. The other book was about a celebrity's, Rob Lowe's, wild lost years before he discovered the joy of family life. I didn't like how much I felt like Harry, always dutiful, compromising to meet everyone else's needs. I already had five kids and a great wife, but I'd never been wild and lost.

"You wrote you wished you were 'happier,' 'more in love' with me. What? You say you want to go 'off the rails,' sow your 'wild oats'? How am I supposed to respond to that?" Emily asked.

I wasn't sure how to respond to her. I didn't know. I was still sorting through my feelings. That's why I keep a journal. Emily didn't pause for a reply. Understandably, she had a lot to say. Her words were quick and pointed, but low enough that she wouldn't wake the kids. "I know I'm not a great sailor. I know I talk about school and church a lot and that can be tedious. But I'm *here*, in the middle of the Bahamas, living on a sailboat with you. How many wives are up for that? I listen. I encourage. I'm affectionate and responsive. I'm inquisitive. I love learning. I'm frugal. I'm a good team player. I'm funny. I can make a meal out of almost nothing. I've had five kids and I'll never be twenty-one again, but I'm healthy and probably stronger and tanner than I'll ever be again." She paused, looking for words. "I mean, if you're not happy with me now, you'll never be satisfied. If you're not happy with this, it's a *you* problem. If you want something else, I won't stop you. I've never stopped you. I want you to be happy. But if you walk away from this, you can't come back."

That escalated quickly. I kept my mouth shut. Emily had been my best friend for twenty-two years and my wife for nineteen years.

She'd always believed in me, encouraged me. I could trust her with my dreams and hopes. She would never laugh at me and tell me I was foolish. There were seasons of greater satisfaction, when communication was clear and we were in harmony. Other times were dissonant, distant, or even lonely. Normally, I sorted my feelings in writing. Once I knew what I was feeling, I discussed it with Emily. She was similar. She tends to talk through her undrafted emotions, and then sorts through them in writing and discussion. It can be a bumpy ride.

She was sharing her raw response. I was still sorting myself out. I knew she hadn't meant to read my journal, but I'd been caught in the stall with my pants down. My natural response was to slam the door. I needed privacy. I didn't have any more answers than when I had fallen asleep the night before.

"If you don't have anything to say, I don't have anything else to say," Emily said. "I'm going to get dressed and eat breakfast." We had an early departure and an all-day crossing to Nassau. In our city life I would have gone to work, Emily might have taken a long walk. Instead, we pulled anchor and headed north.

Our pattern was to work side by side with an easy flow of ideas, insights, and observations. We normally joked and_flirted, but that morning, our exchanges were strictly functional, limited to raising the anchor and setting sail. The kids were still sleeping. Emily sat next to me at the helm, her usual habit, but it wasn't usual because the silence was the uncomfortable silence of two people trying not to hurt each other. We sailed up the chain quietly until the islands veered northeast. I reached out to hold Emily's hand. She didn't pull away.

"What are you thinking about?" I asked, looking at her salty face—a mixture of sea breeze and tears—for clues.

"I'm thinking about how I can provide for myself and the kids," Emily kept looking ahead. "I could recertify as a teacher, but maybe it would be better if I became an orthodontist assistant, like your mom.

Then I could leave work at work." She was making plans for her life without me in it.

"If you want to get a job, I'll support you in that. But I'm not going anywhere," I said.

"We'll see. I know you're still figuring out how you feel. I don't know how long this has been building. I don't know how serious it is. You aren't giving me any information." I didn't have any new information. I'd been sitting at the helm, trying to keep us on course, all morning. The water deepened, there were no more rocks, and the wind carried us forward.

After lunch, Alison took over the helm. Karina read in her cabin with the hatch open. Eli and Lily watched a movie at the salon table, and Sarah Jane was using the bimini as a jungle gym. Emily was sitting on the portside deck, her arms wrapped around her knees, looking out at the ocean. I sat next to her. She looked at me and smiled. I thought it was a good sign.

Emily said, "This is actually really good for me. When things are off between us, I usually try to improve something about myself. Obviously, the only person I can change is me. I certainly can't change you. But I'm realizing that it's not always about me being a better person. I'm far from perfect, and I want to improve because that's my nature. But it's liberating to realize that I am enough right now. I don't have to be all things to you. I can't be. And you can't be all things to me. You are my favorite person. I admire you. But you don't hold my happiness in your hands. It's my happiness. If you don't want me, if you don't choose happiness with me, it's really not my responsibility to make you happy. If you want to be more 'in love' with me, that's your choice."

"That reminds me of a cartoon I saw. Two stick figures stood side by side," I said. "One held a jar that said, 'HAPPINESS.' The other asked, 'Where did you get it?' The first replied, 'I made it myself.'"

"Yeah, that's true." Emily said.

I wanted to make my own happiness *with* Emily. I said, "When I said I'm not as happy as I'd like to be in our marriage, what I meant was I'd like to work on being happier."

"If that's what you meant when you wrote it, you could've told me this morning. Maybe it's what you mean now that I'm upset. Right now you're stuck with me," she leaned her head on my shoulder. "We'll see how you feel when we get to the States."

"We're a great team. I think we're going to figure this out."

CHAPTER 17

SQUALLS

OPEN WATER NORTHWEST OF THE EXUMA CHAIN, BAHAMAS

5 Months, 25 Days aboard *Fezywig*

EMILY

Erik and I were having a marriage squall. I was blindsided by the unexpected storm. We kept sailing. What else could we do? We made our way up the island chain. The tide continued to rise and fall. We ran into lots of squalls, violent gusting winds and driving rain.

I didn't think we would need foul-weather gear in the Caribbean. All the blogs included it on their prep lists, but I'd thought, "It's the Caribbean. How cold can it get? A little warm freshwater sounds nice." And, stupidly, I'd packed only dollar-store ponchos in case we got caught in a sprinkle. As it turns out, the Caribbean can get cold enough to make your lips turn blue and your teeth chatter. It can be more like being thrown in an industrial washing machine than skipping through a sprinkler. The bimini only shaded us from the sun if it was directly overhead. In wind and rain we might as well have been driving a convertible with the top down. Obviously, we tried to avoid storms, but when we couldn't, we were totally exposed and it was my fault.

With Staniel Cay to our stern, I watched tall thunderheads rising up in the distance all morning. Everyone noticed. We lived close to the weather and registered changes in wind or temperature. The sky was full of information. We were also tracking a tropical wave as it moved north from Barbados, clipping Martinique, up through the Mona Passage and into the lower Bahamas. It was on our tail and spinning off lots of nasty weather. We knew enough now that if it got really bad, we would point into the wind, drop the sails, and keep motoring.

Around noon we hit the squall at full sail. The rain was warm and the winds picked up, pushing us farther north quicker. We blazed across the emerald water setting a new speed record for *Fezywig*, eleven knots. The sails got a freshwater rinse, and it was good for the deck, and us. A few hours later we hit a second squall, and then a third. The rain was getting colder. It wasn't fun anymore. Erik pulled out a yellow poncho and I had that recurring pang of guilt. I had let my family down. Really, I let Erik down—the kids stayed dry inside. Erik was the one who captained us through every unusual or uncomfortable situation.

Erik was the one who captained us through every unusual or uncomfortable situation.

He always took care of us. Now, he was essentially wearing a plastic bag, a life jacket, and a snorkel mask as his sole defense in a blustering cold rainstorm. I was dressed the same—minus the snorkel mask. Maybe I wasn't such a great partner. I stood next to the helm holding the iPad. The cold and wet were my deserved penance.

The rain stopped. Erik got us to anchor in Nassau. The girls baked soft gingersnap cookies. Erik picked up some internet and connected with our life back home. We were on track to get the girls to Fort Lauderdale on time for their flights in mid-August. Our close friend, Ros, agreed to pick them up at JFK airport, house them, feed them, and take them to camp. Karina and Alison wrote a song for her that included the line, "We were kind of homeless and you took us in. Ros. Ros. Rosalyn. Dr. Ros Ord for the win." Erik ordered bus tickets to carry them from New York City to his parents in DC afterwards. Their trip was emerging. We'd sort out the next step as it got closer. We were living life in increments, not trying to figure out everything at once.

We wouldn't figure out everything in our marriage at once, either. Erik and I talked on the bow while the kids watched a movie inside. We figured out enough to know we both wanted to figure out the rest. We made love and the sky literally filled with fireworks from the towering Atlantis Resort.

"Fireworks?" I laughed.

"Only the best for my woman," Erik said. We left Nassau at dawn and continued north. It was a forty-mile crossing to Chub Cay, and the weather was clear with lots of sunshine. The tropical wave had a name now, Hurricane Bertha, and she was heading north too. We decided to tuck into the lee of Chub Cay, where a rocky peninsula on the south-west corner could provide protection against the coming storm. We had a head start, but the spawn of Bertha was gaining on us.

"You see that beacon?" Erik asked. "That's our exit. It's gonna be tight." I looked back—for the one thousandth time—at the charcoal clouds. We were a snail racing a turtle. The sky darkened, the water lost its color, and the wind grew cold and fast. The squall boosted the wind, so we moved faster and faster, but the squall was gaining on us. Without breaking stride, we lowered the sails. We were only minutes away when the squall overtook us. That's when it got nasty.

We turned the corner at the peninsula, but the seas weren't calm enough for anchoring. Erik turned the boat 180 degrees to put the wind behind us, which cut its apparent speed in half. This calmed things down considerably, but it almost put us on a course to run directly into a basin of one-foot-deep water. He turned 90 degrees off the wind, cheating away from Chub Cay and the shallow pool. There was a small basin created by a low, long, flat rock that kept much of the ocean swell on the other side.

"I'm going to get behind that rock and do laps until this passes," Erik shouted.

"I see it. Good idea," I said. I didn't have any ideas.

"Oh, great," Erik said once we were doing short laps behind the rock. "The charts show sunken boats everywhere. Let's get out of here. I want to find the back of this thing." He pointed the boat out into open water and straight into the waves. His pathetic storm uniform of a flimsy poncho and a snorkel mask didn't inhibit his resolve. We rode out the squall and broke through to the backside. The rain stopped as quickly as it had started, and the wind faded back to its normal, steady pace. With clear visibility and calm seas, Erik pointed us back to the peninsula and pulled into the channel and we anchored in the lee. The kids started dinner while Erik and I dinghied to shore to scout things out. We were getting better at clearing squalls.

Chub Cay felt abandoned. There was a large protected marina, but only a few boats docked. There was a big hotel, but it was empty. Maybe it was still under construction, but there was a pool full of water lined with lawn chairs. Most of them had blown over in the squall, but you wouldn't put out beach chairs before you finished building the hotel, would you? Two teenagers played tag in the pool, and a man and a woman sat at the bar sipping cocktails. There was no bartender and no sign there had ever been a bartender. We introduced ourselves and learned that Mary and Jay, a friendly couple from Boulder, had brought their own drinks. They called their kids out of the pool to make introductions and told us they were on a fishing trawler called *Merry Yacht*. We were all headed to Fort Lauderdale, but Mary and Jay wanted a few more days on this private island first.

"Maybe we'll see you in Cat Cay," Erik said. Cat Cay was our last stop before crossing the Gulf Stream back to Florida.

"Maybe," they said, and we wished each other well.

Erik and I were up at 3:45 a.m. We wanted to be anchored before sundown and would need the whole day to cross to Cat Cay. We pulled anchor in the predawn darkness and sat side by side at the helm while the kids slept. Eli appeared shortly after sunrise.

"What's for breakfast?" Eli asked, even though we always ate oatmeal.

"What are you making?" Erik replied.

"Can we have pancakes?" Eli asked.

"We can if you make them," Erik said.

"I'll help you," I said, stepping down from Erik's side at the helm. I pulled out the giant metal bowl from *Silverheels* and set the ingredients on the salon table. I measured and Eli poured and mixed. I set the table and Eli flipped the pancakes.

"I want to have really good food when Karina and Alison and SJ are at girls' camp," Eli said.

"I mean, we always want to have good food, but what's the big deal?" I asked.

"They keep saying they're going to take hot showers and have all this good food like hot dogs and hamburgers and treats."

"Are you getting jealous?" I asked.

"A little," he said.

"Let's make a meal plan. What do you want to eat while your sisters are at camp?" I asked. I pulled out a sheet of paper and grabbed a colored pencil. Eli dreamt up meals while he flipped pancakes.

"We could have a taco night, and hamburgers, and macaroni and cheese . . ." he continued. The list grew. He even agreed to help cook everything on his eight-year-old fantasy menu. When he called his sisters up for breakfast he assured them they were going to be jealous of all the good food *we* would be eating while they were away at camp.

As the morning progressed, more and more boats came into view. We were all converging on the little chute of water that led from the deep Tongue of the Ocean back up onto the shelf. We all successfully squeezed back up onto the Bahama Shelf and the deep water widened out again. The boats scattered in all directions, heading for different islands and ports. We'd enjoyed nice fifteen to twenty knots of wind and lots of speed.

"We might get in early," Erik said. Then the squalls crawled up over the horizon.

"Spawn of Bertha," I said. I liked how it sounded. Erik didn't care about dramatizing the situation. He was the one at the helm in a storm. He wanted to get through it as quickly as possible. We missed the first few simply because we were traveling on different vectors.

"Dead ahead," Erik said. It was a big one. A power yacht ahead of us wanted to avoid the same storm. "See how that guy went perpendicular to go around it? That's what I want to do." We followed its lead and turned south. After forever in the pitching cold rain, Erik said, "It keeps going. There is no back."

"I guess we'll have to go through it," I said. We lowered the sails. Erik started up the engines and turned the boat west, directly into the squall.

With a strong headwind, our progress slowed, even with both engines running. Now it was a race to get in before sunset. We soldiered on for hours, the rain continuing in torrents. I stepped out periodically to check in with Erik or offer him a mug of warm beef broth. Our main job was to fend off seasickness. Eli and Lily always fell asleep in a long storm. The rest of us sat around the salon listening to music and VHF chatter about the storm.

We heard a sputtering sound, and then the starboard engine shut down.

"Crap," Erik said. "I think I know what it is. I'll deal with it later." Our speed dropped in half. The tension went up. Visibility dropped to a hundred yards and the seas got heavy. What had started out so beautiful in the morning was now a slog. Without proper foul-weather gear, Erik simply put the boat on autopilot, pointed *Fezywig* toward Cat Cay, and came inside the cabin. We closed the hatches, which made the cabin stuffy and nausea-inducing. We took turns watching through the windows for any ships to avoid.

Over the radio we heard, "*Fezywig, Fezywig*, this is . . ." Then static. "*Fezywig, Fezywig*, this is . . ." Again static. Then we heard, "*Marriot.*" Who? No one had hailed us over the radio in months.

"*Merry Yacht?*" I guessed.

Erik clicked in. "*Merry Yacht*, this is *Fezywig*. It's nice to hear from you!" They switched down to a lower channel and picked up the conversation.

"How you guys holding up out there?" Jay asked.

"Oh, you know, it's gotten kind of nasty, but we're still making headway," Erik said.

"The weather wasn't getting any better, so we decided to head out ourselves," Jay said. "We're right behind you."

"Really? How far?"

"Oh, a couple of miles. I saw a blip on the radar and thought that was you."

"Yup, here we are," Erik said, relieved to be in contact with someone during this squall that showed no end. Bertha was headed out to sea, which we were grateful for, but she spun off some lousy weather.

"We lost our starboard engine," Erik said. "I think it's a clogged fuel line. I've dealt with it before. We should be fine, but I wanted you to know about it in case things get worse."

"We've got your back if something happens," Jay responded.

"I appreciate that."

"We'll probably get to Cat Cay before you, but look for us when you pull in."

"Will do. Thanks for touching base. *Fezywig* out."

Erik and I traded relieved smiles. Someone knew about us and knew what we were dealing with. That made all the difference. We were still in a miserable storm, but we weren't alone.

A few hours later the rain finally broke. We raised the sails and made good time, anchoring as the sun sank over the horizon.

CAT CAY, BAHAMAS

ERIK

We found Mary and Jay the next day. The *Merry Yacht* kids took the *Fezywig* kids out spearfishing and inner tubing. With the kids gone, I opened the engine compartment. It was exactly the clogged fuel line issue I'd suspected. All the jostling from the storm had loosened debris in the tank, which had stuck in the line. I cleared it and reprimed the pump and the engine started up. I felt like I had graduated from the Boat Mechanics' School of Hard Knocks.

I thought back to the first time the engine had conked out on us sailing from the lagoon to Oyster Pond; the despair, the anxiety, the fear. Then it had conked out again, right after the engine had been replaced. I thought back to the first crossing from Saint Martin to the Virgin Islands; how terrified I was. Now we were sailing in hurricane spinoffs, getting hit by three squalls a day and losing an engine in the middle of it all, and I knew we could handle it.

Something was happening to me, something important. It wasn't over yet, but it was happening, to all of us. Now we could pull into a town or anchorage and within an hour we knew the lay of the land. We still welcomed the help of others, but we were self-sufficient. We had become street-smart. You don't see it coming, but one day you look in the mirror and you realize it's the way it is.

The next day we would cross the Gulf Stream. We would leave the water and borders of foreign islands and return to our own country. We would enter another chapter. We were excited to be back. We wanted something familiar. But we knew we would miss this new home. There would be no more remote islands, no more crossings, no more clearing in. It's a beautiful thing to come home. But it also made us sad.

PART

FIVE

5 Months, 29 Days aboard

to

4 Hours off *Fezywig*

CHAPTER 18

STRANGERS IN A FAMILIAR LAND

ATLANTIC OCEAN, EAST OF FLORIDA, USA

5 Months, 29 Days aboard *Fezywig*

ERIK

We motored across the Gulf Stream. All the squalls were behind us. We pulled into Port Everglade, Fort Lauderdale that evening, but we were otherwise lost.

Everything was big. This was the main seaport for tanker ships and cruise ships coming in and out of South Florida. Less than a mile inland from the beach ran the Intracoastal Waterway. The ICW would become a big part of our lives over the coming weeks, but for now we were trying to get past the first drawbridge.

After an hour wait, the bridge rose up like two giant pincers in the sky and opened a path for all the tall-masted ships to pass through and head north up the ICW. I did my best to take in the barrage of sounds I had forgotten existed: police sirens, beeping buses, ambulances.

We motored through the canal neighborhoods. They felt like the love child of a McMansion suburb and Venice. There were hundreds of huge, newly constructed homes butted right up against the waterways, most with a speedboat tied up at the private backyard dock. We made our way back into a little pond grandly named Lake Sylvia and dropped anchor. Lake Sylvia was more of a watery cul-de-sac amidst this surreal neighborhood. Compared to the massively open spaces we'd become accustomed to, Lake Sylvia felt like a fish bowl. We opted to not hang out our laundry. We ate dinner in the cockpit as usual, but exchanged awkward glances with the people on shore sitting around their backyard firepits.

Eventually we made our way to a municipal marina about a mile north of Lake Sylvia, tucking ourselves into the corner slip. There were no other boats on that section of the dock. It was safe, secure, and private; just what we needed as we tried to acclimate to a world that didn't feel as much like home anymore.

We rented a car. We were no longer in a place where people came and went by dinghy. We located a chandlery and grocery store and were off. The chandlery was sensory overload, pure and simple. I bought the small items I needed and stumbled out.

When we stepped foot in the grocery store, we got reverent. We walked in as a family, kind of how a gang of gunslingers saunters into a saloon, quiet but ready to shoot the place up. Emily and I checked prices on a few select items and turned to each other and then to the kids. I told them, "Let's get fat!" We split up into three teams, each with our own grocery cart, and blew that place to smithereens. Before we'd even left the parking lot, we'd cleaned out two entire boxes of Fudgsicles and were just getting started. We were adjusting fast.

Emily called Stacey, our neighbor in New York City. She was excited to hear from us, and it made the "home stretch"-ness of our journey a reality. The girls would need to get into our apartment to get their sleeping bags and other stuff for camp. Stacey wanted to know when we would be home so she could organize a welcome-home party. We couldn't ask for better friends and neighbors. We also learned the marina that was supposed to be built in our neighborhood was, in fact, done. *La Marina* at 200th and the Hudson River was a reality.

We slept for a few hours, woke at 2:30 a.m., and got the girls to the airport for their 5:00 a.m. flight. With white hair and red faces, our little family of tomatoes walked into the Fort Lauderdale-Hollywood International Airport. Our girls' faded clothes and salted backpacks paled next to the crisp roller luggage of the others checking in for their flights.

I've never seen siblings hug each other so tightly. Our little boy and girls gathered up into a circle hug and cried their eyes out as they said goodbye. I knew we'd meet up with them somewhere farther up the coast. I didn't know exactly when, where, or how, but I knew that would emerge. They went through security, waved, and were gone.

EMILY

It was surprisingly easy to operate *Fezywig* with a reduced crew. Usually there was a kid or two lounging in the cockpit. We'd either have to rouse them to help or jump over them. Now, Erik and I sat at the helm. The cockpit was empty. Eli and Lily preferred the salon, where they didn't have to wear life vests. So, while the girls had been a great help and we missed them, four people were simpler than seven.

A few days later we had to pass through Canaveral Lock to get into the ICW.[21] We'd never been through a lock, and I wasn't sure how Erik and I would manage alone. I'm still not sure what happened. First of all, the lock was gigantic. After space shuttle launches, the rocket boosters return to NASA through that lock. I don't remember if I cleated the ropes wrong or if Erik pulled too far forward or not enough. I know the lock keeper stomped out of his control hut to shake his fists at us and yell as we floated away. I tried to apologize and indicate it was our first lock. He kept yelling. Then Lily appeared. She walked along the deck in her life vest, waving and blowing kisses. The lock keeper shrugged, waved back, and went back inside the control hut to close the lock behind us.

"I don't know what he was saying, but Lily took care of it," I said, taking my place at the helm next to Erik.

"She's a keeper," he said. Once in the ICW, we tucked into an inlet to stop for the night. Erik asked me to get the windlass and lower the anchor. The two of us had a smooth system.

Things were smoothing out between us as well. Three fewer kids onboard gave us a lot of time for private conversations. My confidence in our relationship had taken a hit. I knew I couldn't make Erik think, feel, or act a certain way any more than I could control my children or my neighbor. We all do what we want and live with the consequences,

---

21. ICW: Intracoastal Waterway. If I'm going to keep mentioning this thing, I should explain. The history's pretty fascinating: after World War I and II it was clear ships needed to be free to move up and down the U.S. coasts without fear of attacks from U-boats and other submarines. You could move a lot of bulk on land, but you could move even more by sea. Standardized depths and widths were established by the Army Corps of Engineers, and existing channels, bays, inlets, and coves were connected through man-made canals to create one long continuous ribbon of protected water. It is now possible to sail from Brownsville, Texas, on the western edge of the Gulf of Mexico, all the way up to the Manasquan Inlet in northern New Jersey—without ever sailing in open ocean. That's basically from Mexico to New York City. Pretty impressive, if you ask me.

but I knew the grass is greenest where you water it. We watered it. And we started saying "I love you" again.

In the evening, Eli and I made macaroni and cheese from scratch. He sliced and boiled carrot coins while I steamed broccoli. We had a pretty smooth system, too. Erik and Eli knocked back a couple of root beers. Cold soda was still a novel perk thanks to the fridge Erik had installed.

Just past bedtime we noticed some bioluminescence flicker in the water. I spit in the water. It glowed. We all started spitting in the water.

"This really makes me want to pee in the water," Eli said. I told him to go for it. He lit it up—better than sparklers. I pulled out a boat hook to swish the water. Then I dropped the swim ladder. It was an explosion of light and color. Erik turned on one of the engines and ran the propeller. A bright column of rainbow light shot out from under the boat. We killed the engine and Eli and Lily went skinny-dipping. We strictly forbade night swimming on *Fezywig*, but we made an exception. They both wore life jackets and we tied a line to each of them. They jumped in and splashed around.

"I love sparkly!" Lily said.

Eli said, "What if I farted underwater?" Magical. This rave could have gone on all night. Finally, Eli climbed out. Erik had to pull Lily out. I showered both kids with freshwater. Back to back and slippery in our tiny "shower" they did a "lunar landing" dance—featuring their naked rumps. They laughed their heads off. Who needed NASA? With their three older sisters away, Eli and Lily had a chance to shine, and they totally owned it.

The next day was a traveling day, and that night we tied off in *Discovery's* backyard. John and Michelle owned a home on the ICW in New Smyrna, Florida. They had invited us to use it. We tied off the boat, climbed up and over the rail, and walked down the dock.

"Can you believe we're here?" Erik asked. We hadn't even known these people when we started our journey, and now we were docking at their house.

"It's surreal," I said. The house was locked, but there was a small pool in the backyard and some patio furniture. I loved imagining the Alonsos there—all their kids playing, swimming, and dancing and John grilling. What a happy home. Erik swam with Eli and I waded around with Lily on my hip. We wrapped up in our towels and sat at the table until the lights in the other houses started to turn on. We didn't see anyone we knew, but being at the home of someone who knew us and understood us felt a little like home—like we'd closed a loop and come full circle.

We whooped and hollered when we sailed past Jacksonville. We were officially out of the hurricane box. It was August 15, the last day of our insurance provision. That night, anchored in St. Augustine, Eli helped me fry up some juicy hamburgers. We smothered them in ketchup, deli mustard, and cheese.

"Let's take a picture to show my sisters," Eli said. "They're going to be sorry they missed this." Erik took a picture.

"This whole idea of a hurricane box is ridiculous," Erik said.

"You mean because we get hurricanes in New York in the fall?" I asked. He was getting ready to preach to the choir.

"They rarely happen before August 15, but I'll sleep better knowing we have insurance," he said, still working on his burger. "This is delicious. Those girls *are* going to be jealous."

"I miss them," I said.

"I do too," Erik said. "When they get home we can go on the outside and start doing overnights again." Outside meant the open ocean. It wasn't as calm as inside on the ICW, but it would be less tedious and faster.

Camp ended and Karina, Alison, and SJ started working their way south with a stopover at Grandpa and Grandma's. I wondered if they would be content on *Fezywig* after enjoying land luxuries with their friends. Boat life could be cramped, confining, and uncomfortable. Our tentative plan was to meet up somewhere in North Carolina. Whenever, wherever that happened, I hoped the girls would be glad to rejoin our crew.

Before Karina had left, we'd had a conversation that I'd been replaying in my mind. "How have you changed on *Fezywig*?" I had asked.

"I don't think I've changed," she said. "I've become even more myself. I've gone further down the path that I was already on." Astute and articulate, she'd captured a truth I hadn't even considered. When people said something was *life-changing*, what did they mean? Did they become a completely different person? Maybe, but that wasn't my experience. Like Karina, I was myself, only more so. I had gambled on guiding principles. I hoped experiences were more important than things. I hoped making memories would unite us. I hoped struggling together would galvanize our relationships. I hoped trial and error would work. Putting my beliefs on the line led me to deeper self-trust. Through experience, hope compounded into confidence.

As we sailed north toward the girls, I distilled my thoughts in a conversation with Erik. "I think we're cultivating three kinds of confidence. First, confidence that we'll do what we say we'll do. Second, the confidence that comes from learning new skills. Third, and I think most important, the confidence that it will emerge."

"I agree," he said. "Why do you think the last one is most important?"

"Because it lets us get started. We don't have to know everything. We don't have to control everything. It lets us be patient while we're figuring it out."

"Credibility. Competence. Calm. I like it."

ERIK

We motored up to the Savannah River, which marks the border between Georgia and South Carolina, turned east, and headed back out to sea. I was doing my best to stay out of the way of cargo tankers and military battleships coming and going. It was tight quarters. Fortunately, the river widened and we had more breathing room. I went below for a second to make sure the water maker was running. That was when I felt the boat jolt to a stop. "What the . . . ?!" I yelled from below deck.

I came up and looked around. All the channel markers were in the right spot. Then I looked at the charts. I'd gotten the beacons switched around in my head. We were going down the wrong side of the marker and we were in the shallows. I threw the boat in reverse and tried to back off, but it wasn't happening. I tried rocking us forward and backward. I even had Emily and Eli running around moving jerry cans of fuel and water to shift the weight so we could get free. In the end, I checked the tide tables. The tide was going out. We were stuck and getting more stuck with each minute. But we were close to low tide. As much as I wanted to fight and keep revving the engines, I knew I had to wait.

I sat at the helm waiting, watching the clock. As the tide shifted I turned on the engines. After half an hour I started to feel some shifting. We waited, and the water continued to rise. I engaged the prop and gave it some throttle. We budged. I waited another minute and then juiced it a little more. The hull vibrated and we budged some more. Then I gave it full throttle. The boat shook and vibrated again and broke free. Now that we were buoyant, I didn't want to get pushed further onto the shoal. I gunned it out into the middle of the river. We were back into depth and on our way. For some things, we have to wait.

EMILY

We anchored in a basin off the Ashley River near downtown Charleston. We hoped to meet the girls in North Carolina, where they were visiting cousins, but a tropical depression in the Caribbean had turned into Hurricane Cristobal. Cristobal was in the Bahamas moving north, with the possibility of hitting North Carolina's Outer Banks, our next destination. We'd been moving to meet deadlines for weeks. The best thing to do was to stay put until Cristobal passed. But that meant it would be at least another week before we saw Karina, Alison, and Sarah Jane again. Erik's parents came to the rescue and agreed to drive them all the way to my sister's home near Charleston.

My blessed in-laws arrived with our smiling daughters, greeted my sister's family, and then drove back to Virginia the same day. What would we do without them? When the girls left Fort Lauderdale we weren't precisely certain when or how we'd see each other again. Thanks to Erik's parents, it felt seamless. We simply needed to be patient and trust the answers would emerge as we got closer.

"We had the best food while you were gone," Eli said, and he started detailing our menu.

"I *am* jealous," Alison said. Apparently, they'd had no kitchen, no bathrooms except for a portable toilet, and no running water at camp.

"Some big water pipe broke," SJ said.

"But nobody really complained. They rolled with it," Karina said. "It was probably my best year. Everyone was cheerful and got along."

"Not me," Jane said. "My group was obnoxious and told scary stories, which I heard even though I had my ears plugged. And our tent flooded." Whether they loved it or hated it, they did it together, and that's why we'd gone to all the trouble of getting them there. They got plenty of hot showers and goodies at Grandma's house to more than make up for it.

"It was fun to be back, but it was hard," Karina started. "Nobody understood. They would say, 'So how was the boat?' and unless they wanted to sit down for six hours and talk, there was no way to explain it. What am I supposed to say? 'Great'?" Her sisters nodded.

"They would hold the fridge door open *forever*," Jane added. "They would let the water run and run and run."

"They mostly wanted to talk about TV shows and Tumblr posts," Alison said.

"They complained about really basic stuff. Like how life was so hard and uncomfortable when they really had it pretty good," Jane said.

"You can say 'Great,'" I said. "If they really want to know, it will come out in conversations over time." It would be a while before I started unpacking this experience and figuring out what it meant to me. We were still in it.

"I wrote a song about it," Ali said. "It's called, 'I Went to Mars.'"

"It's like how we all watched *Avatar: The Last Airbender*, but Dad never did so he doesn't get our jokes. Nobody really understands us," SJ said.

"But we understand each other," I said.

"I wanna hear your song," Erik said. Alison got her guitar and sang it for us. The chorus went like this:

> *It's like I went to Mars and you weren't there.*
> *It was an experience we didn't share.*
> *But oh how I wish you'd been there*
> *But I'm glad you're here right now.*

"When you're out on the water, people's barriers are down. They're friendly and willing to engage. On land, people are more closed and have their guard up," Alison said.

"It was nice to shower at Grandma's, and have ice, but it wasn't better," Jane said.

"Out on the water you meet all kinds of interesting, quirky people," Alison said. "I think that's partly because you've got to have something kind of *off* to be out here."

"I guess that means there's something kind of *off* about us?" Erik said.

"Yeah, pretty much," Alison smiled.

On shore the French Quarter was close, so we walked into town and strolled past the historic houses with antebellum side porches and cobblestone streets. We walked through the College of Charleston campus. We split up to run some errands. We'd reconvene at the library. Shocker.

Erik went with the big kids to check prices on tours of Fort Sumter. I pushed Lily's stroller through a mile and a half of Southern humidity to a U-Haul store. The guy at the counter looked like he'd never seen a woman pushing a baby stroller with a propane tank hanging from the handles, but there wasn't a line for propane, so we were on our way pretty quick.

This was the biggest library I'd seen in a long time—a sweeping, three-story structure with symmetrical ramps up both sides leading to a vaulted-ceiling lobby. It was as gorgeous on the inside. There were paintings and sculptures and advertising for cultural events. And stacks and stacks of books full of stories, wisdom, and information I don't have yet. I love libraries and their promise of more to learn. I found Erik on the third floor, and he looked down at the bulging Ikea bag.

"Maybe I shouldn't have brought a ten-pound can of propane into the public library?" I guessed the meaning of his look. There was a sign that said, "No Food," but there wasn't anything about explosive fuel. We weren't on Mars anymore.

Cristobal did head out to sea. The next morning we pulled anchor and left with good wind, a full crew, and a full propane tank.

CHAPTER 19

CONNECTING THE DOTS

ATLANTIC OCEAN, EAST OF THE CAROLINAS, USA

6 Months, 21 Days aboard *Fezywig*

ERIK

Morehead City was on the southern edge of North Carolina's Outer Banks. It was a 200-mile jump that would keep us out at sea for two nights and up to forty miles offshore, but with the girls back aboard, we could rotate through watches. It was a bit of an abrupt start for them, but they were good sports.

After all our inland sailing, it was refreshing to be back on the ocean. After two days, we closed in on Morehead. Suddenly we found ourselves sailing headlong into a stampede of boats coming out through the pass.

I stayed on course and let them swerve and weave around us. A sailboat under sail always has the right of way. Fishing boat after fishing boat zipped past us. As the morning progressed, we entered the channel. The stampede continued, but now it was twice as thick and the boats were half the size. It felt like we were in a chase scene heading into oncoming traffic. At one point I counted eleven boats coming directly toward me like a cavalry charge.

We took our sails down and turned on our engines. I held steady and let the smaller boats zip around us. We made it back into a small inlet. As we looked along the shore, lawn chairs and coolers were strewn everywhere. BBQ pits, beer, and umbrellas filled in the rest of the scene. We motored to the far end of the inlet and dropped anchor. After three days at sea and the mob scene coming in, I was grateful to be out of the fray. "What in the world is going on here?" I asked out loud. I'd never heard of Morehead City, but it seemed like the rest of the world had.

It wasn't until the next day that it dawned us. It was Labor Day weekend. We were still on Mars.

After the jostling and bustle of Morehead, our nightly anchorages consisted of pulling off to the shallow side of a bend in the river, everyone taking a swim, and eating dinner while the sun set. Open marshes expanded for miles in every direction, and elegant egrets and darting swallows moved across the silent, cloudless skies.

We sailed up Adam's Creek, the Neuse River, and Bay River. We skirted the open Pamlico Sound and continued to cut up through the salty ICW. The Pungo River and Alligator River were connected by a seemingly endless canal that ran almost perfectly straight for twenty miles. I read a lot of chapters in *Harry Truman* that day.

The pastoral beauty of the marsh lands gave way to rusty bridges and industrial warehouses. The water thickened and the weather turned gray and broody. A storm was churning. Skies turned gunship gray and lightning flickered in the distance. We passed through the Great Lock, which brought us back to sea level and ultimately into Norfolk, Virginia. We entered through the massively tall bridge that frames the southern entrance to the U.S. Naval Shipyard. We moved slowly and reverently past the towering warships that lined both sides of the river and dwarfed *Fezywig* many times over.

It was like sailing through a canyon with metal walls. The darkening sky beyond continued to create an almost enclosed feeling of dread. The condensed space was packed with massive firepower. Lightning began to shoot down. I was grateful we weren't the tallest piece of metal anymore. We prepped the boat and got everyone and everything inside. Once the rain started, I decided we should lower the dinghy to keep it from filling with rainwater and buckling.[22]

I should have brought the big boat to a stop, and not tried some Knight Rider/Evel Knievel launch while underway. But I didn't, because I didn't want to stop the boat right in front of the navy police boat floating nearby. One doesn't want to look suspicious, right? Sometimes I am an idiot. The dinghy flipped on its side and started spilling its contents—fuel canister line, oars, bench—into the water. Emily grabbed the fuel line and saved it, but one oar went into the water. We stopped the boat, leveled the dinghy, got it properly lowered, and tethered for a tow. We then looped around and picked up the oar that had drifted lazily away. Nothing suspicious there.

It's kind of like parallel parking. Plenty of people screw up parallel parking, but it's another matter to do it while the police are sitting across the street watching. They're not going to give you a ticket, but it's embarrassing.

Sorted out, we were on our way. All the kids went below deck so

---

22. I should note here that I'm not an idiot. Every half-savvy cruiser knows that there's a plug at the stern end of a dinghy that is pulled whenever the dinghy is hoisted out of the water. I know this. However, because the dinghy we could afford was not a hard-bottom dinghy, the bottom of our dinghy was supported by a stiff, inflatable pad. This pad covered, and consequently made it difficult to remove, the drainage plug at the stern. It was easier to just lower the dinghy into the water and tow it behind rather than deflate the floor pad each time we wanted to pull the drainage plug. There. I've made my case. I'm not an idiot.

they wouldn't be seen with us. I wanted to go below deck too, but Emily wouldn't let me. I waved to the police as we sailed past.

Two months earlier we had been sitting on the eastern edge of the Virgin Islands. We'd asked our kids if they wanted to go to Anegada or head home. They voted for home. Then we scrawled a short timeline for getting to Virginia. It was almost like some mystical magic that we were now actually in Virginia. All the day sails and overnight passages, sketchy anchorages and overpriced marinas, open sounds and constrained canals strung together, and now we had arrived.

EMILY

When we originally discussed living on a sailboat, I asked Erik, "What's the worst that could happen?"

He said, "We could be financially ruined, never recover, have to send our kids to live with relatives, and all our friends will think we're idiots."

"How likely is that scenario?" I asked. We agreed it wasn't likely and we'd still be young enough to make a comeback if it happened.

We'd spent a day with the Andersons, who lived nearby. We loved them, and they loved *Fezywig*. It felt like a perfect fit. Erik checked email. His former employer had given him definitive word that he was being hired back on. He would start in two months. I'd wanted him to quit that "soul-numbing" (his words) job for years. We were practicing taking life one day at a time and letting it emerge. Now that Erik knew how we were going to pay rent and buy groceries, he was visibly relieved. It didn't seem right for him to return to the same gray graveyard-shift cubicle after living at sea. But if it put his heart at ease, I was on board. Our savings were practically depleted, so our hourglass was almost empty, but we now had an exit strategy.

We could have ended the trip right there in Virginia. We technically didn't need to sail home. The Andersons, who would lease *Fezywig* from us, lived in Virginia. All our stuff in storage was in Virginia. Our minivan was in Virginia. Why sail *Fezywig* all the way up to New York City?

"I want to connect the dots," I said. "I want to travel all the way from Saint Martin to the Dyckman Marina at five miles per hour. I want to see it with my own eyes." Erik liked the idea of sailing under the George Washington Bridge. Our kids were game for anything. The Andersons were willing to come north to get *Fezywig*. So home would be our finish line. Home had been a moving target. It was where we were together. It was where we had friends. It was where we'd been before. But there was no arguing that the two-bedroom apartment where we had lived, loved, struggled and raised our family for fifteen years— where Lily was born in the bathtub—was definitely home. It was our beginning, and it would be the end.

We still had 300 nautical miles to go, sixty hours of nonstop sailing if the conditions were good and we stayed on the outside; longer if we used the ICW or anchored at night. We needed provisions, a charge cord for the phone, and a new line for the dinghy. The old line was small and frayed and brittle from baking in the sun, like our topping lift. It was falling apart. Erik borrowed a car from the Andersons so we could run some errands.

I was gathering the kids to join him when a dinghy pulled up to our stern. It was a family of four. Eli saw the two boys in their dinghy and made his way down the starboard steps to grab their line and cleat it off.

"Hi, my name is Eli and I'd like to play," Eli said, and he proceeded to introduce all of us and ask about our guests. Was all this time in the South turning him into a gentleman? This boy had some manners. The Rabin family was from a large catamaran called *Little Wing*, and their two boys invited Eli to play Legos on their boat. I knew he wouldn't have any fun running errands, so I let him go. The rest of us hopped in our dinghy and met Erik at a parking garage.

"So where's Eli?" Erik asked.

"He's having a playdate with the boys on the kid boat that pulled in," I answered.

"Cool. What are their names?"

I gave him their first names, "Marina and Joseph." I didn't know their last names.

"Do they have a way to reach us if something comes up?"

"I dropped my phone in the ocean a while back," I said. That's when I realized I could've given them Erik's number. I wasn't in the habit of using a phone.

"You guys talked for about five minutes?" Erik asked.

"Maybe three," I said. "Do you think we should go back?"

"It's okay," Erik said as I shrugged. "I was just wondering." Erik smiled and squeezed my hand. We were used to being in a small, safe community where trust was high and goodwill was plentiful. We knew we would have to say goodbye to that soon.

It was weird being so far away from *Fezywig*, zipping around in a car running to Target and Home Depot. I felt like we were playing in somebody else's life. It wouldn't be this convenient even in New York City. Parking was never this easy. We got a lot done quickly. We got the food, the charger, and the new dinghy line. It was made out of material that was stronger and would float. It was a glossy black and silky, which didn't matter, I guess. The main point was we wouldn't have to worry anymore about losing our dinghy or snagging the line under the boat.

After unloading the groceries and ferrying them back to *Fezywig*, Erik and I rode over to *Little Wing* to check on Eli. He was having a grand time making Lego movies with the other boys. Their dad was a filmmaker. He said he would take the boys out for ice cream on shore and drop Eli off later. It was an easy yes. We got a lot of points with Eli.

ERIK

That evening our family was all gathered on *Fezywig*. We went to bed safe and secure. I wrote in my journal:

"So what do I make of all this? Is it too good to be true? Does the Universe really want good things to come my way? I'm a little stunned how things seem to be working out. We seem to have our boat going into the hands of wonderful family, who I'm confident will do their best to take care of it. I seem to have a job that will allow me to take care of my family. Things can go wrong. What I meant was, turn out differently than we want or expect. But right now they're turning out the way I'd hoped. That makes me feel lucky. I suppose this is the moment where I look back at my journey of buying this boat. I think about that email to my dad, the one where I talk about buying my VW Rabbit, and maybe I'd made a mistake. Well, I don't think I did. It's been hard. It's been different than I'd expected. But that's okay. It's not over yet. I still have to sail up the coast to NYC. But I think I'm excited to do that. For now, we're here. We've made new friends. We have food. And transportation. And communication. And our kids are happy. And we're happy. We have a home to go back to. We continue to meet lovely people. Our kids continue to make friends. I guess what I'm saying is things feel good. We're in a good spot."

EMILY

The next morning we joined *Little Wing* for brunch. We had a common friend: *Day Dreamer*. They'd ridden out a hurricane together a few years back. *Day Dreamer* had given us their Swedish pancake recipe, so Karina and Alison made a batch in honor of them. I turned a large can of dried apples into a spicy warm filling. It was an amazing meal and even more amazing conversation. Cruisers have the flexibility to make a new friend and visit for hours at a stretch. That's how new friends become life friends so quickly. Nobody had to be somewhere by a certain time. And if they did, you'd go together and help out. On this particular morning we sat and talked.

Joseph was a successful cinematographer who was represented by a huge global agency. Name any big-time rock star and he had shot their music video. At the time, he was getting more and more offers to work on feature films. He'd taken the work, but it was taking its toll on his family. After a while, he asked his agent a direct question: "How many of your feature film cinematographers are still married?"

The answer: none.

That's when he stopped doing feature films. They sold their house on the north shore of Long Island, bought *Little Wing*, and focused on strengthening their marriage and family.

The boys were in the main salon working on a stop-motion movie on the table. It was like a little miniature film studio made out of Legos. They were completely absorbed. The boys played, we grown-ups talked, and the Bigs listened as they helped clean up the kitchen.

Marina and Joseph were seekers. They shared their journey from one faith to another, one philosophy to another, their exploration of manhood and womanhood and the roles each played in their marriage and family. They ended up where they were now.

We all liked music, so we sang hymns together. It was unusual for us. We loved to play music, but we usually played Jack White or the Decemberists, or our own tunes. We didn't play church music together often.

Joseph taught us the Southern spiritual "I Want Jesus to Walk with Me." We sang it a cappella. Then we sang it a cappella in a round. Joseph and Erik sang the bass call and the ladies sang the soprano response. We repeated the final phrase over and over. Quieter and quieter, and then we stopped. After a moment, we all smiled big and applauded. I would miss all this.

On land, we're insulated. We have our lives, our work, our locked doors. We invite people in, sort of. Sometimes we go out for dinner with another couple, or host a party or take someone a meal when they're sick. But it's never the same. There's something intangible about two or three boats anchored near each other, sharing the load of living on the water, raising children and seeing to the necessities of daily life. I think it has something to do with time and creating more of it.

On land we work our time hard. We squeeze every ounce of productivity out of it. Or we fritter it away on stuff that doesn't matter. Or we think things matter a lot that don't matter at all. I'm looking at you, internet. I think it has something to do with being outside.

On the water, the elements and weather are close. It's like being a farmer. What happens in the sky affects what happens on the ground. It doesn't happen behind two-by-four walls and sheetrock. It's close, always on hand. On a boat, the protective walls are thin, for better or for worse.

Little Wing needed to get south. Once again, they sailed south and we prepared to sail north. We would miss them.

The rain poured for one day, and then two days. The dinghy was resting on the water but it filled up with enough rain that we had to go out twice a day to pump it out to keep it afloat. We read and puttered, waiting it out. We ate breakfast and lunch and puttered some more. We put out bowls to catch the rain that was now leaking through our watertight hatches. This was a lot of rain. The temperature dropped, so we pulled out all the layers we could find to stay warm.

"This is miserable," I said while I washed the dishes. It was something to do.

"What if we got out of here?" Erik said. He gets this mischievous alertness in his eyes whenever he's about to do something impulsive.

"Where would we go? It's raining everywhere," I said.

"It's not raining in my parents' house," he said.

"I love it," I said. "Who wants to go to Grandma's?" It was like a good fairy had woken up the whole kingdom at once.

"When?" Karina asked. It would take us days to sail there, but only hours to drive in the car we were borrowing.

"Right now," Erik said. There was some waffling. Reasonable concerns were mentioned, but the kids were already squealing, cheering, and packing.

"It would be so awesome to show up on their doorstep," Alison said.

"We should probably give them a *little* warning," I said. They had lives. They worked, traveled, and occasionally had houseguests. Seven people couldn't be completely cavalier.

Everything went into our waterproof sack. We locked all the hatches, slid the salon door shut, and lowered into the dinghy. In a moment everyone was completely soaked. The rain pounded without a sign of letting up. We motored ever-so-slowly the short distance between *Fezywig* and the dock. The dinghy was riding low in the water. With the cooler temperature the tubes deflated slightly, but we all made it. We threw ourselves and everything in the truck and sped up I-95.

"Hey, Mom," Erik said into his cell phone. "How you doing?"

"Fine. How are you?" she asked, a bit wary.

"We were wondering if you guys were home."

"Are you standing outside our door?" she asked. She knew Erik well.

"No. But we're on our way. Is that okay?"

"Oh, yes! We'd love to have you!"

It felt like cheating. I could count on one hand the number of nights I hadn't slept on *Fezywig* over the whole year. Eli always referred to Erik's parents' house as the "mansion of happiness and joy." In truth it is a well-maintained home, but pretty typical for the suburbs of DC. To a little kid who grew up in a two-bedroom/one-bath apartment in a sooty city and now lived on a cramped, soggy boat, it did feel like a mansion. At Grandma's we enjoyed warm beds, a dryer for all our wet clothes, a big TV, and a couch from which we watched countless movies. Grandma stuffed us full of warm foods both salty and sweet.

There's so much to love about being on the water. And there's so much to love about being on land. I liked being amphibious. There's a beauty being exposed to the elements. There's a reassurance being protected from them. There's so much meaning and purpose to being out and isolated, yet equally as much being gathered in and together. I think there's a balance that depends upon and requires a shifting from one to the other. Perhaps it's a cycle or rhythm more than a place or location.

When we got back to *Fezywig* the rain had stopped. The dinghy was still tied to the dock and, thankfully, the outboard was still above the water line. The dock was practically submerged because the water had risen so high. It took half an hour to pump out the dinghy, but sitting—essentially—in a tub of fresh rainwater was its own kind of luxury. We were all thrilled to see *Fezywig* again. We'd had our time to sit still. Now we were excited to be on the move.

CHAPTER 20

UNSINKABLE

HAMPTON, VIRGINIA, USA

7 Months, 2 Days aboard *Fezywig*

ERIK

We were ready to be home. It was about three hundred miles to New York Harbor. We were rested and refreshed. We had our full crew and the weather was beautiful. We motored into the wind as the river widened, passed the Chesapeake Bay, and continued out to sea. Once we were far enough out to point north, we raised the sails.

We sailed for two straight days and were heading into our second night on the water. Fifteen miles offshore we passed the Delaware Bay. The outcoming tide pushed us even farther out. The rain returned and the seas got rowdy. I didn't feel well. No one felt good. We had gone soft. All the days motoring up the ICW, being at anchor in Hampton, and the days at my parents' cost us our sea legs. Seasickness returned. Around midnight the lights of Atlantic City came into view and I asked everyone if they wanted to head in. They did. Karina joined me on watch and we motored, finally making it to anchor after 1:00 a.m.

After a long sleep and broody weather all night, we woke up to a clear blue sky, wispy white clouds, and a breakfast of Nutella and bread. The season had turned and the weather cooled off considerably, especially on the water. While at my parents' we had pillaged our stash of clothes under their stairs and come away with several scarves and hats. We put them to full use now. The dinghy sagged because of the cold air. We inflated it with more air, and that solved it for the time being.

Everyone was layered up in fleece pullovers, windbreakers, and stocking caps. We dug deep into our cabin closets and found our socks. Those went on, and then we pulled out the almost-forgotten deck shoes lost under piles of flip-flops and sandals.

The final leg of the ICW started at Atlantic City and continued up to the Manasquan Inlet. I proposed the idea of going slow and easy on the inside, heading back out to sea at the Manasquan Inlet, and then running up to New York Harbor. Everyone thought I was a genius.

As we moved north on our final leg, I couldn't help reflect on the two worlds that sit strangely side by side yet remain so completely separate. There's a thin divide between here and there; land and sea. We use different maps. Land maps don't show water depths, submerged rocks, or shipping lanes. They show malls, neighborhoods, and freeways. Sailing charts don't show roads, town names, or restaurants. They show buoys and channels and marinas. They're two separate worlds.

As we passed through the coastal towns of New Jersey, we knew nothing about them except what color the light was on top of the water or radio tower. Car drivers crossed bridges oblivious to the crucial relationship between the height of the bridge, the height of a mast, and the tide. On land, the world was faster and insulated. On the water, we moved slow and exposed.

We motored all day, snuggled against the crisp air in our sweatshirts, hats, and jeans. It made for perfect end-of-summer sailing. We passed Toms River. I couldn't help but laugh at our first, chaotic family sail there. We'd bounced off channel pylons, dropped sail ties into the water, and generally bumbled around while Eli and Lily screamed their heads off. We still had our issues, but now we more or less had our act together. That first sail felt like another life.

As we moved farther north the channels narrowed and shallowed. I stayed at the helm all day with Emily at my side. We ended up fighting currents, which made for slow going. I took a wrong turn and wound us back into a dead-end inlet. I retraced our wake back to the ICW. I was getting tired and we were running out of daylight.

Each drawbridge required a radio call to coordinate an opening. Some of the bridges were fixed. Either we fit under them or we didn't. If we didn't, we'd have to wait for low tide. The last fixed bridge bent the VHF antenna. We held our breath and cleared it, but we knew we were cutting it close. We would get to our last bridge, the Manasquan Inlet, after midnight. The next day was forecast for rain. I called the crew together.

"Hey guys, we've got a decision to make," I told them. "We'll need to decide whether we push on through the night or anchor, get some sleep, and keep going in the morning."

"Do we have to decide right now?" Karina asked. The sun was getting low in the sky.

"Not yet. We can get through all the bridges and then decide. But we should think about it."

We continued passing through bridges. I realized around 8:15 p.m. that we had to call four hours in advance to schedule the last bridge opening. We were going to get there around midnight, so we were already late. We called and the operator, thankfully, obliged. I felt bad when we got there closer to 1:00 a.m. thanks to the opposing currents. We were grateful he'd waited for us. I hope he got paid for overtime.

Now was the time to decide. There was a marina on our left and a small basin on our right. The marina was lit with big stadium-like fluorescent lights that blinded our night vision and made it hard to see anything on the water. I pulled over into the basin and did a small loop while our eyes adjusted.

"So what do you ladies want to do?" I asked. Emily and the Big girls were on deck. The Littles were soundly sleeping.

"I think I want to keep going," Karina said.

"Me too," Alison concurred.

"I'd like to get home," Jane said.

"If we can make it work, it'd be nice to be home by morning. Maybe beat the rain," Emily said.

"Okay," I said. "I'm really tired and need a break. Here's what I propose. We head out this channel, out to sea, and get some distance from shore. Once we set the sails, we'll turn north. At that point, I'll go below and get some sleep. I'll probably need to sleep from two to six. Can you guys take those watches?"

The girls and Emily nodded.

"Okay, then I'll get up at dawn and sail us into New York Harbor." It was going to be boat rush hour on the water, and I didn't want Emily or the girls to be responsible for that section. That one was on me as captain.

"'All right, everyone clear off the tables and stow everything. It's going to get bumpy." We put away coloring books, boxes of crayons, leftover dishes, the laptop, a bag of pretzels. It had been a flat day in the ICW. That was about to change. This was no Oyster Pond, but we'd gotten savvy. Emily and Alison unzipped the lazy jack and made sure the lines were properly flaked for raising the sails.

I pointed *Fezywig* toward the channel and headed out to sea one last time.

EMILY

We had about twenty-five miles to New York's Lower Bay, then another twenty-five miles to the Upper Bay; then up the Hudson, under the George Washington Bridge, and tuck in at the Dyckman Marina. I'd been dreaming about pulling up to the Dyckman Marina. Once we unloaded the boat our local friends could hang out, dance, maybe play some music. They could see where we'd been living. We'd close the loop. We'd bring our two worlds together. Erik was obviously exhausted, but if he could push through one more hour, Karina and I would take over and he could sleep. We'd be home by 9:00 a.m.

We cleared the breakwater walls and Erik pushed down the throttles. The wind whistled through the shrouds. We were pounding into the oncoming seas, running both engines, our sails aloft but luffed. The rigging rattled like the whole thing was going to come apart, and the slack sails slapped and thrashed with the slippery sound of Dacron. The deck pitched. Then something broke loose, silently. The heavy end of the dinghy, the end with the outboard, broke free. The dinghy was now dragging askew in the ocean behind us, dangling from the engine chain clipped to the lifting line. The contents of the dinghy gradually spilled into the night sea: the oars, the bench seat, the water pump. This was Norfolk all over again but much worse.

"Get a spotlight on that stuff," Erik shouted. It looked like he was going to try to retrieve it in the dark in those pitching waves. I didn't think it was a good idea to chase down the dinghy flotsam. We'd be more likely to retrieve whatever showed up on shore the next morning. I wasn't going to argue under the circumstances. I grabbed the spotlight and stepped up to the transom. *Fezywig* pitched again. My whole body hit the mainsail rigging, and it flung me back on the cockpit table. I scrambled to my feet. If I hadn't hit the ropes, I would be in the water with the oars and the bench seat, drifting away.

"We're turning back," Erik said. We'll regroup and then figure out what to do." Nobody wanted to go back to the inlet. It was only a couple of miles to retrace, but it meant anchoring for the night in the rain and delaying our homecoming another day. We were all exhausted. We all knew it was the smart thing to do. We'd sleep aboard one more night. Erik turned downwind and headed straight back for the rocky entrance to the Manasquan Inlet.

We crossed through the open train bridge, picked a spot in the tight inlet, and dropped anchor. Erik didn't like our spot—still too in the way of traffic—so we pulled anchor and tried to reset ourselves farther out of the channel. With the anchor out, he bore down on the port engine to set it. We heard a quick thud and the engine stopped hard.

"Great," Erik said. "I'm wasted. I can't do one more thing today." He set the anchor with the starboard engine. Then he sat down near our port stern swimming stairs, leaning back against the step where the decals spelled out "*Fezywig*." I sat down next to him as he stared off into the blackness of the night. Karina went to bed.

"I'll take care of the dinghy," I said. I went to work sorting out the chain and lines and collecting everything that hadn't spilled into the ocean. My right foot was suddenly wet. I was standing on the bottom step of the starboard side and my foot was underwater. "That's weird."

"What?" Erik asked.

"Why is my sock getting wet on the steps? It is really warm, though," I said.

Karina called from below, "The bilge is really full."

"Turn on the pump," Erik said.

"It's coming up really fast," she said with some urgency. "I can hear water gushing."

"Okay." Erik slowly lifted himself from the stern steps and lumbered below. "I'll come take a look."

"It's not good. The floorboards are floating," Erik said. "Water is spilling over the door thresholds into the cabins." I went straight to the cupboards and bench seats to pull out bowls, buckets, and whatever could hold water.

"It's coming from the port engine compartment," Erik said. He opened the compartment lid. "It's like there's a spring in here. Water is rushing in. Start bailing!"

Alison came up to grab a bowl and immediately jumped into the engine compartment with a bucket. Karina started bailing in her room. Jane came out to get a bowl as well. I started pulling books and clothing from their lower shelves. I dumped it on the salon seating. Some of it was already soaked. I don't remember who started it, but the girls and I were singing "Shake It Off" by Taylor Swift as we bailed. Then we launched into other favorites. I love my singing family. Alison dumped straight overboard, but Karina and Jane brought their full containers to me. I'd dump them overboard and leave an empty container at the top of the stairs for them to grab. We'd established a solid system at lightning speed. Even in the moment I was proud of my cheerful crew.

"We're pulling anchor," Erik said. "Alison, stay put. The rest of you, I want docking lines and fenders on the port side." The boat was now listing deeply on the port side. A fuel dock stood 100 yards behind us. "We going to lash the boat to those pylons so we don't sink."

Erik got the starboard engine running and edged forward to take tension off the anchor chain. Karina, Jane and I got everything in place quickly and precisely. Eli and Lily stumbled out into the starboard hallway to see what was going on.

"The boat is sinking," I said. "You can sleep in Mommy and Daddy's bed." There was no fear or reassurance in my voice. I simply stated the facts. Eli took Lily's hand and they crossed the hall into our berth.

Erik moved the boat over the anchor and we pulled it up. With one engine, he spun the boat 270 degrees counterclockwise to get momentum and the right approach angle.

"Okay everyone, we've got one chance to get this. As soon as we touch, I want you off the boat and on the dock. Jane, you go and find help. Anyone. Tell them, 'Our boat is sinking and we need help,'" Erik said.

The dock was wide open—plenty of room for our boat. The floodlights that had obscured our vision before now made it easy to see. They lit up the whole length of the dock. It was an easy target. But Erik saw something in the shadows.

"Does everyone see that boat?" he asked. A small boat was tucked along one end of the dock. It was a beautiful Ralph Lauren-type wooden motorboat, standing maybe four or five feet out of the water. Just low enough that it was hidden by the shadow of the floodlights. "We've got no room for error. We have to hit this spot on."

Fortunately, we did. That one move should redeem us from all the missed mooring balls before. He pressed the starboard side against the pylons without ramming the glossy speedboat. Karina and I were off the boat and onto the dock in one smooth motion. We immediately lashed the boat to the pylons that stood over six feet tall. Erik came right behind us, letting the engine still run. Jane jumped off the boat and ran down the dock, barefoot, looking for any signs of life in the marina at 2:30 a.m.

Erik joined us in wrapping the lines around the pylons as many times as we could then tying them off with bowlines—one for the stern, one for the bow. The boat was secure for now. Alison was still bailing the engine compartment. Jane was out there somewhere in the darkness.

Karina, Erik, and I ran a bucket brigade to the deck, where we dumped water over the side. Then we shortened the route, dumping everything into the kitchen sink. Then Karina poured water out the side hatches of the cabins below deck—anything to speed the process and stay ahead of the water gushing in.

Karina took over in the engine compartment and Alison took a break. Her arms hung listless at her sides. The water was still rising, so I worked fast to move books and clothes out of the water, all while trying to keep pace with the inflow. But the water was continuing to rise and our pace was falling off. We were exhausted before this had started. Now all we had was adrenaline.

Erik went to the engine compartment. The water was definitely coming from the sail drive, the underside of the engine where it connects with the propeller outside the boat. Once we were in off the ocean we'd lowered the dinghy down flat onto the water and towed it behind us. The new glossy black line on the front of the dinghy disappeared somewhere under the waterline below the leaking engine compartment. The other end was lashed around the stern deck cleat. The line was tight as a wire, pinched against the hull. We didn't know if that was related to the problem, but it was a good place to start. Erik went below and found his knife. He came above deck and cut the line. Snap!

"Whoa!" Karina yelled from inside the engine compartment.

"What?" Erik asked.

"The engine moved like two inches."

"Okay, that's good," he said.

"The water seems to be coming in slower," she said.

"Good. Keep bailing. I'm going to call for help."

It took him ten minutes or so, but he finally reached the local Sea Tow for the Manasquan Inlet. A guy named Scott took the call.

"I'll be there in twenty minutes," he said, and he hung up.

Erik sent me to the road to meet him and guide him to our boat. I raced out of the marina to a suburban street corner. I paced barefoot. Of course I was barefoot. I'd taken off my wet socks and shoes. I looked up and down the road. I wished I were bailing. Someone else could wait. I wanted to work. I checked the phone. It had been only five minutes. Finally, Scott arrived. I ran ahead of his truck to show him exactly where *Fezywig* was lashed to the pylons.

Scott pulled up in his huge pickup truck, jumped out, grabbed his high-power pumps out of the bed, and ran down the dock with me carrying a giant hose right behind him. His truck stood empty, the door open and engine still running.

Jane was back. She had brought a bleary but willing sailor trailing a few feet behind her. He was probably the only person living aboard in this marina. It was that kind of a place. The poor guy was white-haired and hungover. He asked what was going on. By that time Sea Tow was on the way. Erik had thanked him and recommended he go back to bed. The old guy disappeared back into the night. Scott conferred with Erik. I rejoined the girls. We kept bailing.

Erik and Scott wired up the pumps and shoved them down into the lowest point of our engine compartment. Immediately water was pulled out faster than it was pouring in.

"Do you have any of the foam floaties kids use?" Scott asked.

I pulled out four or five from the cockpit bench seat. With their knives, Erik and Scott sliced them into thin, short strips and shoved them under the engine around the edges of the leak. Once the water level started dropping, Scott got on the phone.

"Hey, Dean, we've got a catamaran here that's taking on water and needs a haul out. It's tied up to the Brielle fuel dock. The beam is twenty-one feet. Can your lift handle that?" He listened.

"Excellent," he continued. "How soon can your guys get here?" It was 4:00 a.m. The marina he was calling was next door to the dock where we were lashed off. The crew came en masse and got everything moving. To make room for *Fezywig*, they had to get a boat out of the lift that was currently hanging in the slings, put it on blocks, and reposition the lift for us. Then came instructions for me from the crew chief.

"You have to sail your boat around to that alley," the chief said, pointing a hundred yards away, "and come straight in. Then stop before you hit the concrete wall, but don't come in too fast." Just stop our twenty-ton boat on a dime. Erik could do it. The more difficult or urgent a situation, the more focused, calm, and decisive Erik was. This kind of pressure brought out his best.

The sky started to lighten. The tide was slack, but picking up. The wind was blowing out of the east, pinning the port side of *Fezywig* against the dock. We had one engine: starboard. Running that engine would spin the boat counterclockwise, the exact wrong direction we needed to go, but it was the only way. Erik started our one good engine.

He tried every trick and angle to get the boat off the dock. Scott, Karina, and I grabbed fenders and moved them between the boat and all the hard objects we were about to hit. Erik couldn't get enough momentum to have control of the boat's direction. Finally, he went backward. He's a genius. One day a stroke of brilliance will kill him, but not that day. It was Fajardo all over again. He put the starboard throttle in reverse.

As the boat moved down past the end of the dock, the bow began to swing around counterclockwise. The only problem was we were surrounded by beautiful, expensive fishing trawlers with long bow sprits jutting out five or six feet off the front of each boat. As our boat pivoted, we moved fast to make sure no additional damage was inflicted. Free of the dock, we picked up speed in reverse and moved toward the lift alley.

Imagine a movie car chase. The car is speeding along in reverse, hits the brakes, swings around 180 degrees, and then peels off in the original direction, but now facing forward. That's what we did, but at four miles per hour. Not nearly as impressive to watch, but nerve-racking to pull off.

Erik turned the corner into the lift alley. We had good momentum now and the boat was moving straight. The tricky part was still stopping *Fezywig* before she ran into the concrete wall dead ahead.

The guys on land were radioing instructions to Scott on the boat, who was standing next to Erik. He needed both hands to drive. He edged this way and that way. *Fezywig* was twenty-one feet wide. The lift pit was twenty-three feet wide.

"It's a good thing we've done all those narrow bridge openings with one engine in Saint Martin," he said. Every part of this journey had prepared us for what would come next. I was preparing for what would come next, too. Once *Fezywig* was in the slings, we'd have to get off, and we couldn't get back on until she was on blocks. I brought Eli and Lily on deck. I told the older girls to pack their go-bags with PJs, toiletries, a regular outfit, and Sunday clothes for church the next day. I packed for myself, Erik, Eli, and Lily. We broke our record set during the surprise trip to Grandma and Grandpa's house. We were focused.

Erik hit the centerline right on. That's when the guys started shouting, "Slow down! Slow down!" This was the "stop on a dime" part.

Erik throttled the boat in reverse, trying not to pivot the boat off its line. The slings slipped under the hull and snugged safely between the rudder and keel fin on both sides.

"Okay, you can kill the engine now," Scott said.

Ten minutes later the boat was out of the water . . .

Erik exhaled.

Ten minutes later the boat was out of the water, the cut dinghy line dangling off the port propeller. The tear in the sail drive was now easy to see. That was the breach. So simple. So small. But so important.

It was about 6:30 a.m. The sun was rising over the Atlantic Ocean.

Scott packed up all his gear and found us by the bench with the kids, our go-bags piled in the gravel at our feet.

"Can I drop you guys at a breakfast diner or something?" he asked. "Rental car offices will be open in a couple of hours, but in the meantime I'm sure you guys would like to eat."

We hadn't thought about it, but he was right. My mind was still spinning. We were supposed to be pulling up to our dock at home in a few hours. Now we were standing in a gravel parking lot some-

. . . the cut dinghy line dangling off the port propeller.

where in New Jersey—I didn't even know the name of the town—and *Fezywig* was on blocks. This was a different world. Erik accepted Scott's kind offer.

He ferried us over to the diner and then disappeared. I'm sure he wanted to get some sleep. We were grateful for him that morning.

It's not overly dramatic to say some of us staggered into the diner, overdressed for the weather on land and a bit blank in the eyes. Erik asked for a couple of booths. They gave us two tucked-away booths facing each other. We all fell into the bench seats.

"Order whatever you want," Erik told the kids. He never said that at restaurants. They started scanning the menus. "I'm sorry if we're a little distracted," he told the waitress. "We were just in a boating accident." She assured us not to worry and went off to place our order with the kitchen. She brought out a round of hot chocolate for everyone. The kids promptly began to fall asleep. Jane crawled under the table and spread out on the floor. Eli and Alison rested their heads on the table. Karina leaned into the corner of the booth and closed her eyes. Lily lay down on the bench. The waitresses didn't bat an eye at the sleeping kids when they carried in trays piled with scrambled eggs, pancakes, waffles, whipped cream, hash browns, and pounds of breakfast sausage. The kids woke up, took a few bites, and fell asleep again.

It was still early, but the diner was starting to fill up. I went to the restroom and found our waitress on the way back.

"I'm sorry our kids are so sleepy. We've been up all night," I told her. "Our boat started sinking around 2:00 a.m. and we just got her out of the water." She came to check on us a few minutes later.

"You all doing okay?" she asked.

"We're waiting for the car rental shops to open up. We don't have a way to get home. Can we sit here for a while?" Erik asked. She seemed reluctant but went to check. This was a busy Saturday morning at a breakfast diner.

She came back a moment later and said, "We'll let you know if there's a line." We waited. The kids took turns waking up and falling asleep. Erik and I made calls. No one had a car big enough for our family. He made more calls. The kids slept.

Another waitress came. "You all stay put as long as you need. We'll let you know if there's a line," she reassured us.

Finally, we found a car. It was expensive, but it was big. A large, black, Ford Escapade. They said they'd be by to pick us up. We thanked the wait staff and went outside to wait in the park.

"Look," I said to Erik. There was a line of customers around the side of the building waiting for a table.

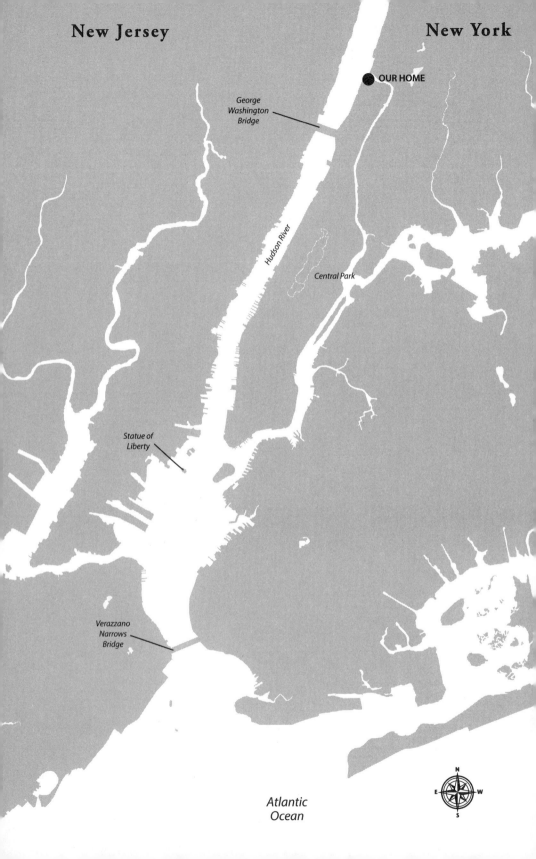

New Jersey

New York

● OUR HOME

George
Washington
Bridge

Hudson River

Central Park

Statue of
Liberty

Verazzano
Narrows
Bridge

Atlantic
Ocean

CHAPTER 21

QUIET VICTORY

GARDEN STATE PARKWAY, NEW JERSEY

4 Hours off *Fezywig*

ERIK

I was jolted from my daze by a tollbooth up ahead. We didn't have an E-Z Pass, and there were no attendants. This was one of those anti-quated tollbooths where you throw in a couple of coins and drive on. We immediately started hunting for change. No one had any. All we had were bills. Then Emily remembered her purse was in the trunk. I didn't want to get a ticket for jilting the New Jersey state government.

I pulled over and she got out and brought up her purse. She tried to open it, but the zipper was stuck. Sea salt had sealed it shut.

"Do you have your buck knife?" she asked. I pulled it out and slit open her wallet. She fished around inside and pulled out coins. They were all coins from other countries. This was getting stupid. I put the car in gear and drove past the tollbooth. They could send me the ticket in the mail.

We drove up I-95 and across the George Washington Bridge,

turned onto Broadway, and pulled into a parking space across the street from our apartment building. For the moment, we sat in the car in silence. Karina offered a prayer for all of us. Then she cried. Emily cried, silent tears running down her face. The rest of us sat silently as rain drizzled down.

Our neighbor waved to us from her fifth-story window. We'd told her we were coming and would need our apartment key. Karina went up ahead to get it.

We walked into our building, a backpack over each of our shoulders. We crammed into the elevator and rode up to the fourth floor. No one said anything.

Karina unlocked the door. It was covered with paper hearts and messages from our friends near and far. Our far-away friends had called our nearby friends and passed on the messages they'd wanted taped to the door.

We opened the apartment door and passed through. We were home, but not really. We opened the fridge. It was filled with food. We didn't know who had put it there. The kids and I fell asleep. Emily didn't sleep.

Our door was covered with paper hearts and messages from our friends near and far.

I woke up twelve hours later. It was 4:00 a.m. Again.

Emily was sitting in the living room. She hadn't slept. She did laundry. "I think we're in shock," she said. I think she was right.

We ate a little pasta—very little. I realized our dishes were gargantuan compared to the boat dishes.

Emily and I talked for a

couple of hours. We stretched. Our bodies were sore. We remembered bailing a lot of water. We fell asleep as the sun was rising.

That afternoon my parents pulled up with our minivan. My dad had driven it while my mom drove their car. They hugged and kissed us, said they loved us, and—just like in Charleston—turned around and drove back to Virginia.

By evening all the kids were awake. They remembered the marina, the diner, and the car. They were trying to piece it all together in their minds. We were too. We gathered around the table, ate dinner from the food in our fridge, and cried.

Fezywig was steadied on wooden blocks in a gravel parking lot. We pulled ourselves up the swim ladder and went inside. It still had everything in the same places, but instead of being surrounded by water, it was surrounded by parked cars, a chain-link fence, and houses. I felt disoriented.

We took the groceries out of storage and moved them to the trunk of the minivan. We gathered the schoolbooks and packed them, too. We collected the clothes and stuffed animals that had been left behind. We'd run an extension cord to the boat, so it still had power. We opened up the fridge and found some leftovers and sausage. Emily turned on the stovetop and cooked us all some lunch. We washed and dried the dishes and put them away. Then we climbed down the stern, down the swim ladder, walked across the crunchy gravel, got in our minivan, and drove home.

The first time we went with everyone. Emily and I needed the help, but more importantly, we needed to see *Fezywig* again. We needed to see she was okay. We needed to remind each other we were okay. We patted her hull and took a few pictures. Good boat. We walked to the dock with all the kids and noticed the sunset. We hadn't realized how pretty this place was when we were here last.

After that it was usually Emily and I driving out to collect and clean the boat, like scuba divers gradually stripping an old wreck. We took down pictures, quotes, and drawings taped up in the cabins and main salon. I tidied the nav desk. Emily swept the floors. We sat down and took a break.

"So do we hand the boat off here, or sail it back to the city?" I asked Emily.

"There's no practical reason to sail it back to Manhattan," she said. We both knew our friends could just as easily come and pick *Fezywig* up in New Jersey.

"But I kind of want to sail it all the way home," I said.

"Me too. We are getting a fair bit of work done. Maybe another shakedown cruise makes sense?"

"Yeah. I'd hate to turn it over and then discover any issues."

"The kids would be up for it. It'd be a day sail."

Emily and I smiled at each other. We were talking ourselves into it.

After two and a half weeks on blocks, *Fezywig* was back in the slings, ready to launch. We packed the kids in the car and drove to New Jersey. We got there a little later than planned, but as usual with boats, there was a delay. The starter motor needed to be replaced. It had finally rusted out as a result of the flooding. The part would be delivered in a few hours. We could wait. We cleaned the boat.

There's a certain catharsis in cleaning something. Emily scrubbed the deck with Soft Scrub and was thrilled to see it revert to its brilliant white color. It was probably good we had a few hours to mentally acclimate. It'd been two and a half weeks on land. The starter motor arrived a few hours later, the mechanic quickly installed it, and the engine started strong. Even though I could now install a starter motor in under ten minutes flat, it was nice to have someone else do the job. I had nothing to prove.

We turned on all the systems and stowed our stuff. We called the kids back from the playground as we let the engines warm up. The slings lowered into the water, *Fezywig*'s keel went under, and we were floating once again. No water in the engine compartment. That was good. We reversed down the alley that had been our gauntlet of death two weeks prior. It was slack tide. The perfect time to go.

Gray clouds. Wind out of the north. We motored. It calmed our nerves to safely pass the few miles of water that had been so treacherous before. The kids sang and danced to their favorite *Fezywig* playlist. We sat around the salon table. We took some pictures. It all felt nostalgic, even though we'd moved off only three weeks earlier. We were dressed more for sledding than sailing, but the kids' faces were rounded out with rosy cheeks and genuine smiles. We settled into the eighty-percent-boring part. The kids went below to take naps, and Emily and I snuggled up on the helm bench.

We pressed our feet against the bulkhead and sat back. When we'd started this journey, we were sweating from heat and nerves. Now we wore beanie caps and winter coats. It was getting dark.

As the evening wore on, we watched the Jersey Shore pass along our port side. In a few hours we came up on Sandy Hook and passed under the Verrazano Bridge. It rose tall. In New Jersey, our mast had scraped the underside of one bridge, but here we had acres of space. It was like a cathedral for boats; high, lofty beams conveying the grandeur of where you were. The waters calmed as we entered the Lower Harbor. Tankers passed us in both directions. We actually saw a sailboat coming out in the darkness, headed out to sea. *Brave soul*, I thought to myself. Coney Island. The lights. The comfort of lights. The water flattened further. Around the bend: the Freedom Tower, the Statue of Liberty, the Battery. Brooklyn and Queens on the starboard side. It was happening so fast and so slow.

We were hoping to get in at a reasonable hour. Many generous friends wanted to meet us at the dock, welcome *Fezywig*, and help us celebrate. But the tide was against us. With our late start we'd missed the current. We would get in late—around midnight, I estimated.

We posted updates to Facebook and Instagram. Friends and loved ones cheered us on silently with their likes, hearts, and comments. We took pictures, but none came out well. The light was beautiful, but not enough for good pictures. We would have to remember this one in our minds.

Emily and the kids turned on music and danced on deck. This was definitely something worth celebrating.

The southern tip of Manhattan. It felt like the Macy's Thanksgiving Day Parade except in reverse. The skyline stood still, and we floated past. It had been dark for hours.

We moved slowly, like a child stopping and looking at everything. Slow, slow, slow. Our engines purred. We all stood in the cockpit and on deck, looking, taking it in with our eyes. The tall lights, the black water, the steady progress.

We sailed past the basin where we had first learned to sail. Even before Toms River, there was this place. I was a different person now. So was Emily. We all were. I could see my old office from the river. I called Mark on the phone.

"Mark, look out the window. That's us sailing up the Hudson."

"No way!" he said. After a few moments and some muffled sounds, he came back on. "I've got everyone here are the window. I think we see you." The building was tall and far away and we were small. I waved, but I was sure they couldn't see that. So many nights at work I'd sat at my desk, looking at boats, drafting budgets, "building bombs," as Mark had called it. Now we were sailing past, with everything behind us.

"We'll talk when you're back in the office."

"Yeah, sounds good," and I hung up.

It all drifted past in the cold night as we continued up the river.

We came around the bend at Chelsea Piers. The river straightened in front of us. The George Washington Bridge rose full into view, like an entrance gate, a string of lights draped over two tall towers.

A laugh jumped up and out my mouth. It was as if my body had to respond to the amazing fact: we were here. After all the miles, all the distance, the people, the islands, the storms, the sweat and worry and spilling and spending of blood, treasure, and energy, there it was in front of us: our gateway. I never thought we'd make it this far.

It was almost midnight. The water traffic thinned as we pushed above Central Park. The 79th Street Boat Basin. Columbia Cathedral. The West Side Highway. Places we knew so well. Comfortable, familiar to us. We'd gotten comfortable being uncomfortable. We were used to being outside our comfort zone. It felt strange to be back in it. The bridge was closer. The tide was easing. We moved faster. Soon it would carry us. But it would be too late.

Our friends were in bed. We came up to the bridge. One last red beacon marked the bank on our starboard side. The marina came into view. We put our fenders and docking lines out. The river went dark. No buildings along the banks.

We pulled up alongside the low dock. Alison hopped off and attached the stern line first and then the bow line to one of the cleats. I remembered telling her in Oyster Pond, when we scuffed the bow after our first trip to Tintamarre, "It's just a boat." I turned off the engines.

I hopped down, tied a spring line, and walked to the marina. The restaurant was closed. I spoke with the night guard. In broken English he asked me what was wrong with our boat. Why were we arriving so late? In Spanish I told him nothing was wrong. We'd just sailed up from the Caribbean. We lived a few blocks away. We were going to walk home and come back in the morning.

He was confused. I assured him we'd be back in the morning and gave him my card. He agreed, reluctantly. I walked back to the boat. Emily and the kids got their bags. I got mine and we walked down the dock, bid the guard a good night, and walked through the gate down 200th/Dyckman Street. In the silence we walked east toward Broadway. We all wore coats, hats, and scarves. We'd left in January, when it was cold. It was October and cold again. Ten months. Everyone walked, even the little kids. 1:00 am. The night was quiet.

There was no one there to greet us, and we were fine with that.

We stopped and took a picture under a streetlight. We laughed a little amongst ourselves. *We were walking home from the boat.* How many years had we talked about doing this? We'd started sailing six years earlier. We'd gotten the idea for this trip four years ago.

What a crazy idea.

How unlikely.

How impossible.

We walked some more. Warm beds awaited. There was no one there to greet us, and we were fine with that. "It's nice," Emily said. "It's a quiet victory." I agreed and we walked along, holding hands. The kids had their arms around each other, bulky bags and coats swishing as we ambled. We walked behind the church, past the bike shop, through the gas station. We stopped at the crosswalk at Riverside. The light turned and we crossed, quietly. Then we turned down Broadway. Three more blocks.

Sometimes home was us together, sometimes it was our destination, sometimes it was what we missed, sometimes it was how we felt in a new place or with our friends.

The night was cold, but home was close. We crossed Broadway and cut into the courtyard. I unlocked the lobby door, up two stairs. Into the lobby, then up three more stairs. Someone pushed the button to call the elevator. It arrived and we opened the outer door. We all pushed inside, fitting tightly with our bags. Up four flights, and then we pushed open the elevator door again. Down the hall. First the top lock, then the bottom lock. We opened the door and stepped inside. We were home.

We shall not cease from exploration
And the end of all our exploring
Will be to arrive where we started
And know the place for the first time.

—*T. S. ELIOT*

EPILOGUE

EMILY

1 day after *Fezywig*—Erik sailed with the Andersons back to the Chesapeake Bay.

7 days after *Fezywig*—Erik went back to his glass tower, cubicle job.

21 days after *Fezywig*—Erik and I talked about a new unconventional job opportunity.

Erik said, "Look, we've had enough risk for a while. We have to pay off the haul-out and repair expenses on the boat. Karina is going to college soon. We're going into the expensive years when we're launching our kids."

"But this could take care of all of that," I said.

"If I don't succeed, we don't eat. I'm responsible for you and these kids."

"So am I."

Fezywig sailing in the Hudson River under the George Washington Bridge. Photo by Kendra Cope.

"I know it's both of us."

"Okay," I said. "Why don't we ask the kids?" I opened the door from our bedroom/office into the dining/living room where Eli and Lily played plushies.

"Family meeting," I called, and the older girls gathered. Erik and I filled them in.

"So it's a choice between a risky job with unlimited potential or a stable job that you know you don't like?" Alison confirmed.

"I would think there was something wrong with you if you stayed where you are," SJ said.

Karina said, "Do we really even need to discuss this?"

3 months after *Fezywig*—Erik quit his cubicle job.

6 months after *Fezywig*—The Andersons returned.

9 months after *Fezywig*—We sold her. She's sailing still. Let us know if you see her.

1 year after *Fezywig*—Karina went to college on academic scholarship.

2 years, 6 months after *Fezywig*—Erik and I sailed in French Polynesia.

3 years after *Fezywig*—Back-to-back hurricanes Irma and Maria, the two most powerful hurricanes that year, pummeled many of the islands we traveled. The resilient people and places we loved are recovering and rebuilding. The islands are as vibrant and welcoming as ever. Consider visiting. Life goes on. Alison went to college on academic scholarship. Karina hiked from Scotland to Wales with a study-abroad group and then traveled solo through France, Switzerland, Germany, Finland, and Iceland. She is majoring in film. The rest of us downsized into a minivan for two multi-month, cross-country rock climbing trips. Erik spent three days climbing the largest granite cliff in the world, El Capitan in Yosemite.

3 years, 6 months after *Fezywig*—We have house sat for two months in Hawaii. Erik, SJ, and I scuba certified (sixty feet deep!) and learned to surf. SJ is a dedicated longboarder. Lily cliff jumped. It was a low cliff. Eli is an animator on YouTube (eli26). Erik raced a sailboat from Annapolis to Bermuda. We've had multiple land reunions with *Day Dreamer* and *Discovery*. As of this writing, Karina is studying in Finland. Alison is going to Japan for eighteen months to serve as a missionary. The rest of us are planning to sail in the Mediterranean with *Discovery* and road trip across Europe while this book is printed.

But these adventures are not the "life-changing" part of living aboard *Fezywig*. If we are a tree, these adventures are the fruit. The real changes are inside the tree, inside of us.

We know we can learn new skills. We have done what we said we would do. We know the details will emerge. Competence. Credibility. Calm.

Drop us a line. We'd love to stay in touch.

www.sevenatsea.com

hello@fezywig.com